D0216583

The Bomber
in British Strategy

The Bomber in British Strategy

Doctrine, Strategy, and Britain's World Role, 1945–1960

S. J. Ball

Westview Press

A Division of HarperCollins*Publishers*

Published in 1995 in the United States of America by Westview Press, Inc., 5500 Central Avenue, Boulder, Colorado 80301-2877, and in the United Kingdom by Westview Press, 12 Hid's Copse Road, Cumnor Hill, Oxford OX2 9JJ

Library of Congress Cataloging-in-Publication Data
Ball, S. J. (Simon J.)
The bomber in British strategy : doctrine, strategy, and
Britain's world role, 1945–1960 /
S. J. Ball.
    p.   cm.
Includes bibliographical references and index.
ISBN 0-8133-8934-8
    1. Nuclear weapons—Government policy—Great Britain.   2. Bombers—
Great Britain.   3. Great Britain—Military relations—United
States.   4. United States—Military relations—Great Britain.
I. Title.
UA647.B567   1995
355.8'25119'0941—dc20   95-18392
                                                                    CIP

The paper used in this publication meets the requirements of the American National Standard for Permanence of Paper for Printed Library Materials Z39.48-1984.

10   9   8   7   6   5   4   3   2   1

To My Parents

Contents

Acknowledgments

In researching and writing this book I have incurred many debts for the kindness shown to me.

Research was financed by the British Academy and the Prince Consort and Thirwell Fund. I would like to thank the trustees and administrators of those bodies. I am also very grateful to the University of Glasgow, and in particular the Department of Modern History, for granting me the academic leave during which this book was completed.

My first and greatest personal thanks go to David Reynolds, who read virtually every draft and from whose incisiveness and scholarship I learnt a huge amount. Michael Dockrill, Ian Clark and Philip Towle all read all or part of the manuscript in various stages of its gestation: each made a number of much-valued suggestions which have been incorporated in the final work. Hew Strachan and Evan Mawdsley read the work and gave a great deal of personal encouragement to the author. Dennis Showalter not only offered encouragement but was instrumental in this publication. Martin Navias very generously allowed me to use his copies of documents from American archives and a transcript of a witness seminar on the 1957 Defence White Paper he organized at King's College, London. I also learnt a great deal from his book *Nuclear Weapons and British Strategic Planning, 1955-1958* (Oxford, 1991), which he allowed me to read in draft form. Sebastian Cox, of the Ministry of Defence's Air Historical Branch, gave me a great deal of assistance, especially in guiding me around the Slessor papers of which he was custodian. Andy Vallance, the Royal Air Force's Director of Defence Studies at the time I was researching this book, allowed me access to certain archives at the RAF Staff College, Bracknell, and also the use of his thesis on RAF doctrine. Elliot V. Converse kindly arranged for copies of documents to be sent from the USAF's Historical Research Center at Maxwell AFB, Montgomery, Alabama, and also made available his own thesis on United States planning for a postwar military base system.

I have been extremely fortunate in my Cambridge contemporaries. Sean Faughnan helped me set this book in a wider context through discussion of his work on Churchill's foreign policy. My understanding of British missile policy was greatly enhanced by John Elliot, who allowed me to use his thesis on Blue Streak. Richard Aldous provided me with numerous insights drawn from the preparation of his book on the foreign policy of Harold Macmillan; he also gave me the opportunity to test out some of my ideas at a conference he organised, under the auspices of Cambridge University's Centre for International Studies, at St. John's College, Cambridge. Richard has been a constant interlocutor and constructive critic; as such he was instrumental in the completion of this book.

The late Viscount De L'Isle granted me an interview from which I learnt more about the internal politics of Sir Winston Churchill's administration than I could ever have hoped to glean from written archives. Cecil James also took a great deal of time and trouble to talk to me. His comments were doubly useful: As an Air Ministry civil servant from the 1940s to the 1960s he was an invaluable primary source; as the author of the Ministry of Defence's own classified official history of the period 1956 to 1963 he was able to give me many invaluable clues and leads for my own work.

I have been greatly assisted throughout my research by the efficiency and kindness of the staff at the Public Record Office, Kew; the Air Historical Branch, London; Churchill College Archives Centre, Cambridge; the Royal Air Force Museum, Hendon; the RAF Staff College, Bracknell; and the USAF Historical Research Center, Montgomery. Material drawn from records found in the Public Record Office is Crown copyright; permission to quote this material is gratefully acknowledged.

Mike Black, Ann Lee, Don Spaeth, Astrid Wissenburg and Christelle Le Riguer, all at Glasgow University, gave me indispensable assistance with computer equipment and advice.

Although this work would have been impossible to complete without the assistance of those mentioned above its weaknesses are, of course, entirely my own.

S. J. Ball

1

Nuclear Strategy and the Central Organisation of Defence

Nuclear Strategy and the Central Organisation of Defence

To understand how and why nuclear strategy developed as it did it is necessary to understand the nature of the system which formulated it and the processes by which that system operated. The component parts of the British security policy system in the 1940s and 1950s, the 'defence establishment', can be easily identified. It comprised a relatively small number of elected politicians, senior civil servants and high ranking military officers. Each was served by a number of lower ranking civil servants and officers. This system was not, of course, hermetically sealed. It is best regarded as the inner ring of three circles. Outside it was a second circle consisting of other groups and individuals with a direct interest in defence policy; parliamentarians, retired or serving officers not in senior staff positions, journalists or self-appointed military thinkers such as Liddell Hart. From the mid-1950s onwards there was an attempt by some of these individuals to create a more organised framework for extra-governmental thinking about strategy, an attempt symbolised by the formation of the Institute for Strategic Studies in 1958.[1] The outer ring consisted of the British electorate; important both because defence decision-makers were not divorced from their own society and because governments always had some conception of what the 'people' would accept in terms of economic self-sacrifice or threat of nuclear devastation. Party politics could have a direct effect on defence policy. For instance, the decision taken by the Macmillan government in 1957 to phase out national service was strongly influenced by the desire to enhance the electoral prospects of the Conservative Party. On occasion popular movements, drawn from the second and third 'circles', did attempt to exert a direct influence on defence policy-making, the most notable example being the Campaign for Nuclear Disarmament. Yet their influence was minimal.[2] Although the 'strategic studies' commentators of the second circle gained in influence during the 1960s any attempt to reconstruct British strategy and its influence in the 1940s and 1950s must focus on the ideas and relationships of important decision-makers within the British government.

The first point to note is that although the British defence establishment in the 1940s and 1950s functioned on almost continuous strategic debate all participants held certain views about the international system in common. These views could be described, using Martin Ceadel's classification system, as 'defencist'. They believed that war could be prevented and that diplomacy as well as military force played a part in achieving this. They believed that war could never be abolished, since states were always in conflict. The best to be hoped for was a diplomatic compromise among states which reflected the prevailing distribution of power: an anarchical society or an armed truce. This position was based on two fundamental propositions. First, a moral intuition, that defensive intent was not only a necessary but also a sufficient condition for war to be just. Second, an empirical generalisation, that strong defences were the best way to prevent war.[3] Less abstractly, it can be argued that a set of core beliefs existed in the political and defence establishments based on an interpretation of the causes and course of the Second World War and articulated by 'Churchillian historiography'.[4] Alternative views existed in British political and public life but these implicit beliefs underpinned all the strategic decisions of the British defence establishment.

Defence policy-making was carried out by vigorous, strong and unified service staffs and ministries with weak central direction. The result was that strategy tended to be incoherent and conservative. British strategy was incoherent in the sense that Britain did not have one military strategy it had several, although they were linked by a series of agreements and compromises. Conservatism was apparent in two respects. First, it was a generally accepted proposition that Britain should retain three services each with the full range of military capabilities. This position was only seriously challenged by Duncan Sandys and his failure to find any allies in government demonstrated its strength. Second, there was a lack of any institutional outlet for dissent, about either national security policy or military strategy, other than that officially sponsored by a ministry or department. These problems were exacerbated by the lack of co-ordination between defence and foreign policy departments.[5]

Each of the post-war governments had a different style in defence policy-making. The Attlee government, which introduced the post-war system with the 1946 White Paper on the Central Organisation for Defence, generally operated the system well enough with senior ministers, particularly Bevin and Attlee, using the Defence Committee of the Cabinet to take major decisions. The 1946 reforms created a small Ministry of Defence to co-ordinate the existing service ministries and a Minister of Defence with Cabinet rank. The Secretaries of State for War and Air and the First Lord of the Admiralty were removed from the Cabinet. The wartime position of the Chiefs of Staff Committee as the government's chief advisers on strategy was formalised. The 1946 White Paper, although explicitly a compromise, was seen as radical at the time.[6] Although the formation of a unified Ministry of Defence was discussed in 1945 and 1946 such an outcome was never likely.

The post-war Labour government was faced with a 'concatenation of crises' and the disorders of the changed world created by the war. In addition it was generally assumed that there was little probability of a major war for at least ten years. This meant that although inter-service disputes and intra-governmental debates about the overall size of the defence budget were fierce the government concentrated more on pressing short-term problems and crises rather than on long-term planning. Even the Korean rearmament programmes involved an increase in expenditure on equipment and service establishments which were already available rather than a rethink of strategy.

The long haul was left to the incoming Conservative government which was peculiarly ill-equipped to deal with it. Part of the problem rested with Winston Churchill himself. Churchill was immensely interested in problems of defence and initially took the Defence portfolio for himself and then passed it on to the easily controlled Lord Alexander. Churchill was by far the most powerful figure in the field of defence policy. Yet his interventions and attention span were uneven and his opinions often irrelevant to the main thrust of strategic debate.[7] His successor Eden showed little interest in or aptitude for strategic policy-making although he did make some attempt to strengthen central direction by creating a Chairman of the Chiefs of Staff Committee and issuing a directive increasing the authority of the Minister of Defence.[8] No further attempt to reform defence decision-making was undertaken by the Eden government. The Minister of Defence, Sir Walter Monckton, who had strongly criticised the existing machinery,[9] was offered a further increase in powers in 1956 but he considered that substantive changes in defence policy were more important than any defence reorganisation.[10]

These years of drift produced great frustration in other Conservative ministers involved in defence and formed the background to the convulsion in the defence establishment caused by the appointment of Duncan Sandys to the Ministry of Defence by Macmillan in January 1957. Macmillan equipped Sandys with a directive instructing him to formulate a new defence policy and intended to show that that the minister would exercise much greater personal authority in decisions 'on all matters of policy affecting the size, shape, organisation and dispositions of the armed forces'.[11] The Macmillan/Sandys period could be described as one of 'personal rule'. The main problem with this new dispensation was the lack of any institutional backing. Although relatively clear policy could emerge in areas where Sandys and Macmillan had definite ideas, such as the abolition of national service or the scaling down of air defence, Sandys' personal direction was little more effective than that of the Chiefs of Staff when there was a balance of arguments.[12] Sandys himself recognised these problems and pressed for properly formalised policy-making in a unified Ministry of Defence.[13]

In June 1957 Macmillan instructed Sir Norman Brook to conduct a detailed study of defence policy-making since the war.[14] Brook's report was highly critical of the government's performance. Its tone demonstrated the loss of confidence felt by politicians and civil servants in the advice of the military because of its inability to agree coherent strategic and force-structure plans. This loss of confidence was particularly apparent amongst senior civil servants in the Ministry of Defence.[15] Brook was one of the architects of the post-war organisation for defence[16] and had been constantly involved in it since 1945. His comments are thus particularly pertinent to the working of the system between 1947 and 1957. Brook made three main points. First, defence expenditure was not based on any coherent or agreed strategy. It was not clear whether Britain was wholly committed to nuclear deterrence or was preparing to fight a major war. Second, it had originally been envisaged that the Cabinet Defence Committee would make all major strategic decisions. This system had broken down: the Defence Committee met rarely and often dealt with minor matters of detail. Policy-making had been shifted to ad hoc groups of ministers but they had also dealt with problems piecemeal without any overall strategic appreciation. Third, the failure of ministers to give firm guidance had meant that the Chiefs of Staff had become largely responsible for defining the needs of national security. Brook believed that they were ill-equipped for this task.[17]

Brook, who was Macmillan's most influential adviser on defence reorganisation, nevertheless opposed Sandys' proposal that the Ministry of Defence absorb the other four defence ministries and carry out their roles on a functional basis. Even when he had defeated Sandys on the unified Ministry of Defence he continued to oppose the latter's attempts to increase his power on the grounds that 'the present Minister wishes ... to substitute for leadership the power of arbitrary decision'. According to Brook the divorce of policy from execution was dangerous, removing inbuilt checks and balances and risking the confidence in the conduct of military operations, if not long-term planning, between the civilians and the military which he felt was the best aspect of the World War Two system.[18] Macmillan, Brook and John Hare, the Secretary of State for War, who Macmillan consulted, agreed that the most pressing problem was to restore the morale of the forces and ensure that regular recruitment was successful enough to prevent the decision to abolish national service from becoming an embarrassing political disaster. In the end any major attempt to reform defence organisation was regarded as too disruptive at a time when major policy decisions had to be worked through.[19] Brook's solution was to make 'greater use of ad hoc bodies of Ministers, officers and civil servants to solve problems in the size and shape group.'[20]

Any attempt to reorganise the defence machinery was actually a much more overtly political exercise than strategic policy-making, involving as it did not only the defence establishment but also other ministers, the Conservative Party and Parliament.[21] As a result the July 1958 White Paper on the Central Organisation for Defence was a tame affair.[22] Sandys certainly felt he had been let down by Macmillan. The Prime Minister's view was that to continue the controversy would damage the government as a whole.[23] The changes introduced were a more powerful Defence Committee, a new Defence Board in which the Minister of Defence was to work out policy with the service ministers and the creation of a Chief of the Defence Staff. Macmillan and Sandys soon made it clear that they saw the Defence Committee[24] and Board[25] as little more than talking shops in which they would hand down policy directives which they had already decided on after informal consultation with advisers of their choice.

Britain's central organisation for defence has been discussed intensively.[26] The central issue in the context of the present work is whether a different organisation would have produced significantly different decisions about British military strategy and national security policy. At one level this is a question of 'efficiency'. Policy implementation, especially over a period as long as fifteen years, was bound to feed back into the decision-making process. It could certainly be argued that the much commented upon phenomenon of 'overstretch' was equally a function of an inefficient higher organisation for defence and military industrial complex as of an excess of military and political commitments. The 'inefficient' failure to effectively review and reduce such commitments in the late 1950s and early 1960s contributed to the precipitate nature of the withdrawal of British forces from the Far East and the Persian Gulf in the financial crisis of 1967-8.[27]

Despite the obstacles presented by the conservatism and fragmented organisation of the defence establishment, however, defence policy did undergo significant change. Military strategy shifted towards a much greater reliance on nuclear weapons for both deterrence and war-fighting. National strategy changed from the maintenance of worldwide power through a colonial empire to the attempt to maintain worldwide power with a much smaller number of colonies, a system of bases and bilateral and multilateral alliances. The geographical centre of interest also shifted from the Mediterranean to Europe, the Gulf and the Far East. It is conceivable that with a different defence organisation decisions relating to national, military and nuclear strategy could have been challenged in the 1950s as they were to be in the the the 1960s. Yet given the views of key policy-makers including Macmillan, Sandys and his most influential adviser, the Permanent Secretary at the Ministry of Defence, Sir Richard Powell it seems unlikely that even if Sandys' proposal for a unified Ministry of Defence had been accepted in 1958 radically different decisions on strategy would have been taken between 1957 and 1960. Defence organisation was important in shaping strategic concepts but the concepts themselves were the determinants of the broad shape of defence policy.

As Aaron Friedberg has suggested, in his study of Britain's response to relative decline between 1895 and 1905, 'change agents' partially explain shifts in strategy and the limits of such shifts. According to Friedberg: 'shifts are likely to result not simply from exogenous shocks or random personnel changes but rather from a prolonged process of bureaucratic discussion and, sometimes, public political debate. This process is driven by gradual developments in the thinking of "change agents", middle- and upper-level officials whose views begin to deviate from the norm and who are able to receive a wider hearing only at moments of intense crisis.'[28] The first important 'change agent' discussed in this book is Sir John Slessor, Chief of the Air Staff from January 1950 to December 1952. Slessor's period in office straddled the change-over from Attlee's to Churchill's government. The exogenous shock which brought him a hearing was the Korean War and the subsequent strain on the British economy caused by the the rearmament programme. Slessor made a vigorous case during the six months he was in office before the war for a change in British defence policy towards a firmer commitment to nuclear deterrence balanced by real rather than 'shop window' conventional forces. He also argued for priority to be given to Europe rather than the Middle East. Although his views shifted even more towards a belief in deterrence as a result of the economic strain of rearmament he had adumbrated his approach to strategy fairly clearly in 1949-50. Slessor was undoubtedly the most persuasive strategic advocate to hold high military office during this period but the influence of his ideas was greatly increased by the mismatch of British economic resources and military commitments during a period when a direct threat from the Soviet Union was believed to be real if just 'over the horizon'. Yet although Slessor wanted to change military strategy and reapportion the attention given to certain geographical areas in national strategy he was an outspoken advocate of Britain's role as a world power.

The other striking example of an exogenous shock allowing certain officials to implement their views was the production of the 1957 Defence White Paper in the aftermath of the Suez crisis. As Sir Richard Powell, one of the main architects of the paper, has put it: 'The aftermath of Suez ... was not the most important element in this situation [although] Suez was certainly the proximate cause of the White Paper, in the sense that it led to a change of Prime Minister and Minister of Defence. If these things had not happened the White Paper would not have happened in the form that it did.'[29] Once again the reassessment of defence policy was propelled by 'change agents' from within the establishment. Macmillan and Sandys had been important ministers before Suez and officials such as Powell and Sir Norman Brook simply continued in their posts. Much of the thinking which underlay the White Paper could be found in a paper, 'The Future of the United Kingdom in World Affairs', produced under Brook's auspices in mid-1956. It had argued that the advent of the hydrogen bomb meant that much more emphasis should be placed on nuclear deterrence and that if government spending was not rationalised Britain would be incapable of maintaining a global role. Added to these general concerns were Macmillan's conviction that the fighter defence of the United Kingdom was pointless and Sandys' belief that the ballistic missile would soon make most manned aircraft obsolete. As in the case of Slessor and the Korean War, however, although important changes to military strategy were introduced, the aim was to make Britain function more efficiently as a world power not to change its status to that of a regional power.

There were those in the 1950s defence establishment who wanted to greatly reduce Britain's commitments. At a lower level middle-ranking potential 'change agents' were smothered by the organisation of the defence machinery. Michael Carver, War Office Director of Plans in 1958-9, 'wished to give greater emphasis to our being good Europeans and involving ourselves in the European Economic Community, pulling in our horns in the Middle and Far East'[30] but found that 'it was very difficult to inject my own ideas or views at any stage, particularly if they ran counter to official War Office thinking.'[31] This was not necessarily the case in the 1960s following the embodiment of the service ministries in the Ministry of Defence in 1963 and the setting up of such bodies as Denis Healey's Programme Evaluation Group in which officers from all the services were 'instructed to look at the problems in the interests of the country's defence as a whole, ignoring pressures from the individual services.' Even after 1964, however, officers risked their careers if they were seen to act against the interests of their service.[32]

The fate of attempts to provide some unified assessment of national power and strategy such as the Future Policy Study Group set up by Macmillan in 1958 is instructive. In the case of the FPSG Macmillan had wanted a study 'answering the questions: "What will the world be like in ten years' time? What will Britain's position in it be? What should be done about it?" The body charged with the duty of providing the answers should be drawn from the principal ministries, but not subject to direction from them.' Departments did, however, apply pressure to their reprentatives serving on the the study group. In addition the report was significantly watered down by a steering committee made up of the Permanent Under-Secretaries and the Chiefs of Staff chaired by Norman Brook.[33] It was perhaps symbolic that Macmillan was unable to attend the Chequers meeting at which the FPSG's final report was considered.[34] Friedberg's judgement on British policy-making in 1905 that 'although efforts to overcome them are possible, there would appear to be strong organizational forces acting to push modern states away from from a unified assessment process [of relative national power] and towards a more fragmented approximation of that ideal' is actually a valid description of the situation half a century later.[35]

In these conditions the concept of strategy presents problems. Barry Posen has suggested that strategy is 'a political-military means-ends chain, a state's theory about how it can best "cause" security for itself.'[36] In other words strategy, in the context of the governmental decision-making of modern states, consists of the identification of national interests and threats to national security combined with decisions on the manning, equipment, deployment and employment of armed forces to support the interests and meet the threats. Such formal definitions would suggest that the British government dealt with strategy on three distinct levels: first, deciding on national strategy, second, framing a military strategy to support these national aims and third, building a strategy or doctrine on nuclear weapons into this military strategy. But this is not, of course, what happened. First, national, military and nuclear strategy interacted; each helped to define the other. Second, the British defence establishment developed a number of competing military strategies; government policy was a compromise between them.

The importance of these competing strategies, their similarities and differences and the compromises arrived at should not be underestimated. Although Britain's position was to a large extent structurally determined, by geographical position, economic power, technical development, social organisation and by the relative strengths of potential allies and enemies, a structural interpretation does not satisfactorily explain the tenacity with which Britain maintained a global military role.

If a structural interpretation is insufficient to explain national strategy it also fails to provide a complete explanation of the development of nuclear policy. At one level the rapidly increasing importance of nuclear weapons in British defence policy can be seen simply as the result of technical development. A consideration of the chronology of the development of nuclear weapons shows why they became more important in British planning in the mid-1950s. In the winter of 1946/7 the Attlee government decided to develop a British atomic bomb and the long-range jet bombers to deliver it. In November 1952 the first British atomic device was tested and the first operational atomic bomb was delivered exactly a year later. In July 1954 the Churchill government decided to develop a British hydrogen bomb and the first long-range jet bomber capable of carrying nuclear weapons entered service at the beginning of the next year. In 1958 the first British hydrogen bomb was tested and in the same year deliveries of advanced long-range jet bombers reached their peak. Thus before 1955 Britain had no operational nuclear capability. Policy was limited to planning and reliance on the United States. From 1955 onwards, however, Britain could attempt to use its possession of nuclear power to further national ends on an independent, bilateral and alliance basis.

Parallel to the physical development of nuclear weapons and their delivery systems was the relative decline of Britain's non-nuclear armed strength. In 1948 Britain's defence expenditure was £740 million, 7.1% of GNP, in 1959 expenditure was £1561 million, 6.4% of GNP.[37] Yet whereas in 1948 British defence expenditure amounted to approximately 31% of the United States' and 26% of the Soviet Union's by 1959 it was only 9.5% of the United States' and 12% of the Soviet Union's.[38]

The combination of a relative decline in British power and the belief in the pervasiveness of the Soviet threat placed constraints on British policy. British governments could not, it seemed, follow Lord Lansdowne's example and seek rapprochement with major military rivals. Neville Chamberlain had, in any case, discredited appeasement in the eyes of the governing elite. The summit policies of Churchill, Eden and Macmillan, whether born out of Britain's military over-extension, personal hubris or genuine fears of nuclear Armageddon, were pale reflections of the policies of the 1900s or 1930s.

The failure to whittle away the threat was matched by the failure to build up British power. The loss of India left Britain defending Curzon's 'barbicans and toll-gates' of Empire. Withdrawal from Palestine and Greece publicly demonstrated Britain's weakness in relation to America. In the Far East ANZAM was a geographically limited planning organisation whilst Australia and New Zealand looked mainly to American power in ANZUS, from which Britain was deliberately excluded, for their security. Britain failed to renegotiate the 1936 Anglo-

Egyptian Treaty and the replacement of the 1930 Anglo-Iraqi treaty was wrecked by popular unrest in Iraq in 1948. Britain's impotence in Iran was demonstrated by the 1951 Abadan crisis. Britain failed to organise a Middle East defence organisation because of Egyptian hostility or to secure the deployment of large American or Dominion forces in the region. Following the abrogation of the Anglo-Egyptian treaty in 1951 the British were harried from their Canal Zone base. The 1956 Suez crisis was the culmination of a decade of failure for conventional military strategy. Nuclear weapons seemed to be the only option open to Britain in the the mid-1950s.

At another level the increasing dominance of nuclear weapons in British strategic debate can be traced through the processes of British defence policy-making. It can be argued that since British strategy would not have developed as it did without the exogenous shock of the Suez crisis the policy decisions taken by Macmillan and Sandys in 1957 should be given more prominence than the often deadlocked strategic debates of the Churchill and Eden governments. Yet nuclear weapons would have achieved much greater prominence in British strategy with or without Suez. Both before and after Suez the physical and psychological investment in nuclear weapons seemed to offer a new factor in the assessment of national power and thus delayed any fundamental review of national strategy. To argue that nuclear weapons served as a substitute for declining power is not unusual. This book suggests, however, that the phenomenon can be equally well explained by the nature and organisation of strategic debate in 1950s Britain as by reference to 'nuclear totemism'.

In the defence establishment choices were made on strategic grounds. Procurement and deployment were decided on such grounds. Even if a visceral preference for highly sophisticated, high performance and high cost aircraft lay behind the RAF's commitment to the manned bomber it could never openly state such a proposition. Equally, a military organisation of this type could not have functioned effectively if its officers had been unable to equate service with national interest. As part of their job staff officers had to think strategically; the military bureaucracy had to argue strategically. Although many decisions were taken on the basis of tradition or sectional self-interest each had to have at least a veneer of strategic justification.

The ability to argue strategically was therefore vital to the decision-making process. From 1945 one of the most pressing fields for strategic argument was nuclear weapons. Within the defence establishment they were considered not only in their own right, as weapons which could cause previously unthought of damage to the world in general and Britain in particular, but also in relation to procurement decisions, British national power and service self-interest. Indeed the lack of concern shown by military planners for the internal logic of their proposed nuclear strategies in the 1950s led to them being partially outflanked by their civilian counterparts in the 1960s.

Within the British government two kinds of strategic argument can be seen at work. The first was hardly argument at all since it consisted of the transmission of instructions down a chain of command. At the military level this could take the form of a direct order. For instance, the service Directors of Plans, of Brigadier rank and equivalents, were usually instructed to argue the position of their own ministry, and in particular that of their Chief of Staff, on the Joint Planning Staff whatever their personal opinions; even though the JPS was supposed to be a body capable of independent thought giving collective advice to the Chiefs of Staff Committee. At a governmental level a similar process can be seen when ministers decided to disregard the advocacy of their relevant military advisers. The decision of Macmillan and Sandys to abandon the air defence of Great Britain whatever the views of the Air Staff is an example of this process.

In a diffused decision-making system the second form of strategic argument was both more common and more influential. It was the argument by proposition. This procedure had quasi-legalistic aspects. A proposition was advanced and an attempt was made to have it accepted by an authoritative body or person. If it was accepted it became a precedent upon which other propositions could be built. Any person or body wishing to challenge a policy decision would have to attack either the particular decision or the precedent proposition. This could be done by having a superior body overrule an inferior one or by getting a body to reverse its own decision. An example of such a 'proposition line' can be seen in British nuclear planning from 1945 to 1960. In October 1945 the Chiefs of Staff accepted the proposition that nuclear weapons would, in future, deter all forms of war. On the basis of this proposition the Air Staff put forward the further proposition two years later that a nuclear force should be the first priority for British defence policy. This second proposition was formally accepted in the Cabinet decision to adopt the 1952 Global Strategy Paper. The proposition that nuclear weapons deterred all forms of war was challenged by the War Office and the Admiralty in 1956 and again in 1958. From 1955 onwards the same two ministries challenged the proposition that a nuclear force should be given first priority in the defence budget. Each of these challenges was turned down by the Cabinet or one of its committees. The Air Ministry meanwhile combined the proposition that nuclear weapons deterred all wars with the priority already accorded to the strategic nuclear force and proposed that Britain should acquire the capability to deploy its nuclear forces worldwide. This proposition was accepted by the Chiefs of Staff and the Cabinet Defence Committee in 1955. On the basis of the desirability of global force projection the Air Ministry further proposed a nuclear air base in the Far East and the Cabinet Defence Committee endorsed the concept in 1958. When the Air Ministry attempted to go even further by proposing the construction of nuclear facilities in Borneo as well as in Singapore it was successfully blocked by the the Ministry of Defence which argued that such facilities would be too costly in light of the limited usefulness they would have for British foreign policy in the region. In the period after that covered by this book the proposition that nuclear weapons deterred all war was successfully challenged by Lord Mountbatten, Solly Zuckerman, Denis Healey and, from without, Robert McNamara. The proposition that the strategic nuclear force should have first priority in the defence budget, on the other hand, has been consistently reiterated by successive governments.

Military bureaucracies were particularly important in this system of propositional argument since they had long-term vested interests, an institutional memory and a pool of staff officers and civil servants to prepare their case. Ministers could and did override the bureaucracies but they were at a disadvantage since they relied on the informal and personal development of ideas and were in office for relatively short periods. Although the parameters of the defence debate were set by the proportion of GNP governments were willing to allocate to external policy the most important component of decisions on resource allocation was strategic argument. These strategic arguments tended to be decided by propositional debate over a number years.

The RAF, the Air Staff, the Air Ministry
and Nuclear Strategy

The Royal Air Force was a large military institution. It was also a small club in which all senior officers knew each other, sometimes from before the founding of the RAF in April 1918, from service in peace and war. Service socialisation based on common experience and training played an important informal role in policy-making. The core beliefs of senior RAF officers in this period which had a direct impact on policy-making are clearly summarised in the published work of Lord Tedder and Sir John Slessor. In 1947 Tedder gave the Lees Knowles lectures at Cambridge and they were published in book form as *Air Power in War* the following year. Sir John Slessor published his memoirs, entitled *The Central Blue*, in 1956. Tedder and Slessor believed that first, the threat of war was ever present, second, that airpower was the dominant factor in warfare, third, that airpower had to have the greatest possible offensive capability and that reliance on defence was potentially disastrous[39] and fourth that 'for our Empire and Commonwealth there is no decline and fall. ... The Empire will last ... as a creative, dynamic partner and exemplar in the English speaking community of the Commonwealth and United States.'[40]

Such views underpinned the RAF's approach to both military strategy and national security policy. They were essentially those of a generation which reached the top of the defence establishment in the 1940s and 1950s. British strategy, especially nuclear strategy, did not remain static; a process of reassessment and adaptation did take place but its parameters were set by this generational perspective.

Formal policy-making lay in the hands of two bodies; the Air Ministry and the Air Staff. The Department of the Chief of the Air Staff was, in administrative terms, merely one department of the Air Ministry but it was by far the most important strategic policy-making body. The governing body of the RAF was the Air Council, chaired by the Secretary of State for Air, and made up of the departmental heads and ex officio members such as the Deputy and Vice-Chiefs of the Air Staff. It was serviced by a Standing Committee which had been retained from the Air Ministry's wartime post-war planning machinery.

Policy formulation was in the hands of a mixed group of RAF officers, civil servants and politicians. The officers and the civil servants co-operated closely and there were few examples of policy debates within the Ministry splitting on civil/military lines. The influence of the Permanent Under-Secretary was determined largely by personality. Sir James Barnes, PUS from 1947 to 1955, was almost invisible in terms of strategic policy-making. His successor Sir Maurice Dean had a much higher profile. The Secretary of State for Air and the Parliamentary Under-Secretary of State for Air were in a more anomalous position with their loyalties to ministry, service, party, government and political patrons. Their influence also largely rested on personality. Arthur Henderson, Air Minister for most of Attlee's governments, was usually ignored by the Chiefs of the Air Staff who were his titular subordinates. The question of 'who rules?' politician or service chief could cause very considerable personal friction as between Sir John Slessor, Chief of the Air Staff from 1950 to 1952, and Lord De L'Isle and Dudley, Secretary of State for Air from 1951 to 1955. Anthony Seldon suggests, on the basis of an interview with Slessor, that he retired in 1952 largely because of his inability to work with Churchill even though De L'Isle wanted him to stay on.[41] Viscount De L'Isle's recollection was that he himself would have considered resignation if Slessor had not gone.[42] Yet these personal animosities had relatively little influence on policy. The Air Council proved a successful forum for ironing out major divisions.[43]

The real engine room for strategic policy in the Air Ministry was the Air Staff. The Air Staff was effectively ruled by a triumvirate of the Chief of the Air Staff, the Vice-Chief of the Air Staff and the Deputy Chief of the Air Staff. They were served by a number of Assistant Chiefs of the

Air Staff who were in turn serviced by various Directorates. The lines of responsibility between the Vice- and Deputy Chief were somewhat blurred but it usually fell to the VCAS to deal with questions of strategic planning. Research, advice and the preparation of position papers usually came from the Directorates of Plans and Policy and was channelled through the Assistant Chief of the Air Staff (Policy). The most important civil servants in this advisory process were the Assistant Under-Secretary attached to the Air Staff and the head of its secretariat. This system came under criticism from time to time as having too many tiers and was reformed in 1958 with the post of Assistant Chief of the Air Staff (Policy) being amalgamated with the Assistant Chief of the Air Staff (Operations) and the Directors of Plans and Policy reporting directly to VCAS with a separate Briefing section serving CAS.[44]

Probably the most important weakness in policy terms was highlighted by Sir Arthur Sanders, the DCAS, in 1951. He argued that

> there is a very important aspect of the work of the Air Staff which is not at present covered, i.e. the evolution of really long-term policy for the size, shape and role of the RAF in the period beyond that covered by current plans. ... The pace of scientific discovery is now such that revolutionary changes in weapons, e.g. the atom bomb, or the guided missile, may be introduced in the space of a few years. These weapons will exert a far reaching effect on the whole organisation and structure of the Air Force, and this requires someone who can see the problem as a whole and ensure that timely attention is paid to all its many aspects.[45]

Sanders's ideas were rejected because of the distrust of 'planning cells' without executive responsibility.[46] The Air Staff policy directorates remained mired in practical detail. In addition the possibility that the views of senior officers would be seriously challenged was never allowed to arise.

In terms of strategic policy-making the Air Ministry could be viewed as a unitary actor. Internal debates did take place but once decisions had been taken by either the senior officers of the Air Staff or more formally by the Air Council they were fully accepted as ministry policy to be wholeheartedly worked for - not constantly challenged. Thus it is usually accurate to talk of Air Ministry policy or the Air Staff view and equate them with the position of the RAF even if many of the officers of the service doubted the wisdom of a particular decision. This is in stark contrast to any discussion of British strategy as a whole which often amounts to a historical rationalisation of constantly evolving compromises.

Throughout the 1940s and 1950s the RAF was an important and, on the whole, a skilful bureaucratic player. Its primary concern was with airborne weapons systems. Nuclear strategy was shaped by the fact that a powerful and self-interested organisation served by talented officers, civil servants and, especially in the Conservative administrations, ministers, was charged with developing and elaborating it.

The RAF's commitment to an independent bomber force went back to the inception of the service in 1918. The concept of the bomber as a deterrent to war had played a large part in Air Ministry planning in the 1930s. Yet the 1930s and the experience of wartime Bomber Command did not seem to provide clear pointers to the future. In 1945 Air Ministry certainty about the need for an atomic bomber was matched by uncertainty about its exact role.

Wartime experience had shown that an independent heavy bomber force could operate in a wide range of roles: against cities, naval targets in port, submarine pens, industrial targets and oil targets. Despite failures earlier in the war a large degree of success, at least in terms of destruction, had been achieved against each of these target systems by 1945. Some thought was given to each after the war but it was the central concept of an independent heavy force rather than a specific target system which was of overriding importance.

The atomic bomb had been dropped on two cities and thus could be portrayed as the final form of an 'area' attack, rendering the experience of wartime conventional bombing a matter of only historical interest. As Sir Arthur Harris said of his own report on Bomber Command's wartime operations, delivered in December 1945, 'it may ... be of use to service students for a year or two, and to the Archaeologists thereafter.'[47] Although any lessons to be drawn for the atomic era were certainly not an unproblematical acceptance of a 'Trenchardian' legacy the RAF's commitment to the manned bomber underpinned its development of nuclear doctrine. The concept of the nuclear-armed bomber prefigured any detailed thought about nuclear strategy. Nevertheless, the Air Ministry did play a major role in formulating four propositions about nuclear strategy between 1945 and 1949 which were developed and embroidered in the 1950s in ways which seemed to obviate the need for a fundamental recasting of national strategy.

The first proposition was that nuclear weapons deterred war but that if war did break out between the Soviet Union and an Anglo-American alliance nuclear weapons of all kinds would be used. In the 1950s the Air Staff developed a primitive version of 'mutually assured destruction' arguing that the threat of thermonuclear retaliation would deter even a Soviet Union which had achieved nuclear parity with the West from taking any action which risked a major war. At the same time it rejected any concept of an 'escalatory ladder' on the grounds that it was impossible to predict Soviet wartime decision-making and that any doubts about the willingness of the West to use nuclear weapons would weaken the whole concept of deterrence. This rather Manichaean view of nuclear strategy, it was impossible to have the 'God' of nuclear deterrence without the 'Satan' of potential thermonuclear cataclysm, had an appealing simplicity for the political establishment and remained government policy throughout the 1950s. It enabled both the Air Staff and many politicians to follow their natural inclination of adopting a policy of 'limited liability' in Europe whilst maintaining armed forces around the world.

The second proposition was that a stable alliance with the United States was the most important aim of British nuclear security policy. According to the Air Staff American nuclear weapons would be a deterrent to war whilst Britain developed its own. British nuclear weapons enhanced the chances of Anglo-American security and technical co-operation. British nuclear weapons strengthened and guaranteed America's deterrent posture. Until the mid-1950s it was feared that America would be too ready to employ nuclear weapons and risk the destruction of the United Kingdom. Once America itself became vulnerable to nuclear attack the Air Staff started to argue that there was also a danger of the United States becoming explicitly reluctant to use nuclear weapons in the defence of Europe thus undermining deterrence. The RAF vision of a British nuclear force as a 'trigger' became influential in the late 1950s and reinforced the belief that Britain would remain indispensable to the United States.

The third proposition was that the possession of nuclear weapons inevitably gave a nation great power status and strengthened its foreign policy but that, conversely, the lack of nuclear capability would automatically reduce a nation to insignificance, especially in times of international crisis. This belief was essentially intuitive rather than a formal component of strategy and in the 1950s was accompanied by 'totemistic' attitude to the nuclear force. That Britain should be a 'member of the H-club' was a commonplace of the mid-1950s defence establishment.

The fourth proposition was that the advent of nuclear weapons constituted a revolution in the nature of warfare. The negative side of this strategic revolution was Britain's unique vulnerability, as a small, densely populated island within easy reach of the European mainland, to atomic attack. Whilst Britain's increased vulnerability greatly strengthened the belief in deterrence rather than defence, a view clearly stated by the Air Ministry in 1947, it is possible to overrate the emphasis the RAF laid on finding a military solution to this threat. In the 1950s the positive aspect of the military revolution, offsetting British disadvantages in other fields such a relative lack of economic power and conventional military resources, was more influential. In the 1950s the replacement of conventional with 'tactical' nuclear weapons contributed to the policy of 'limited liability' in Europe already being pursued under the umbrella of the thermonuclear deterrent. The Air Staff also supported a policy of cementing overseas alliances with nuclear forces and deterring and threatening non-nuclear powers outside Europe.

Although it is clear that each of these propositions originated in the 1940s the relative importance and chronological development of each has been a matter of historical controversy. The nuclear-armed bomber has been regarded as a functional military weapons system and as a political symbol, substituting for a decline in imperial power. The latter view was prevalent in the histories of the British nuclear force produced in the 1970s. Andrew Pierre wrote: 'For a nation in the "habit of power" it does not come naturally to recognise diminished status. ... The creation and maintenance of the British nuclear force has been closely intertwined with the nation's self-image and the reduction of her power and influence.'[48] This was a view shared by Margaret Gowing: 'This decision [to design and manufacture atomic weapons] was not the result of careful strategic calculation but rather the reflex action of a still great power with great military commitments. The atomic bomb was the last word in weapons so Britain must have it, the more so since the only defence anyone could see against the enemy's bombs was the threat to retaliate in kind.'[49] More recently this thesis has been challenged by Ian Clark and Nicholas Wheeler who write: 'The idea of a once great power scuttling to hide its imperial nakedness with the fig leaf of the atomic bomb, whatever relevance it might have to the 1950s and beyond, is a wholly inadequate account of British perceptions in 1945.'[50]

This work argues that Clark and Wheeler overstate the importance and coherence of strategic thought about the atomic force in the 1940s, especially in the period between August 1945 and January 1947 when the decisions to build an atomic bomb and the bombers to carry it were actually taken. On the other hand it shows that from 1950 onwards strategic debate played an important role in marshalling and maintaining support for the bomber force. The existence of the bomber force in turn maintained support for Britain's role as a world power. However true Pierre's remarks remain as an historical judgement, contemporaries believed that the bomber force had an important military, as well as a symbolic, role in maintaining British power. At the begining of the 1960s the nuclear force was seen as a key element of Britain's continuing global military role rather than a replacement for it.

Notes

1. Healey, *The Time of My Life*, pp. 237-39; Buchan, 'The Institute for Strategic Studies', pp. 16-17.

2. Taylor, *Against the Bomb*, passim.

3. Ceadel, *Thinking about Peace and War*, pp. 72-3.

4. Wiggershaus and Foerster (eds.), *The Western Security Community*, p. 430.

5. For a review of the problems in the Foreign Office and foreign policy formation see Young (ed.), *The Foreign Policy of Churchill's Peacetime Administration*, pp. 1-29.

6. PWD(45)1st, 24 October 1945, London, Public Record Office (P.R.O.), CAB127/38.

7. Gilbert, *Never Despair*, pp. 707-16; Seldon, *Churchill's Indian Summer*, pp. 295-306.

8.Minute to Prime Minister, 29 Oct. 1955, London, Public Record Office (P.R.O.), PREM11/2352.

9.Sir Walter Monckton to Prime Minister, 9 April 1956 and Sir Walter Monckton to Prime Minister, 12 June 1956, London, Public Record Office (P.R.O.), PREM11/2352.

10. Prime Minister to Minister of Defence, 13 June 1956, London, Public Record Office (P.R.O.), PREM11/2352.

11. 'The Minister of Defence and the Armed Forces' Directive by the Prime Minister, 18 Jan. 1957, London, Public Record Office (P.R.O.), PREM11/2352

12.For a fuller discussion of these issues see Ball, 'Harold Macmillan and the politics of defence', passim.

13. Prime Minister to Sir Norman Brook, 27 Dec. 1957, London, Public Record Office (P.R.O.), PREM11/2352.

14. Unofficial Minutes of Meeting between the Prime Minister and the Chiefs of Staff, 20 June 1957, London, Public Record Office (P.R.O.), PREM11/1179.

15. Sir Richard Powell to the Prime Minister, 14 March 1958, London, Public Record Office (P.R.O.), PREM11/2352.

16. 'Committee on the Post-War Defence Organisation' L.C. Hollis/Norman Brook, 11 Oct. 1945, London, Public Record Office (P.R.O.), CAB127/38.

17. 'The Central Organisation for Defence' Report by the Secretary of the Cabinet, December 1957, London, Public Record Office (P.R.O.), AIR19/679.

18. Sir Norman Brook to Prime Minister, 29 May 1958, London, Public Record Office (P.R.O.), PREM11/2352.

19. Sir Norman Brook to Prime Minister, 14 May 1957, London, Public Record Office (P.R.O.), PREM11/1179 and Prime Minister to Sir Norman Brook, 27 Dec. 1957, London, Public Record Office (P.R.O.), PREM11/2352.

20. Sir Maurice Dean (PUS Air Ministry) to Secretary of State for Air, 7 Oct. 1957, London, Public Record Office (P.R.O.), AIR19/679.

21. Sir Norman Brook to Prime Minister, 30 June 1958, London, Public Record Office (P.R.O.), PREM11/2353.

22. Cmnd. 476 Central Organisation for Defence (July 1958).

23. Macmillan to Sandys, 8 July 1958, London, Public Record Office (P.R.O.), PREM11/2353.

24. Prime Minister to Chancellor of Exchequer, 17 July 1958, London, Public Record Office (P.R.O.), PREM11/2228.

25. DB/C(58)1st Conclusions, 31 July 1958, London, Public Record Office (P.R.O.), DEFE13/154.

26. Useful recent surveys include: Seldon, *Churchill's Indian Summer*, pp. 295-335; Broadbent, *The Military and Government*, pp. 15-27; Dillon (ed.), *Defence*

Policy Making, pp. 9-52; Edmonds (ed.), *Central Organisations for Defense*, pp. 85-107 and Smith, 'Command and control in postwar Britain: defence decision-making in the United Kingdom, 1945-1984'.

27. Ponting, *Breach of Promise*, pp. 40-60, 85-106, 306-9 and Healey, *The Time of My Life*, pp. 249-300.

28. Friedberg, *The Weary Titan*, p. 18.

29. Sir Richard Powell, 'King's Seminar', p. 2.

30. Carver, *Out of Step*, p. 289.

31. Ibid., p. 279.

32. Healey, *The Time of My Life*, pp. 268-9. The head of the PEG, Neil Cameron, nearly had his career blighted by the posting. Subsequently, however, he became Chief of the Air Staff and finally Chief of the Defence Staff.

33. Carver, *Out of Step*, pp. 288-289.

34. Darby, *British Defence Policy East of Suez*, p. 144.

35. Friedberg, *The Weary Titan*, p. 282.

36. Posen, *The Sources of Military Doctrine*, p. 13.

37. Dockrill, *British Defence since 1945*, p. 151.

38. Percentages derived from figures in Kennedy, *The Rise and Fall of the Great Powers*, p. 495.

39. Tedder, *Air Power in War*, pp. 123-4.

40. Slessor, *The Central Blue*, p. 1.

41. Seldon, *Churchill's Indian Summer*, p. 318.

42. Interview with Viscount De L'Isle.

43. Cooper, 'The Origins and Development of the British Strategic Nuclear Deterrent Forces 1945-1960', p. 27.

44. 'Memorandum on Organisation of Air Ministry and RAF Commands, and RAF Methods of Training' Air Ministry, 27 Feb. 1947, London, Public Record Office (P.R.O.), AIR20/7268; Organisation and Manpower Review of Air Staff Organisation, August 1951, London, Public Record Office (P.R.O.), AIR20/7603; Air Ministry Form 1702, December 1957; Sandford Report (1958); Sandford Committee Progress Report, London, Public Record Office (P.R.O.), AIR2/15040.

45. 'Some thoughts on the organisation of the Air Staff' Air Chief Marshal Sir Arthur Sanders, May 1951, London, Public Record Office (P.R.O.), AIR20/7603.

46. DCAS to VCAS, 2 Feb. 1952, London, Public Record Office (P.R.O.), AIR20/7603.

47. Harris to Tedder, 12 Dec. 1947, London, Public Record Office (P.R.O.), AIR2/9726.

48. Pierre, *Nuclear Politics*, p. 67.

49. Gowing, *Independence and Deterrence*, p. 209.

50. Clark and Wheeler, *British Origins of Nuclear Strategy*, p. 40.

2

Air Staff Nuclear Doctrine: 1945-1949

The Air Striking Force and Air Staff Nuclear Doctrine

Two decisions central to British nuclear defence policy were taken in the winter of 1946-7. In January 1947 a small Cabinet committee decided that Britain would design and manufacture atomic bombs. In December 1946 the Air Ministry had issued an operational requirement for advanced jet bombers which would take seven to ten years to develop and bring into service.[1]

The RAF had wanted an advanced long-range bomber three years before the atomic bomb was dropped on Japan.[2] By 1944 the Air Staff had clearly decided on an aircraft which would take a relatively long time to develop, would have a range of about 2500 miles and would be very high flying.[3] Within this framework it responded quickly to the use of atomic bombs against Japan. In August 1945 the Air Staff argued that a bomber with the maximum performance that could be achieved was needed in order to overcome defences much more hostile than Japan's.[4] In September 1945 the Air Staff issued a preliminary requirement to the Ministry of Aircraft Production for a long-range bomber which was to be an 'unarmed, high speed, high altitude aircraft to carry the new weapon'.[5] Even without taking into consideration the exact role of the bomber armed with nuclear weapons it would have taken a huge political defeat to stop the RAF from procuring one.[6]

Nevertheless, in analysing the RAF's response to the atomic bomb it is not enough to speak of its commitment to strategic bombing.[7] There was a tendency to propose a wide range of roles for the bomber in case one was rejected. Not only did the RAF emerge from the war fearing that the heavy bomber's importance to victory in Europe would be disparaged and that the morality of attacks against cities would be questioned[8] but within the Air Ministry there was no clear agreement on doctrine.[9]

The Air Staff did, however, believe, that 'it [is] difficult to imagine ... a permanent situation in which deep penetration bombing attacks will be too costly to maintain over a long period'.[10] In the long term warfare would be revolutionised by the atomic bomb, especially when it could be mounted on a missile. As Sir John Slessor observed:

> Whether this will render warfare itself as obsolete as the duel without first destroying civilisation, is clearly the most vital question in the world ... which we ... must solve satisfactorily or perish. If our cities could be attacked by this weapon without any defence or risk of sufficiently immediate retaliation, we would be wasting our breath discussing other means of warfare.[11]

The Air Staff produced its first full assessment of the relationship between the RAF and nuclear weapons in December 1945. Looking forward to 1955, it concluded that atomic weapons would be used in any major war despite moral objections. It argued that Britain should pursue a deterrent strategy. Deterrence was understood to mean that atomic weapons could deter war. The Air Staff argued that once a major war had broken out both sides would resort to atomic weapons since they both multiplied the power of air attack and increased the vulnerability of countries to it. Since no solution to defence against atomic air attack was foreseen an Air Striking Force was proposed as the best deterrent to war. The Air Staff paper clearly identified the Soviet Union as the enemy and pointed out that it was less susceptible to atomic attack than the United Kingdom because it lacked high densities of vulnerable areas. It argued, therefore, that the size of the bomber force had to be calculated on the basis of its ability to cripple the enemy not on parity between Soviet and British capabilities. The Air Staff also believed that in a major war Britain would be devastated; the only solution it offered was a system of imperial defence which did not rely on the United Kingdom as the main base.[12]

The development of strategic thinking in the RAF during 1945-6 simply confirmed existing policy: that the possession of a large, modern bomber force was vital. This had been a major part of the service's planning for the post-war period and the advent of atomic weapons did not challenge it. The exact role of the bomber in the nuclear age was a matter of more doubt although there was a clear realisation that the atomic bomb had revolutionised warfare and that future policy could not be wholly dictated by wartime experience.

The Air Staff argued that deterrence would be achieved by threatening Russian cities. Although it acknowledged that wartime experience had demonstrated the enormous effort needed to destroy a city and the difficulty of disrupting industry in urban areas it argued that attacks on other target systems would not necessarily lead to a decisive result. In the meantime defeat could be forced on the much more vulnerable United Kingdom by a nuclear armed Soviet Union. In the light of this analysis it concluded that:

> Attacks must therefore be directed against objectives whose destruction will lower enemy morale, reduce their industrial capacity, and dislocate a large part of the centralised administrative machinery of the country. The only objectives that fulfil these requirements are large cities, and it is our considered opinion that our only chance of securing a quick decision is by launching a devastating attack upon them with absolute weapons.[13]

Although it espoused deterrence as early as 1945, until 1947 the Air Staff was equally concerned with the maintenance of defensive forces. Air Staff reactions to the first concerted attempt to work out a nuclear policy, the revision of the Tizard Report by the Joint Technical Warfare Committee which was approved by the Cabinet Defence Committee in July 1946,[14] showed its cautious attitude towards the atomic bomb. The Air Staff agreed with the proposition that the next war could be of very short duration and argued that it certainly would be if 'our air defence and our deterrent striking force is not fully developed, deployed and effective right from the beginning'. Yet although the Air Staff assumed that it was Russian cities, and specifically the morale of its citizens, which would be targeted it actually doubted the efficacy of this policy. The Air Staff regarded any estimate of the number of atomic bombs needed to bring about the collapse of Russia as purely speculative. It pointed out that conventional attacks on German cities had been ineffective, despite being concentrated, because the German authorities were able to isolate affected areas. Such isolation was harder under atomic attack which, it was assumed, would lead to wholesale chaos and attempts at evacuation but the Air Staff believed that Russia's size might allow the government to isolate the knowledge of the effects of attack.[15] Some senior RAF officers worried that the Russians were already making preparations against atomic attack in the form of vast underground shelters and enormous schemes for the dispersion of industry thus making it dangerous to assume any war would be short.[16]

In the summer of 1947, however, the RAF set out radical new proposals for Britain's defence posture. Initial caution about the role of nuclear weapons was abandoned because of a recognition of a weakness in the RAF's existing position. By 1947 the British government was under great pressure to reduce the defence budget. The Air Staff realised that Chiefs of Staff plans called for resources of manpower and money which were not likely to available in forthcoming years. The RAF was contributing relatively little to immediate peacetime requirements and the other services, especially the Army, were seen as having a better chance of getting short-term programmes accepted. The Air Staff believed it would need strong arguments about the nature of future war to prevent politicians forcing 'arbitrary' cuts on the RAF.[17]

The Air Staff developed the case that the primary aim of British defence policy, both in the short- and long-term, should be to deter war. The most important task was to achieve a close alliance with the United States, without whom it would be impossible to win any war. Within that context British forces should also be reorganised to provide a deterrent to war. In the long-term defence policy would have to reconcile a deterrent against aggression with the nature of Britain's post-war commitments. In the short-term defensive forces would have to drastically cut since they were unlikely to deter an enemy. Britain would have to gamble on preventing war as the best means of defence. The Air Staff acknowledged that such decisions were painful but argued that 'if we are to pursue our course as a first class power, we must maintain our forces in a form likely to deter any potential aggressor. This can only be done by accepting grave risks and drastically reducing elements of our defence forces which we can ill afford to do without.'[18]

The Air Staff presented the case to the Chiefs of Staff that for the next fifteen years the bomber force would be the best deterrent to war. The 1946 target had been for 960 front-line bombers. This was reduced to 528. All the cut was to fall on long-range bombers and it was now proposed that 48 would be acquired from America as a specialised nucleus of the force for attacks on a few specialised targets. The bulk of the force would remain 480 medium-range bombers capable of reaching most targets with atomic weapons.[19] The exact purpose of this force remained unclear. In the paper submitted to the Chiefs of Staff it was described as 'firstly, calculated to constitute the most powerful deterrent to any potential aggressor, and, secondly, to give us the best chance of survival if war comes, by hitting the enemy the hardest where it hurts most.' These were not very precise formulations and one suspects they were not meant to be. The Air Ministry was providing proposals for both the 1948/9 Defence Estimates and for a 1957 target force. The aim was not only to argue for the primacy of the atomic jet bomber force but for the role of Bomber Command as part of an 'effective deterrent' in the interim.[20]

These considerations lay at the root of a further RAF attempt, in December 1947, to force planning to concentrate on forces nine to twelve years in the future. The Air Staff argued that two overriding factors governed defence policy. First, the possibility that by 1957 Russia would have sufficient atomic and biological weaponry to wage absolute war on a large scale. Second, Britain's economic difficulties meant that for the next ten years defence expenditure 'must be very severely limited if we are to survive as a first class power'. Given the destructive nature of all-out atomic and biological war, which could destroy Britain in a matter of days, and Russia's ability to wage it by 1957 priority had to be given to war prevention rather than war fighting. Since the Soviet Union was deemed to be unlikely to consider war without the possession of enough weapons of mass destruction to destroy Britain it was pointless to plan to fight a nuclear war in the short-term. In the interim Britain would have to rely on American atomic power and any conventional forces the United Kingdom could deploy. Of paramount importance, therefore, was a bomber force armed with atomic bombs as the main deterrent and the 'principal offensive defence if war comes'.[21]

The development of thinking by the RAF about the bomber force and nuclear weapons in 1947 was significant. It raised nuclear deterrence of the Soviet Union by a British nuclear force above all other defence priorities. The short-term aim of the campaign was achieved. The case made by the RAF proved influential with ministers.[22]

Within the Air Staff the bomber force was elevated from a very important part of the RAF to having paramount importance to the service, rhetorically if not yet in terms of resource allocation; it took three or four years for the logic of these arguments to work through into all areas of Air Staff planning.

Policies developed in 1947 have been seen as having further importance for the development of nuclear strategy. The words 'offensive defence' used by the Vice-Chief of the Air Staff, Sir William Dickson, have been interpreted by Ian Clark and Nicholas Wheeler as evidence of the evolution of a doctrine of damage limitation within the RAF.[23] Yet there is little evidence that clarity of thought lay behind such vague phrases. At the beginning of the year the planners had suggested that the obliteration of Soviet cities was the quickest method of stopping a war; a means of 'offensive defence'. Discussions of counter-military targeting are usually found as rhetorical points in the disputes over the allocation of the defence budget.

In February 1949, for instance, the Harwood Report proposed a 208 aircraft Medium Bomber Force.[24] The Air Ministry's alternative proposal was for 320 strategic bombers. It argued that, although traditional Soviet air strategy had concentrated on a large tactical air force supporting the army, by 1957 the Soviet Union would have developed a long-range bomber force capable of mounting a major air war over Europe and attacking the United Kingdom with nuclear and conventional weapons. In these circumstances the only initially effective attack would be the strategic air offensive against Russia, mainly carried out by the USAF. To ensure that this offensive would be immediate and effective the RAF would aim for a small technically superior force to complement the USAF. The possible uses of this force were cited as: attacks on enemy territory, operations in defence of the United Kingdom and operations against threats to sea communications. It was clearly stated that a 320 strong Medium Bomber Force would be unable to attack all these targets simultaneously.[25]

The Air Ministry's decision to argue for a smaller more specialised force did not lead them to a counterforce solution. The Air Staff believed that it would be impossible to beat off a conventional land/air offensive in Europe and the Middle East whilst trying to defend against Soviet strategic bombers as their bases moved ever closer. In this situation:

> The only hope of the Allies is to bring about the collapse of the Russian war making machine, by means of a bomber offensive. This bomber offensive can only be effective if its bases in the UK and the Middle East are secure. Essential parts of the defence of these bases are (a) the long range offensive itself, which obliges the enemy to divert a substantial part of his resources to defence, and (b) the medium range offensive against the communications, etc. that he is using in his land campaigns.[26]

'Offensive Defence' simply meant that the scale of the attack on the United Kingdom would be reduced because the Russians would divert so much of their effort towards homeland defence. The Air Ministry also claimed that the United States could not guarantee an effective offensive. According to the Air Staff it was too much to take on trust that at all times the United States would be able to provide a bomber effective against Russian defences. The British role in a joint offensive could be to make sure it succeeded.[27]

The strategic reasoning behind the bomber force was a reaction to an awareness of its vulnerability in the defence programme. In 1947 this had led the Air Staff to argue that the bomber as deterrent was of paramount importance to British strategy. In its arguments thereafter it continued to imply that the main attack would be on Russian cities but that the deterrent effect would be strengthened if it was shown that an easy victory could be denied. Counter-military targeting was therefore cited as a desirable second role for the bomber force but this could take the form of support for land forces. In 1949 it had not turned into a counterforce mission in the sense of nuclear attack on Soviet strategic bomber bases in an attempt to limit the damage of a nuclear attacks against Britain.[28] This strategy was developed between 1950 and 1952 under the leadership of Sir John Slessor and refined during the defence debates of 1953-7 by his successors.

The difference in dating the adoption of counterforce targeting is important since it demonstrates that the official RAF line on the strategic bomber force was as much political as military. Not only was it designed to demonstrate that Britain needed advanced jet bombers as a deterrent but also to protect the existing Bomber Command from being virtually wound-up.[29] This latter objective may well have rested on fears that if Bomber Command came to be made up of Canberra light bombers in the early 1950s its strategic role would be challenged. Sir Henry Tizard was already waging a vigorous campaign within the defence establishment against Britain's pretensions as an independent atomic power[30] and Aidan Crawley, the Under-Secretary of State for Air, was publicly suggesting that Britain should leave the strategic bombing role to the United States[31]

Even within the RAF there were doubts about the prominence being given to the bomber force because of the way it dominated resources.[32] The most formidable RAF critic of Air Staff policy was Sir John Slessor. He called for particular attention to targeting Soviet submarine pens,[33] criticised the acquisition of B-29s, the retention of a sizable Lincoln force and the concentration on the use of the bomber as part of the land battle. Nevertheless, Slessor was in complete agreement with Lord Tedder about the need for a jet bomber force to complement that of the USAF. Tedder felt that 'the argument about leaving the bombing to the Americans ... has been one of the most dangerous developments. If we deprive ourselves of an air striking force we are not merely ... relegating ourselves to being a second class power, but writing ourselves off completely as a power.'[34] Slessor proposed that Britain should plan a force to carry the A-bomb against Russia, plan a complementary offensive in Europe on the 'Overlord' pattern and try to get co-operation with the USAF in order to wean them away from long-distance 'stunt flights'.[35] His ambitions for the British atomic force were actually fairly modest. 'And when we come to a true Strategic bomber-Atom force then about 150 is formidable'.[36] This was not a force for an extensive counter-military campaign. Although Slessor had shown a public interest in counter-military targeting this should be understood in the context of his belief that Royal Navy plans for securing sea communications with carrier based air power were a misguided use of resources.[37]

Slessor like Tedder had a fundamental belief that possession of a nuclear bomber force was essential to Britain's status as a great power. In 1949 there were seemingly dangerous critics of that force both inside and outside the defence establishment. As well as developing his own thoughts on strategy Slessor was attempting to construct a role for the bomber which would be politically attractive. A damage limitation role through attacks on Soviet nuclear forces, the existence of which became much more immediately threatening with the detonation of the Russian A-bomb in August 1949, fulfilled this criterion.

RAF-USAF Nuclear Relations

The response of British policy-makers to nuclear weapons worked on two levels during the the 1940s. The decision to become a nuclear weapons power looked necessarily to the long-term. It was clear to military planners that for some years the United States would be the only power with nuclear weapons and their means of delivery. Even after Britain and the Soviet Union developed their own weapons America would remain the dominant nuclear power. Yet in 1945-6 Britain was faced with a breakdown of Anglo-American nuclear relations symbolised by the passing of the McMahon Act. Since the way forward in co-ordinated inter-governmental relations was blocked residual bilateral relations such as those which existed between the RAF and the USAAF took on an increased importance.

During the war there had been informal contacts about post-war American involvement in Europe and the Middle East[38] and the RAF became convinced that the USAAF desired a major presence in post-war Europe. Indeed United States thinking *was* in the process of change and overseas base plans began to be recast in spring 1945.[39] Such contacts were important since at this time the RAF was uncertain about American aims.[40] Although it hoped for a post-war alliance no clear information on American plans was available.[41] This dearth was rectified to some extent when General Carl Spaatz took over as head of the USAAF. In June 1946 Spaatz visited England and held talks with Tedder on the 25-8 June and 4-6 July. An informal agreement was reached that the RAF would prepare four or five bases in East Anglia by mid-1947 for American use in time of emergency.[42] The RAF also promised co-operation in preparing at least two of these bases for atomic operations. In August 1946 Colonel E. E. Kirkpatrick of the Manhattan Project arrived in England with personal instructions from Spaatz to supervise the construction of support facilities for 'Fat Man' type atomic bombs.[43] It seems that such facilities together with four heavy bomber airfields were available in the United Kingdom by mid-1947 the British government, citing the belief of a Foreign Office official that Attlee was unaware.[44]

Simon Duke has suggested that the importance of the Spaatz-Tedder agreement was probably kept from ministers. He cites the observation of a Foreign Office official that Attlee was ignorant of the arrangements to support his view.[45] The actual deployment of B-29s in Britain at the time of the Berlin Crisis does not altogether bear this belief out.[46] As the crisis was building up the JCS were meeting with British representatives to discuss plans for the deployment of bombers in the event of war. Tentative agreement had been reached in early April.[47] On the day the airlift began, 26 June 1948, Bevin met the American Ambassador, Lewis Douglas, and a proposal to deploy B-29 squadrons in the United Kingdom was discussed. The Minister of Defence and the Secretary of State for Air were consulted on the same day.[48] On the 27th Bevin wrote to Douglas approving the plan and calling for immediate co-operation to work out the administrative details.[49] Lord Bullock, Bevin's biographer, puts the granting of landing rights on the 28th and notes that the decision was formally taken by the Berlin Committee of the Cabinet which in effect meant Bevin and Attlee.[50] Certainly the Secretary of State for Air, Arthur Henderson, was left trailing in the wake of events and it was not until the end of August that he plaintively suggested the matter should be put to the Cabinet.[51] Bevin delivered a short report to the Defence Committee on 13 September.[52]

The Foreign Office report of the Bevin/Douglas discussions gives the impression that both sides understood that they were discussing long-term deployment.[53] The picture in 1948 is of a policy run by Bevin and Attlee and the speed of policy making suggests that they did not start completely from scratch. The most useful question to ask, however, is how could the Spaatz-Tedder agreement, which was known to so few individuals, have had an important effect on British defence policy between July 1946 and July 1948? It was obviously impossible for it to have an overt impact on British policy debates. Nevertheless, the awareness of a few vital decision-makers that Britain was a key area in American plans and the realistic hope that a threat to the United Kingdom would be met by the deployment of nuclear armed bombers is important to an understanding of British planning. The British certainly overestimated American atomic capability but so too did American planners.[54] No 'Silverplate' B-29s were deployed in the United Kingdom until the summer of 1949[55] and no bombs arrived until at least 1952.[56]

The possibility of relying on American nuclear capability to protect British interests was seemingly strengthened by the 1947 'Pentagon' talks called by Bevin to secretly discuss the extent to which the United States would support British economic, cultural and strategic interests in the Mediterranean and Middle East. These talks took place between 16 October and 7 November 1947 and were preceded by informal military discussions.[57]

Whilst in Washington RAF representatives held detailed talks with senior USAF officers and the Air Planning Staff.[58] Initially it seemed that American planning would give little encouragement to reliance on atomic weapons in Europe and the Middle East. The American side was much exercised by the danger of air attack on the continental USA.

Operations from Soviet North-East Asia against the Pacific seaboard were viewed as a long-term threat.[59] Accordingly, the USAF felt that a large proportion of its effort would go on air defence and that the British could not expect American resources to be diverted to bomber operations from the United Kingdom and Near East.

The USAF was very interested in the trans-polar route for offensive strategic air operations using Alaska as a base. It hoped to send bombers to operate from Britain and the Middle East but pointed out that forces would be limited and certainly not enough to justify cuts in British bomber plans. Indeed it indicated that if detailed Anglo-American planning took place it would press for the British to put more effort into heavy bombers.

There were vague discussions about nuclear targeting from which the RAF drew the conclusion that the USAF did not feel altogether justified in planning to use the A-bomb since supply was nowhere near enough to meet needs, it was considered unsuitable for many targets, there was a reluctance to attack the civilian population and doubts about the effectiveness of attacks on civilian areas (i.e. cities). The USAF's preference was for attacks on oil and transportation targets.

Many of these points were not attractive to the RAF. Emphasis on the trans-polar route, Alaska and the Pacific seaboard diverted attention away from areas the British were interested in. The USAF seemed unsure about the role of the A-bomb. Even support for a British heavy bomber force was of limited comfort since the issue of advanced jet bomber specifications in December 1946 ruled out any short-term British capability.

Nevertheless, the eventual outcome of the talks produced strong support for the RAF view of strategy. This outcome must be understood in the context of changing United States policy during 1947 which gave the United Kingdom and the Middle East a greatly enhanced role. Although a Short Range Emergency War Plan with an atomic air offensive from England and the Khartoum-Cairo-Suez area was not approved by the JCS until May 1948 the USAF was ahead of formal planning in the importance it attached to North Africa. At the end of October 1947, whilst talks with the British were in progress, Secretary of the Air Force Symington told its Vice-Chief of Staff, Hoyt Vandenberg, that work should begin immediately to establish a base in Africa. The USAF began preparing to reopen Wheelus Field, Tripoli. In December 1947 the British were formally asked to agree to continued use of this air base. At an important meeting in January 1948 between the Secretary of Defense, James Forrestal, Symington, Spaatz and Vandenberg it was agreed that decisive air action over the polar ice cap was not practical and that the USAF's objective should be to become established in North Africa and then look for bases closer to the USSR. General Al Gruenther also made it clear to Forrestal that the military regarded air bases in North Africa as too narrow an aim and would be looking for further airfields around the East Mediterranean and Middle East.[60]

Thus in October 1947 the USAF was encouraging about the idea of strategic bomber bases in the United Kingdom and Middle East and wanted the RAF to provide the necessary facilities, although they believed Cyrenaica to be a reasonable substitute for Egypt. Its greatest interest was in the development of Cyprus since it wished to block access to the Iran/Iraq oilfields by air attack on the Baku-Tiflis-North Iran area.[61]

Reliance on the United States became much more overt from July/August 1948 when three groups of B-29s arrived in Britain to occupy the airfields prepared for them by the RAF.[62] It was clear from the outset that such deployments would be a long-term factor in British defence planning. In September 1948 Tedder held discussions with USAF General Norstad who stated that the USAF wished to keep at least one B-29 group and one fighter group in the United Kingdom irrespective of emergency.[63] Indeed the RAF and the USAF agreed to expand the available facilities. As early as May 1947 the USAAF had identified four airfields, beyond those in East Anglia covered by the Spaatz/Tedder agreement, suitable for conversion for heavy bomber operations.[64] In October 1948, probably as a result of the talks with Norstad, the Air Ministry stated that four extra bases would be granted to the USAF in Oxfordshire because the East Anglian bases, which were to be turned over to fighter operations, were too exposed to attack.[65] In the spring of 1949 the JCS conducted a major review of overseas base requirements. As 'a matter of urgency' they asked for the right to supplement the British effort to improve bomber bases at Abu Sueir in the Canal Zone, Khomaskar in Aden and four bases in Oxfordshire. In April 1949 the National Security Council urged the President to approve funding negotiations with the British.[66] On 11 May Truman told the State Department to start negotiations and two days later the bases were approved in principle by the Cabinet Defence Committee if the United States funded them.[67]

Overt and increased reliance on the American atomic deterrent brought to the fore the inherent tensions in British policy. Strategic thinking had to balance the important role of the United States with Britain's desire to keep its independence of military action. These two aims were bound to be difficult to reconcile when even individual officers combined a desire to see a greater American role in the defence of Britain with doubts that the American strategy was working in Britain's best interests. In addition tensions were heightened by quarrels over the funding of American bases in Britain as both the RAF and the USAF became embroiled in domestic budgetary battles.[68]

The conflict between the desire for independence and the desire for co-operation is best illustrated by the acquisition of B-29 bombers for the RAF. The decision to introduce these aircraft into Bomber Command must be understood in the context of RAF commitment to an independent atomic bomber force, fears about political support for such a force, differences of opinion within the RAF about the role of the bomber and unease about American policy. In late 1948 the Air Staff became interested in obtaining 'lend-lease' B-29s. The senior RAF representative in the United States was instructed to approach the USAF and put forward the case that a gift of B-29s would both increase the striking power of the RAF and the size of the B-29 force available at short notice to operate from the United Kingdom and Middle East. Tedder specifically instructed that the USAF's chief of staff, General Hoyt Vandenberg, should be promised that Bomber Command would come under Strategic Air Command orders as soon as war broke out.[69]

Vandenberg soon replied that any British approach to the United States government would receive the full and wholehearted support of the USAF.[70] The deal was hurried through and approved by the Defence Committee in February 1949.[71] Even though the 70 B-29s were a gift the difficulty and cost of operating them meant there was more to their acquisition than an improved conventional bombing capability. There were two main reasons for their procurement. In order to maintain the front-line of Bomber Command, as the Air Staff considered desirable in 1948-9, the RAF would have had either to retain some Lancaster squadrons, expand Lincoln production or accept a Command largely made up of two-engined bombers. None of these options was appealing.[72] More important, as Tedder admitted, was the hope of acquiring an aircraft which could drop an A-bomb on Russia.[73] It seems that, however crudely, the Air Staff hoped to form an independent nuclear force. When Slessor became CAS he was told that with 60 operational B-29s 'we should have enough to put into the air a force capable of delivering an independent atomic bomb attack rather than it should be amalgamated with a USAF force for the purpose.'[74] Slessor thought the whole idea was fairly pointless and only acquiesced to it because he felt the deal with the Americans had gone too far to stop.[75] As the C-in-C Bomber Command in 1950 has recalled there was no serious attempt to form a nuclear force with the B-29s. 'We spent a great deal of time talking about it, but we never did anything practical about it. We just nattered'.[76]

Even though initial ideas about making the aircraft nuclear capable never came to fruition, as the carriers of the A-bombs dropped on Hiroshima and Nagasaki these aircraft were highly symbolic at a time when voices in the government were raised against an independent bomber force. In October 1948 Sir Stafford Cripps, the Chancellor of the

Exchequer, had told James Forrestal that Britain should place reliance on the development of fighters for its own security whilst serving as the main base for the deployment of American air power.[77] The Under-Secretary of State for Air, Aidan Crawley, claimed publicly in newspaper articles that it would be better to leave the development of strategic bombing to the Americans.[78]

There were also disagreements within the RAF. Sir John Slessor, the CAS-designate, opposed the B-29 acquisition.[79] Tedder's response to Slessor's criticism made quite clear the problems for British policy-making.

> is it wise or indeed safe to rely on the Americans, who are concentrating on the technique of A-bombing vital to targets at long range, to intervene in operations in Germany or other areas calculated to help the land campaign to defend the UK? Knowing how reluctant they were to "divert" the Eighth Air Force from its "strategic" task to help "Overlord" directly, I think we would be writing a cheque on the American Air Force which would almost certainly be R.D.'d. Secondly, are we satisfied that their new types of bombers are suitable for the role envisaged for the RAF bomber force? In order to meet the US Navy's argument about carrier borne A-bombers the USAF have gone for enormous aircraft which in theory could operate from the Western Hemisphere. There will be relatively few of them (because even the Americans have limits to their pockets). There will be few, if any, airfields in this country from which they can operate and are we satisfied that they are likely to penetrate against effective defences.[80]

Tedder was having doubts about American policy at the same time as he was offering to subordinate Bomber Command to SAC. At the ABC (American-British-Canadian) Planners conference held in Washington during September 1949 an effort was made to deal with some of these problems. A detailed plan for large scale conventional and atomic USAF operations out of the United Kingdom was drawn up and codenamed 'Offtackle' by the Americans and 'Galloper' by the British. This plan added a new objective in addition to attacks on Russian war making capacity: the retardation of Russian advances in Western Europe.[81] The British remained ambivalent about American intentions and the next two years saw a sustained effort to tie British and American nuclear planning more firmly together.

The nature of Anglo-American nuclear relations as they were to develop in the 1950s was determined by the events of the immediate post-war period. British military planners came to believe that the United States could be relied on as a firm ally particularly in providing, on Britain's behalf, a nuclear deterrent against major Soviet aggression in Europe. Twinned with this belief was the recognition that American strategy was largely determined by debate in the United States and that it would often not accord with British interests. Britain should therefore pursue a defence policy which ensured that it would remain a powerful military ally armed, as quickly as possible, with nuclear weapons. The ideal to be aimed at was a re-emergence of the wartime alliance. Progress in this direction seemed possible when relations were modified by the outbreak of the Korean War in 1950 and the ensuing militarisation of NATO. Despite a much greater emphasis on Europe, however, the heart of the RAF-USAF relationship remained bilateral and air atomic. In the long-term the RAF saw the militarisation of NATO leading to the nuclearisation of NATO strategy and ensuing nuclear co-operation.

Nuclear Weapons and the Continental Commitment

The long-term goal of a British nuclear bomber force and the interim reliance on American nuclear weapons seemingly validated the preference of the British Chiefs of Staff for pursuing a policy of 'limited liability' rather than a full continental commitment in Europe. In 1949-50 the decision to commit large conventional forces to the European continent was taken for political reasons against the balance of military advice. The Air Staff was never convinced that this decision was militarily correct and looked to nuclear weapons to reverse it.

It was a recurring dilemma of British strategy whether to concentrate defence resources on the Empire, relying on naval superiority to keep Britain itself secure, or whether to commit land forces to the European continent in order to ensure that it never came under the dominance of a hostile power. In 1945 British military planners had to decide how far Britain should be committed to the military defence of Europe in an age of nuclear airpower rather than pursuing their preferred goal of keeping the maximum military force available for the defence of the Empire. According to Michael Dillon: 'Britain's continental commitment became dominant because it was the one most directly concerned with the physical protection of the British Isles against a novel strategic danger.'[82] However true this judgement may be of the whole post-war period it took over twenty years for British policy-makers to draw such a conclusion. In 1946 the RAF's position was that Britain did not need a continental army, that the Soviet Union would be deterred from military aggression by nuclear weapons and that if war did break out it was bound to be nuclear. In 1960 its position was essentially the same.

These attitudes can be explained by the contempt in which the fighting abilities of the continentals were held, attachment to the idea of empire and, in the RAF's case, the fear of becoming an army support force in Europe at the risk of losing its own independence. Yet none of these factors seems a sufficient explanation for the lack of any serious thought about a military strategy based around large conventional forces in Europe. The most convincing explanation is that the RAF and many others in the defence establishment believed in the twin propositions that nuclear deterrence would work and that if war did break out between two blocs each possessing nuclear weapons it was inconceivable that they would not be used. The debate about Britain's long-term military role on the European continent got under way in late 1947 when economic weakness had already forced Britain to put greater emphasis on a policy of nuclear deterrence.

The role of the air force as an occupation force in Germany did not reflect changing perceptions of the Soviet threat in 1946-7 but neither did the RAF see the further commitment of military forces to the continent as the correct response to any threat.[83] It was written into the Joint Planners study of the continental commitment in 1946 that an expeditionary force to Europe was impossible and that if attacked British forces should be quickly withdrawn.[84]

In only one area, that of air defence, did the RAF feel it necessary to explore military arrangements with continental countries.[85] Despite agreement in early 1948 that the French, Dutch and Belgian air defence systems would be patterned on Britain's and complementary to it and the existence of the Dunkirk Treaty the RAF were worried lest these arrangements might commit the British government unintentionally to continental defence.[86] Tedder, Attlee and Alexander agreed that the British government need only take note of these conversations and not initiate any action. Their main concern was that any Anglo-French defence co-operation might complicate the 1948 Pentagon talks about the formation of an Atlantic alliance.[87] The concept of an integrated air defence for Europe was rejected by Britain on the grounds that the continental fighter forces would be negligible and the result would be the loss of defence for the United Kingdom to bolster the defence of Europe.[88]

As far as the RAF was concerned the military options for the defence of Europe were concentrated on American airpower and in the summer of 1948 the British were in discussion with the American military about a strategy for Europe which virtually ignored continental defence.[89] This position was not, however, unchallenged within the Chiefs of Staff. In December 1947 the chiefs had been warned of Bevin's discussions with Marshall about some kind of security system in Europe and asked to consider the role of the continental commitment.[90] This sparked off a vigorous debate between January and May 1948 since Montgomery pushed strongly for such a commitment. His paper presented to the Chiefs of Staff on 2 February 1948 stated: 'The political difficulties of forming the Western Union and ensuring that the countries concerned present a united front from the outset, will be considerable. ... Our aim must be to build up a Union which has the necessary economic and military strength in the initial stage. ... There is only one hope of achieving this object. We must agree that, if attacked, the nations of the Western Union will hold this attack as far East as possible e.g. on the Rhine. We must make it very clear that Britain will play her full part in this strategy and will support the battle on the Rhine'.[91]

Tedder and the First Sea Lord, Sir John Cunningham, strongly opposed Montgomery's ideas and advocated that Britain should rely on a strategy based on maritime and nuclear air power for her security. At a meeting with Attlee, Bevin and A. V. Alexander on 4 February 'the Prime Minister ... weighed in very strongly against a commitment to send our Army to the Continent, but he was counter-attacked by the Foreign Secretary and Minister of Defence, both of whom ... supported the CIGS's view.'[92] Yet even Montgomery, who believed that the Western Union should raise 45 to 50 divisions for its own defence was looking ultimately to the United States; in the first instance to abandon its plans to withdraw existing forces in the event of war and eventually to appoint a Supreme Commander.[93] The result of Montgomery's advocacy was a decision to draw up plans for British forces to fight in Europe,[94] but these new plans did not amount to a real change in policy.[95]

It was clear that British strategy would create political problems in the wake of the Pentagon talks, Truman's election victory and the agreement of a draft North Atlantic Treaty by the Brussels Powers in November 1948.[96] The new CIGS, Field Marshal Slim, insisted that the Chiefs of Staff would have to make some fundamental decisions over the continental commitment. Yet Slim was far from being a continentalist, he was primarily concerned with the political problems being caused by British duplicity and confusion over their own strategy. At the heart of his case was the belief that Western Europe was incapable of resistance to Russia. He argued that it would take several years for a viable military force to take shape even with American assistance. Unless American divisions were stationed in Europe there was no chance of holding the Rhine and he believed 'the prospect of American forces being forthcoming is so remote that it can be discounted.' France would be quickly overrun and the allies forced beyond the Pyrenees. Until the Western Union could produce sufficient forces to hold the Rhine, 50 to 70 divisions and 4000 tactical aircraft, any further British commitment would endanger the safety of the United Kingdom and the Middle East and would in any case be militarily ineffective. At the same time it was essential to maintain the morale of France and the Benelux countries and this would not be possible if they thought they were going to be abandoned. Slim's solution was to stress the idea that possession of the atomic bomb by the United States made war very unlikely and to provide training and equipment for continental forces.[97] The Chiefs of Staff agreed that a paper based on Slim's ideas should be presented to the Cabinet.[98]

By the end of 1948 no significant change in British strategy towards Europe had taken place. Although the Chiefs of Staff were aware of the political importance of the Western Union they did not believe that the commitment of British forces to the continent was desirable. There was a predictable disagreement between the Army and the RAF over the size and shape of the armed forces based on traditional service belief and interest, the Army favouring large land forces the RAF a strategic bomber force. The possibility of German rearmament had been aired but was regarded with extreme caution. Above all the emphasis was on the futility of any attempt to defend Europe without American land forces which, unlike an American heavy bomber force, were not regarded as likely to be forthcoming. The need to maintain the continental will to resist the Soviet Union was acknowledged but only produced cosmetic changes in strategy. The really important factor was the role of the United States. There was no military constituency of support for a European commitment.

In January 1949 Montgomery recommended to the chiefs that a firm commitment should be given to the Western Union to reinforce BAOR with one brigade group in the event of war. His case was that the continental countries were only impressed by land force commitments. Unless support was given their will to defend themselves would be irreparably impaired. Although a brigade group had little military value it was a vital token of willingness to be involved in the defence of Europe. The Chiefs of Staff expressed strong reservations about Montgomery's arguments but reluctantly accepted his political analysis.[99] They proposed to ministers that the brigade group commitment should be made and that decision should be taken about the long-term consequences for British strategy on the Western Union.[100] The Defence Committee rejected the brigade group proposal as a fruitless gesture.[101]

Field Marshal Slim concluded that, on military grounds, there was little justification for sending British land forces to Europe and that they would be of more use in the Middle East.[102] He had however been convinced that such a stance was no longer politically sustainable. He proposed that Britain should offer the deployment of two divisions and a tactical air force within three months of the outbreak of war.[103] In May 1949 he forced the issue and insisted that Britain had to make a choice. It could either commit itself to a long-term policy of contributions to the Western Union with the aim of matching Russia militarily on the Rhine or it could concentrate on the Cold War and, whilst agreeing to some long-term force goals, fail to promise any reinforcements for Europe. In Slim's eyes the first option amounted to a full blown continental commitment, the second risked the collapse of the Western Union. He felt ministers should be faced with these options and forced to make a clear decision.[104]

Tedder agreed that the commitment to Europe was the central question for British strategy and that any major change would affect Britain's worldwide position. He argued that the Western Union countries failed to understand the importance of the Middle East and that nothing should be done to endanger the threefold strategy of defending the United Kingdom, the Middle East and sea communications. He acknowledged that if the Western Union was in danger of collapse Britain would have to consider a larger contribution but he doubted that Britain's refusal to do so would have any such effect. Tedder made clear that the most important factor governing British strategy would be the policy adopted by the United States.[105] He pointed out that forces already in Europe had a necessary occupation role. If extra forces were sent it would be impossible to limit further commitments. Britain would therefore be locked into a continental campaign and this would undermine her position as a global power. He pointed out that it was difficult to predict the course of military operations in Europe. He envisaged a scenario in which the Soviet Union would act like Germany in 1939 and stand on the defensive in the West for several months. Forces would then be tied up in Europe whilst the Soviet Union took over the Middle East. He further argued that it was wrong for the chiefs to be influenced by the French who, he believed, did not understand that the Commonwealth had a vital role in global strategy and were out of touch with modern warfare; concentrating completely on land forces rather than air and sea. He ended by claiming that twice in the century the continental strategy had led to defeat and that if Britain committed forces a third time their loss could incapacitate the defence of the United Kingdom.[106]

The chiefs agreed that a presentation should be made to ministers making clear that any increased contribution to the Western Union would prejudice Britain's position in the Middle East.[107] Their submission to the Defence Committee in June 1949 made three main points: the defence of the Western Union was impracticable without American involvement; reinforcements for Europe would risk the security of the Middle East; and the position of the European allies was that a lack of contributions would be disastrous to the will to resist communism. The chiefs stated that political and military logic pulled strategy in different directions.[108]

Tedder presented the Chiefs of Staff case to the Defence Committee, making clear their disagreements. He said that they had been given to believe that without the promise of two British divisions the Western Union would collapse. His two colleagues accepted this as true, he regarded it as French blackmail to which it was unwise to submit. He stressed the far reaching effects any such decision would have on British strategy. A.V. Alexander argued that French pressure was very strong and urged that a decision be reached before the Western Union Ministers of Defence meeting in July 1949. Bevin's view was that the French government were not really concerned with the British position and it was unlikely that a failure to earmark two divisions for Europe by 1951 would lead to the collapse of the Western Union. The European governments were much more concerned with the assistance the USA was capable of providing and this was the principal factor in European defence. Following this forceful statement the general feeling.of the meeting was against making the European commitment central to British strategy and that it was wrong to enter into binding commitments with one group of Britain's allies. Attlee made it clear that the most important aspect of British policy was to consult with the JCS and to try and work out a joint Anglo-American strategy.[109]

By September 1949, although the French once more pressed for a British commitment as soon as the tripartite talks in Washington on the formal military organisation of NATO were complete, the British had been unable to elicit a clear statement on proposed strategy from the Americans.[110] Slim now argued that it was clear that the Americans were not, in the near future, about to make a direct contribution to land or air forces beyond their occupation forces in Germany and some diversion of the heavy bomber effort. Britain would therefore need all its own forces for the Middle East. He wanted to tell the French that for the next three years there would be no prospect of a successful defence of the Rhine. According to Slim the American monopoly of the atomic bomb made the risk of war so remote that the economic burden of large scale rearmament was not justified. If war did break out it would be fruitless sending British forces to Europe to be destroyed. The Army was already fully deployed fighting communism so the only extra forces available would be four territorial divisions which would be better employed in the Middle East. Continental countries should plan to fight with any forces they could extract. Britain should only reconsider this position when there was a realistic prospect of holding the Rhine which in effect meant not until there was an American commitment.[111] Tedder was instructed to hold discussions with the Americans about holding a bridgehead around Brest or Cherbourg and the chiefs agreed that Britain should stall any commitments until they had detailed knowledge of United States plans.[112]

As late as September 1949, when news of the Soviet A-bomb reached the West, there was no support for a continental commitment except in the event of a major shift in United States strategy, which British military planners did not expect to happen. The alliances Britain entered into in 1947, 1948 and 1949 must all be seen in this light. It could be argued that

Bevin and the Foreign Office were ahead of a conservative and cautious military thought but the Foreign Secretary's intervention in the defence debate suggests he too was looking to the Americans not for any European option. Alliances not backed by military power were of only limited usefulness so the debate about strategy was in many ways as important as the formation of the alliances themselves. The shift in British policy towards Europe was a major change not the inevitable result of the formation of the Western Union.[113]

This shift can be explained in terms of three major developments. First, the end of America's atomic monopoly, with the explosion of the first Soviet A-bomb in August 1949, turned attention once more to the conventional defence of Europe. Indeed the swift development of British strategy after September 1949 would suggest that the military establishment were psychologically unprepared for the Soviet achievement even though their own sources had warned that Russia might soon 'have a stock [of atomic weapons] capable of neutralising small areas such as the United Kingdom.'[114] Second, it seemed possible, even before the outbreak of the Korean War, that the United States might consider sending its own troops to Europe[115] so a British commitment to lead the way seemed more important politically. Finally, there was also a significant change of personnel in the defence establishment. The forceful Shinwell replaced Alexander as Minister of Defence and Sir John Slessor replaced Tedder as Chief of the Air Staff. Both were convinced of the political importance of committing some British conventional forces to the continent.

Notes

1. In the first major work on British nuclear strategy in the 1940s and 1950s to be based on declassified government documents Ian Clark and Nicholas Wheeler sought to offer an account that is 'revisionist in so far as it questions Gowing's rather dismissive attitude towards the role of strategy in the formation of British atomic policy.' They suggested that from the autumn of 1945 the Attlee government clearly identified the Soviet Union as the main threat and swiftly developed a strategy of nuclear deterrence to meet that threat. For them, therefore, procurement decisions were based on agreed strategy. Clark and Wheeler, *British Origins of Nuclear Strategy*, p. 4 and Wheeler's essay in Deighton (ed.), *Britain and the First Cold War*, pp. 130-145.

2. Churchill to Cripps, 6 Nov. 1943, London, Public Record Office (P.R.O.), AIR20/1734; PS to VCAS to ACAS(TR), 17 Nov. 1943, London, Public Record Office (P.R.O.), AIR20/1734; Sinclair to Cripps, 27 Nov. 1943, London, Public Record Office (P.R.O.), AIR20/1734; Cripps to Churchill, 30 Nov. 1943, London, Public Record Office (P.R.O.), AIR20/1734; ACAS(TR) to CAS, 12 Dec. 1943, London, Public Record Office (P.R.O.), AIR20/1734; OR(F) to ACAS(TR),

undated, London, Public Record Office (P.R.O.), AIR20/1734; OR(F) to ACAS(TR), 2 Nov. 1944, London, Public Record Office (P.R.O.), AIR20/1734.

3. Minutes of Meeting to discuss Future Bomber Policy, 12 April 1944, London, Public Record Office (P.R.O.), AIR20/1734; CAS to ACAS(TR), 26 July 1944, London, Public Record Office (P.R.O.), AIR20/1734.

4. ACAS(TR) to DOR, 11 Aug. 1945, London, Public Record Office (P.R.O.), AIR20/1734.

5. ACAS(TR) to DTD(MAP), 13 Sept. 1945, London, Public Record Office (P.R.O.), AIR20/1790; CRD Meeting at MAP, 26 Sept. 1945, London, Public Record Office (P.R.O.), AIR20/1790.

6. DAT to D.of Plans, 1 March 1945, London, Public Record Office (P.R.O.), AIR20/3767.

7. Clark and Wheeler, *British Origins of Nuclear Strategy*, pp. 92-3.

8. CAS to ACAS(G), 11 April 1945, London, Public Record Office (P.R.O.), AIR2/5737; Note by Air Staff on WM(44)85th Conclusions, 3 July 1944, London, Public Record Office (P.R.O.), PREM3/12; Churchill to Ismay (for COS), 23 March 1945, London, Public Record Office (P.R.O.), PREM3/12.

9. Tedder, *With Prejudice*, pp. 491-687 esp. p. 659; Zuckerman, *From Apes to Warlords*, pp. 216-324, 337-8, 366; 'Preface to The Strategic Air War against Germany, 1939-45 Overall Report BBSU 1946', cited in Zuckerman, *From Apes to Warlords*, pp. 420-1; Harris to Tedder, 12 Dec. 1947, London, Public Record Office (P.R.O.), AIR2/9726; Supplementary Brief for Secretary of State for Air on COS(45)154, 4 Oct. 1945, London, Public Record Office (P.R.O.), AIR8/799.

10. The 1945 Tizard Report had expressed doubts about the ability of the long-range bomber to penetrate modern defences. These views were rejected on the somewhat spurious grounds that they emanated from known critics of the RAF, such as Patrick Blackett, on the Joint Technical Warfare Committee.

11. 'Comments on Tizard Report', AMP (Slessor) to VCAS, 16 July 1945, London, Ministry of Defence (Air Historical Branch), Slessor Papers, XIVA.

12. 'Effect of Atomic Weapons on the Structure of the Post-War Air Force', Director of Staff Duties to ACAS(P), 6 Dec. 1945, London, Public Record Office (P.R.O.), AIR20/2233.

13. 'The RAF in 1956', Report by the Future Planning Staff, 6 Feb. 1947, London, Public Record Office (P.R.O.), AIR20/7063.

14. Gowing, *Independence and Deterrence*, p. 174.

15. A/ACAS(P) to ACAS(TR)/ACAS(Ops), 15 May 1946, London, Public Record Office (P.R.O.), AIR20/4658.

16. ACAS(TR) to ACAS(P), 15 May 1946, London, Public Record Office (P.R.O.), AIR20/4658.

17. The American loan was running out, the Cabinet could not agree on measures to control the civil economy such as cutting food imports, convertibility was introduced in July and abandoned in August, senior ministers considered a political coup against Attlee. An initially rejected cut in service manpower from 1,007,000 to 937,000 in 1948 was adopted with a further cut to 700,000 in 1949 also agreed. Darwin, *Britain and Decolonisation*, pp. 75-6; ACAS(P) to CAS, 15 Aug. 1947, London, Public Record Office (P.R.O.), AIR20/7198.

18. ACAS(P) to CAS, 15 Aug. 1947, London, Public Record Office (P.R.O.), AIR20/7198.

19. COS(47)180(0), 29 August 1947, London, Public Record Office (P.R.O.), AIR20/7198.

20. Ibid.

21. VCAS to Minister of Defence, 15 Dec. 1947, London, Public Record Office (P.R.O.), AIR8/1587.

22. DO(48)2, 5 Jan. 1948, London, Public Record Office (P.R.O.), AIR8/1587; Extract from *The Times*, 25 Oct. 1947, London, Public Record Office (P.R.O.), AIR20/7198.

23. Clark and Wheeler, *British Origins of Nuclear Strategy*, p. 98.

24. In December 1948 the Chiefs of Staff set up the the 'Inter-Service Working Party on the Shape and Size of the Armed Forces' usually known as the Harwood Committee after its civilian chairman. Its aim was to produce a defence programme over three years from 1950 budgeted at £700 million per annum. The working party delivered a unanimous report in February 1949 and its findings were formally considered by the Chiefs of Staff and the Defence Committee in June 1949. 'Expansion and Equipment of the Strategic Bomber Force' Draft Note to Air Council by VCAS, 11 Jan. 1949, London, Public Record Office (P.R.O.), AIR20/7010; COS(49)48th, 28 and 30 March 1949, London, Public Record Office (P.R.O.), AIR20/7938; COS(49)113 Summary of the Report of the Inter-Service Working Party on the Shape and Size of the Armed Forces, 14 June 1949, London, Public Record Office (P.R.O.), AIR20/7938; COS(49)214, 16 June 1949, London, Public Record Office (P.R.O.), AIR20/7938; DO(49)47, 21 June 1949, London, Public Record Office (P.R.O.), CAB131/7.

25. Air Ministry Paper, 29 Aug. 1949, London, Public Record Office (P.R.O.), AIR20/6599.

26. 'Size and Shape of the Armed Forces' AUS(G) to ACAS(P), 14 Oct. 1949, London, Public Record Office (P.R.O.), AIR20/9135.

27. Ibid.

28. Clark and Wheeler, *British Origins of Nuclear Strategy*, pp. 101-2 and 106-7.

29. The Air Staff argued that the RAF could not wait for an advanced bomber and then build up a force to man it. Long-range attacks needed high skill and long preparation. It was dangerous to undertake a rapid expansion and introduce revolutionary types at the same time. Therefore the present Bomber Command would have to be maintained and found a useful role, the most promising of which was cited as being a contribution to air superiority in Europe by attacks on such targets as airfields. It might seem strange that so much time and effort was expended on the Lincoln force which the Harwood Report labelled as useless. This was certainly the view expressed by Sir John Slessor. He argued that the Lincoln force was not worth much militarily and should be cut back to help pay for contributions to the Western Union. He also pointed out that a force of 200 Lincolns in 1953 was not going to convince the Americans that Britain was a serious military ally. Nevertheless, this was the problem the Air Staff were addressing when it talked of counter-military targeting in 1949. The issue was also one of internal Air Staff politics. Tedder's preferred candidate as the next CAS Sir Ralph Cochrane, a senior figure in wartime Bomber Command, supported the Air Staff view but Slessor was appointed on Attlee's insistence. He and Cochrane, who became VCAS, worked out a compromise in 1950. The strength of feeling was such that Slessor had to give way to Cochrane's argument

that the Canberra would not provide an effective bomber force and that although the Lincoln was vulnerable, slow and only had the range to reach the fringes of Russia it did carry a heavy bomb load which could be used to attack targets presented by the Soviet advance west and submarine pens in East Germany. Slessor made the best of this compromise and took the opportunity to make the gesture of committing Bomber Command to the Western Union in order to divert attention from the Middle East to Europe. By February 1950 he was refusing to countenance doubts about the usefulness of this force of the kind he had expressed the previous year. All the attention given to a counter-military role for the Lincolns was probably influential in later thinking about the use of the V-bombers but the two processes had not merged by 1949. Slessor, *These Remain*, p. 15; Note on MISC/P(49)6 Report of the Inter-Service Working Party by Air Chief Marshal Sir John Slessor, undated, London, Ministry of Defence (Air Historical Branch), Slessor Papers, XIVA; Slessor to Tedder, 7 April 1949, London, Ministry of Defence (Air Historical Branch), Slessor Papers, XIVA; 'Size and Shape of the Armed Forces' AUS(G) to ACAS(P), 14 Oct. 1949, London, Public Record Office (P.R.O.), AIR20/9135; Slessor to Cochrane, 6 Jan. 1950, London, Public Record Office (P.R.O.), AIR8/1590; ACAS(P) to CAS, 5 Jan. 1950, London, Public Record Office (P.R.O.), AIR8/1590; CAS to VCAS, 3 Feb. 1950, London, Ministry of Defence (Air Historical Branch), Slessor Papers, XIVA; Slessor to CIGS/VCNS, 6 April 1950, London, Ministry of Defence (Air Historical Branch), Slessor Papers, XIVA.

30. Gowing, *Independence and Deterrence*, pp. 229-30.

31. Tedder to Slessor, 6 April 1949, London, Ministry of Defence (Air Historical Branch), Slessor Papers, XIVA.

32. B.H. Liddell Hart to Slessor, 2 May 1949, London, Ministry of Defence (Air Historical Branch), Slessor Papers, XXVC.

33. Clark and Wheeler, *British Origins of Nuclear Strategy*, p. 106.

34. Tedder to Slessor, 6 April 1949, London, Ministry of Defence (Air Historical Branch), XIVA.

35. Slessor to Tedder, 7 April 1949, London, Ministry of Defence (Air Historical Branch), Slessor Papers, XIVA.

36. Note on MISC/P(49)6 Report of the Inter-Service Working Party by Air Chief Marshal Sir John Slessor, undated, London, Ministry of Defence (Air Historical Branch), Slessor Papers, XIVA.

37. CAS to Air Staff, 3 Jan. 1950, London, Public Record Office (P.R.O.), AIR8/1590.

38. CAS to ACAS(P), 3 Aug. 1944, London, Public Record Office (P.R.O.), AIR20/3749; ACAS(P) to CAS, 7 Aug. 1944, London, Public Record Office (P.R.O.), AIR20/3749; RAFDEL to ACAS(P), 16 Aug. 1944, London, Public Record Office (P.R.O.), AIR20/3749; Converse, 'United States Plans for a Postwar Overseas Military Base System, 1942-1948', p. 73; Duke, *US Defence Bases in the UK*, p. 16.

39. Converse, 'United States Plans for a Postwar Overseas Military Base System, 1942-1948', p. 131 and pp 182-183; AMP (Sir John Slessor) to ACAS(P), 30 June 1945, London, Ministry of Defence (Air Historical Branch), Slessor Papers, XLIIIH.

40. VCAS to RAFDEL, 21 June 1945, London, Public Record Office (P.R.O.), AIR8/798.

41. RAFDEL to VCAS, 14 July 1945, London, Public Record Office (P.R.O.), AIR8/798.

42. Duke, *US Defence Bases in the UK*, pp. 19-21; Converse, 'United States Plans for a Postwar Overseas Military Base System, 1942-1948', pp. 216-217.

43. Duke, *US Defence Bases in the UK*, p. 21.

44. Ibid.; Converse, 'United States Plans for a Postwar Overseas Military Base System, 1942-1948', p.217.

45. Duke, *US Defence Bases in the UK*, p. 31; Zuckerman, *Monkeys, Men and Missiles*, p. 270.

46. Worcester, *Roots of British Air Policy*, p. 27; Interview with T. C. G. James.

47. Herken, *The Winning Weapon*, p. 251.

48. Frank Roberts (FO) to R. F. Wood (MoD), 26 June 1948, London, Public Record Office (P.R.O.), AIR2/14027.

49. Bevin to Douglas, 27 June 1948, London, Public Record Office (P.R.O.), AIR2/14027.

50. Bullock, *Ernest Bevin, Foreign Secretary*, p. 577.

51. Henderson to Bevin, 31 Aug. 1948, London, Public Record Office (P.R.O.), AIR2/14027.

52. Bullock, *Ernest Bevin, Foreign Secretary*, p. 577.

53. Frank Roberts (FO) to R. F. Wood (MoD), 26 June 1948, London, Public Record Office (P.R.O.), AIR2/14027.

54. Herken, *The Winning Weapon*, pp. 239-241.

55. Duke, *US Defence Bases in the UK*, p. 24.

56. CAS to VCAS, 13 August 1952, London, Ministry of Defence (Air Historical Branch), Slessor Papers, XLIIIH.

57. Price to Hollis, 19 Sept. 1947, London, Public Record Office (P.R.O.), AIR20/2461; ACAS(P) Minute on JP(47)130(Final), 29 Sept. 1947, London, Public Record Office (P.R.O.), AIR20/2461; COS(47)122nd, 1 Oct. 1947, London, Public Record Office (P.R.O.), AIR20/2461; COS(47)209(0) (Revise), 2 Oct. 1947, London, Public Record Office (P.R.O.), AIR20/2461; Secretary, COS to Secretary, C-in-Cs Committee, Middle East, 12 Dec. 1947, London, Public Record Office (P.R.O.), AIR20/2463; Bullock, *Ernest Bevin, Foreign Secretary*, pp. 471-3; Converse, 'United States Plans for a Postwar Overseas Military Base System, 1942-1948' p. 215 and p. 240.

58. VCAS to Secretary of State for Air, 25 Oct. 1947, London, Public Record Office (P.R.O.), AIR20/2462; ACAS(P) to VCAS, 31 Oct. 1947, London, Public Record Office (P.R.O.), AIR20/2462; Air Chief Marshal Sir Guy Garrod to VCAS, 7 Nov. 1947, London, Public Record Office (P.R.O.), AIR20/2463.

59. Interview with T.C.G. James. RAF officers played a part in helping the USAF drawing up their air defence plans in 1947 and 1948. James was part of the Air Ministry team which visited the USA in 1948.

60. Converse, 'United States Plans for a Postwar Overseas Military Base System, 1942-1948', pp. 214-30.

61. ACAS(P) to VCAS, 31 Oct. 1947, London, Public Record Office (P.R.O.), AIR20/2462.

62. Bullock, *Ernest Bevin, Foreign Secretary*, p. 475.

63. CAS to AMSO, 24 Sept. 1948, London, Public Record Office (P.R.O.), AIR8/1606.

64. Converse, 'United States Plans for a Postwar Overseas Military Base System, 1942-1948', p. 217.

65. Duke, *US Defence Bases in the UK*, p. 51.

66. Converse, 'United States Plans for a Postwar Overseas Military Base System, 1942-1948', pp. 230-231.

67. Duke, *US Defence Bases in the UK*, p.52.

68. Ibid., p.51.

69. CAS to Air Chief Marshal Sir Charles Medhurst (Head, BJSM(AFS)), 18 Nov. 1948, London, Public Record Office (P.R.O.), AIR8/1796.

70. Medhurst to CAS, 4 Jan. 1949, London, Public Record Office (P.R.O.), AIR8/1796.

71. DO(49)13, 15 Feb. 1949, London, Public Record Office (P.R.O.), AIR8/1796.

72. 'Expansion and Equipment of the Strategic Bomber Force' Draft Note to Air Council by VCAS, 11 Jan. 1949, London, Public Record Office (P.R.O.), AIR20/7010.

73. Clark and Wheeler, *British Origins of Nuclear Strategy*, p. 109.

74. ACAS(P) to CAS, 5 Jan. 1950, London, Public Record Office (P.R.O.), AIR8/1590.

75. Slessor to Air Chief Marshal the Hon. Sir Ralph Cochrane, London, 6 Jan. 1950, Ministry of Defence (Air Historical Branch), Slessor Papers, XIVA.

76. Brookes, *V-force*, p. 33.

77. Duke, *US Defence Bases in the UK*, p. 35.

78. Lord Tedder to Slessor, 6 April 1949, London, Ministry of Defence (Air Historical Branch), Slessor Papers, XIVA.

79. Slessor to Air Chief Marshal the Hon. Sir Ralph Cochrane, 6 Jan. 1950, London, Ministry of Defence (Air Historical Branch), Slessor Papers, XIVA.

80. Lord Tedder to Slessor, 6 April 1949, London, Ministry of Defence (Air Historical Branch), Slessor Papers, XIVA.

81. Duke, *US Defence Bases in the UK*, pp. 86-88.

82. Dillon (ed.), *Defence Policy Making*, p. 21.

83. The actual ease of occupation led the air force to concentrate its thoughts on army support air forces. In October the Air Staff proposed that these forces should be stationed in Germany for the foreseeable future but would eventually return to the United Kingdom. It was not expected that these forces would be particularly large and there was some discussion whether they would warrant a separate command or should be made up of detached forces from Fighter and Bomber Commands. This solution was rejected on grounds of administrative complexity and the Second Tactical Air Force was retained as a separate composite command and renamed British Air Force of Occupation (BAFO). By the end of 1945 BAFO comprised thirty-six operational squadrons. In 1946 it was reduced to fifteen squadrons and by the end of 1947 to ten. Edmonds (ed.), *The Defence Equation*, pp. 157-8.

84. 'The RAF in 1956' Report by Future Planning Staff, 6 Feb. 1947, London, Public Record Office (P.R.O.), AIR20/7063.

85. 'Statement on Military Aspects (Air) of Western European Pacts', 6 April 1947, London, Public Record Office (P.R.O.), AIR20/10343; ACAS(I) to ACAS(P), 13 Jan. 1948, London, Public Record Office (P.R.O.), AIR20/10343.

86. ACAS(I) to ACAS(P), 13 Jan. 1948, London, Public Record Office (P.R.O.), AIR20/10343; A/ACAS(Ops) to CAS, 5 Feb. 1948, London, Public Record Office (P.R.O.), AIR20/10343; COS(48)46th, 31 March 1948, London, Public Record Office (P.R.O.), AIR20/10343.

87. Minister of Defence to Prime Minister, 14 April 1948, London, Public Record Office (P.R.O.), PREM8/749.

88. Air Vice-Marshal Hudleston to ACAS(P), 19 May 1948, London, Public Record Office (P.R.O.), AIR20/10343; COS(58)1st, 2 Jan. 1958, London, Public Record Office (P.R.O.), DEFE4/103.

89. COS(48)114(0), 13 May 1948, London, Public Record Office (P.R.O.), AIR20/10513; COS(48)68th Confidential Annex, 19 May 1948, London, Public Record Office (P.R.O.), AIR20/10291; BJSM to COS, 17 June 1948, London, Public Record Office (P.R.O.), AIR20/10513; COS(48)85th Confidential Annex, 23 June 1948, London, Public Record Office (P.R.O.), AIR20/10513; COS(48)88th Confidential Annex, 28 June 1948, London, Public Record Office (P.R.O.), AIR20/10513; BASIC 121 General Robertson to COS, 15 July 1948, London, Public Record Office (P.R.O.), AIR20/10513; BASIC 126 General Robertson to COS, 15 July 1948, London, Public Record Office (P.R.O.), AIR20/10513.

90. Baylis, 'Britain, the Brussels Pact and the continental commitment', pp. 615-29.

91. Hamilton, *Monty: The Field Marshal, 1944-1976*, pp. 700-1.

92. Ibid., p. 699.

93. Ibid., p. 702.

94. Baylis, 'Britain, the Brussels Pact and the continental commitment', pp. 615-29.

95. In April 1948 Montgomery had met with the British Military Governor in Germany, General Robertson, and had ordered him, with Attlee's full approval, to prepare a British war plan. Christened 'Doublequick' this plan envisaged no withdrawal of British forces in the event of an attack but also that no reinforcements would be sent. Since the forces under Robertson's command amounted to an armoured division and a weakened infantry division in the British Zone and a brigade in Berlin supported by ten RAF squadrons this amounted to no more than a symbolic and sacrificial defence effort. The successor to 'Doublequick', codenamed 'Congreve', estimated that the Russians had a ten to one superiority in armoured and air forces, better trained and under a unified command and that tank columns supported by large tactical air forces would strike deep into Allied territory in a form of *blitzkrieg*. 'Congreve' was issued with bogus cover versions in an attempt to fool the Europeans about how little faith the British and Americans had in their defence. John Young, 'The Military Origins of the Western Union' Paper given at ICBH Conference 1990; BJSM to COS, 17 June 1948, London, Public Record Office (P.R.O.), AIR20/10513; Edmonds (ed.), *The Defence Equation*, p. 158; General Sir Brian Robertson to Secretary, COS Committee, 1 July 1948, London, Public Record Office (P.R.O.), AIR20/10513.

96. Bullock, *Ernest Bevin, Foreign Secretary*, p. 643.

97. COS1988/25/11/8 Personal Note by CIGS to COS, 25 Nov. 1948, London, Public Record Office (P.R.O.), AIR20/10291.

98. COS(48)178th Confidential Annex, 13 Dec. 1948, London, Public Record Office (P.R.O.), AIR20/10291.

99. COS(49)2nd Confidential Annex, 5 Jan. 1949, London, Public Record Office (P.R.O.), AIR20/10291.

100. DO(49)3, 7 Jan. 1949, London, Public Record Office (P.R.O.), AIR20/10291.

101. DO(49)2nd, 10 Jan. 1949, London, Public Record Office (P.R.O.), AIR20/10291.

102. The Air Staff came to the same conclusion. They did, however, acknowledge that the defence of the Rhine should be kept open as an option since 'the atom offensive must have some effect on Russia's desire and ability to go on fighting' and its forces might be willing to stop on the Rhine if the crossings were well defended. A joint planners study of strategy in 1957, the official year of maximum danger in British plans, saw Russia posing much the same threat but with reconstructed forces. They postulated an attack by 83 Soviet divisions on a 400 mile front. They assumed it would be impossible for the west to hold the whole line with conventional land and tactical air forces. The solution offered was for part of the strategic bomber force to be diverted to assist land operations for the first six months of a war twinned with a light bomber force operating from the United Kingdom. The aim would be to interdict the Soviet offensive in order to reduce by 50% Russian land forces available. ACAS(P) to CAS, 5 July 1948, London, Public Record Office (P.R.O.), AIR20/10513; ACAS(P) to CAS, 13 Dec. 1948, London, Public Record Office (P.R.O.), AIR20/10611.

103. COS(49)57th, 20 April 1949, London, Public Record Office (P.R.O.), AIR20/10291.

104. COS(49)75th, 20 May 1949, London, Public Record Office (P.R.O.), AIR20/10291.

105. Ibid.

106. COS(49)86th Confidential Annex, 13 June 1949, London, Public Record Office (P.R.O.), AIR20/10291

107. Ibid.

108. DO(49)45, 17 June 1949, London, Public Record Office (P.R.O.), AIR20/10291.

109. DO(49)16th, 21 June 1949, London, Public Record Office (P.R.O.), AIR20/10291.

110. COS(49)298, 12 Sept. 1949, London, Public Record Office (P.R.O.), AIR20/10291.

111. Ibid.

112. Ibid.

113. The RAF was only too glad to reject moves towards the deployment of greater conventional forces in Europe. Its attitude towards the formation of a tactical air force had been dilatory throughout 1949. The Western Union Commanders-in-Chief committee under Montgomery produced a requirement for 4200 tactical aircraft and the Air Advisory Committee drew up interim plans for 1800 aircraft by 1954 of which Britain's contribution would be 792. The United Kingdom delegation to the Western Union Ministers of Defence insisted

on the primacy of a Western Union tactical air force over the land forces preferred by the continental allies. In April 1949 the Western Union Defence Committee endorsed a report calling for a 400 strong WUTAF by 1951, with Britain making the largest contribution. Although the RAF drew up plans for four squadrons to be contributed to this force they were dropped during the Harwood defence review. Throughout the year British officials talked enthusiastically about the WUTAF in order to divert criticism away from their lack of land forces so by the end of 1949 they were faced with the messy situation of explaining that Britain had no intention of making a contribution to it. The role of a tactical air force as a political counter is notable since even when it was built up in ensuing years RAF commitment to its existence was barely skin deep. AUS(G) to VCAS, 22 Sept. 1949, London, Public Record Office (P.R.O.), AIR20/7085; AUS(G) to ACAS(P), 14 Oct. 1949, London, Public Record Office (P.R.O.), AIR20/9135.

114. JP(48)117(Final), 19 Jan. 1949, London, Public Record Office (P.R.O.), AIR8/999.

115. Jervis, 'The impact of the Korean War on the Cold War', p. 571.

3

Sir John Slessor and Nuclear Strategy: 1950-1952

Sir John Slessor, the Medium Bomber Force and Nuclear Strategy

The contribution of RAF policy on the nuclear armed bomber to British strategy in the early 1950s revolved around three major issues. The first was the degree of substitution which could be achieved by replacing conventional land and sea forces with a nuclear armed bomber force. Although the need to address this issue was apparent to RAF planners in the 1940s its full consideration was effectively delayed until late 1951. This was partly because Sir John Slessor, who became Chief of the Air Staff in January 1950, believed that in the short-term a conventional air force with a smaller front-line but backed by reserves was of more use than a 'shop window' force. More importantly the outbreak of the Korean war caused the Attlee government to authorise rearmament programmes of such a size that each service could pursue its own objectives without trying to alter the proportional distribution of the defence budget. In 1952 the RAF began to argue vigorously that since SAC and Bomber Command would provide an effective deterrent to war, conventional forces, especially in Europe, could be drastically reduced. Despite the approval of the Lisbon force goals this was a policy accepted by the Churchill government almost from the outset. The exact size of the reduced conventional forces was, however, not agreed.

The second issue that exercised the RAF was the fear that the argument for nuclear deterrence and reduced conventional forces would be accepted by the government but that it would then be decided to leave nuclear deterrence to the USAF. This fear was an important determinant of its approach, even though the history of the British atomic programme leads one to doubt whether it was ever under serious threat. The RAF's worries were not, however, completely without foundation. Churchill returned to office in 1951 with an unrealistic understanding of the state of Anglo-American nuclear relations and expressed the opinion that he had 'never wished ... that England should start the manufacture of atomic bombs. ... We should have the art rather than the article. ... There is however no point in our going into bulk production even if we were able to.'[1]

The third main development in 1950-2, the emergence of a specifically counter-military targeting policy, was largely a product of the perceived threat to the independent bomber force from within the defence establishment. The RAF needed a convincing military argument for its existence. The selection of Soviet bomber bases, submarine pens and land forces as target systems of choice, with the emphasis very much on the former evolved quickly in 1950-1 under the guidance of Slessor.

In early 1950 Sir John Slessor led his senior colleagues and staff in a reappraisal of RAF strategic policy. This provided a starting point for a process which led to the British bomber achieving a much enhanced role in British strategy. Although Slessor became CAS with strongly held views about the importance of the bomber force he initially saw it as the central element of a policy balanced between defence and deterrence.[2]

Starting from the premise that 'the basic weapon of the Air Force is the bomber and the basic strategy of air power must be offensive' he argued that realities had to be faced. The RAF was primarily responsible for preventing Britain being subject to atomic blackmail by providing a strong defence. This did not mean Russia was likely to attempt aggressive war in the face of American nuclear weapons but it was necessary to remain on guard. Defensive developments would therefore have to have the same priority as atomic weapons, especially the guided weapons programme. Second, he reached 'the inescapable conclusion that the defence of Western Europe is vital to the survival of this country ... a biggish change from our present accepted strategic policy of the "three pillars"'. This meant that Britain had to maintain a Continental army. Although such an army would be virtually useless in wartime it might prevent a war from breaking out.[3]

As befitted a successful wartime leader of Coastal Command he was also concerned with the 'second pillar' of strategy, the protection of sea communications.[4] He was highly critical of the Royal Navy's intention of building up to thirteen aircraft carriers and equipping them with 250 aircraft. This compared with a planned Coastal Command anti-submarine force in 1952-3 of 42 aircraft. Slessor challenged this situation by attacking both the overall cost of the Naval Estimates and the navy's plans as an ineffective and uneconomical method of securing the sea lanes.[5] His interest in using the bomber to attack Russian submarines at source should be seen in this context. Moreover, in 1950 he was equally concerned about the strength of Coastal Command.

His most immediate attack was on the plans agreed by the Chiefs of Staff in 1949 for the development of the RAF between 1950 and 1953.[6] These plans admitted that 'the Air Force would be a shop window Air Force, and in the event of war it could not survive more than about a month of intensive fighting.' Slessor considered even such an estimate too optimistic. He described the policy of the 'visible deterrent' as a dangerous nonsense. The only deterrent was the atomic bomb delivered by SAC. According to Slessor an RAF 'shop window' force, of whatever size, was no more effective than the RAF at the time of Munich; he believed that a major role in the events of Munich had been played by Chiefs of Staff advice to the government that Britain could not be defended. He warned that if NATO was to oppose Russia Britain would have to take a strong diplomatic line in support of the United States; this would be impossible if the government knew its defence preparations to be a sham.[7] He rapidly persuaded the Defence Committee to allow him to recast policy[8] and put in hand measures to stop front-line units being expanded without the adequate provision of reserves.[9]

Slessor's next move was to put in motion a wider strategic review in the Chiefs of Staff. He presented his Defence Policy and Global Strategy paper to his colleagues in March[10] and once they had met to discuss it at the RAF Staff College, Bracknell it was approved by the Defence Committee in May.[11] The exact balance of Global Strategy 1950 is hard to define. It called for Russian communism to be confined to the Soviet Union by worldwide co-operation with the USA and an increasingly offensive Cold War strategy.[12] It described priority areas for defence as only those things which contributed to the survival of the United Kingdom or the prosecution of Cold War. These were divided into three categories in descending order of importance. In the first category was the air defence of the United Kingdom, protection of the sea link with the USA and the defence of Europe by land. In the second category was the provision of an adequate deterrent including weapons to replace the manned bomber and secure bases within range of the Soviet Union. In the third category were minimum air, sea and land forces, including garrisons and occupation forces, in Europe, the Middle East, the Far East and the Pacific to fight the Cold War. Nuclear air power was thus ranked as important but not of the highest priority. Yet in Slessor's original draft atomic air power had been described as the key to strategy both as a deterrent and the main offensive weapon. Slessor claimed the only chance of Allied survival and victory was through an air strategy and argued that the deterrent would not be lessened as Russia built up a stockpile of atomic weapons as long as the West made clear that it would respond to any major aggression with nuclear arms. The failure of the nuclear striking force to play a prominent role in the final Global Strategy paper can partly be explained by the effects of inter-service debate: neither the CIGS nor the First Sea Lord was willing to concede the paramount military role to the RAF. Slessor's original proposals demonstrate, however, that he had not tried to insist on the primacy of nuclear forces. The thrust of his proposals was dictated by the lack of a British atomic capability and Slessor's belief that all that could be done in the interim would be to create well found defences and to rely on the Americans. At the same time it seems he envisaged a continuing role for defensive forces even when a British bomber force came into existence.[13]

This is best demonstrated by the the results of the full review of RAF force structure plans presented to the Chiefs of Staff in July 1950. They were completed before the Korean War but submitted after its outbreak. By unexpectedly freeing the defence budget from its previous constraints Korea distorted strategic thinking. Force plans were based on available manpower and production capacity. Yet until the £4700 million defence programme was approved in January 1951[14] the rearmament programme conformed to the plans presented in July 1950.[15] This plan was divided into two parts: proposals if the defence budget for 1951-54 remained at the level of £800-900 million a year and for a rearmament programme.

The first stage of the proposals were built round the statement in the 1950 Global Strategy paper that 'an efficient air defence is so essential to the safety of the main base in the UK that all necessary measures to ensure its early development must be given the highest priority.' The major modifications from the 1949 proposals were the increase in Fighter Command by 190 aircraft, Coastal Command by 84, since 'the Russian U-boat force forms a considerable and growing menace, and to combat it a strong maritime air force will be necessary', and the reduction of Bomber Command from 304 to 208. The rearmament programme advocated another 680 front-line aircraft and a full three months reserve. Throughout it was made clear that the enhanced role for fighters and maritime aircraft and the reliance on USAF strategic bombers was due to the technical limitations of British equipment.[16]

It was thus explicitly stated in the plans drawn up on the basis of a limited defence budget that strategic priorities would be reordered once a British bomber became available. One of Slessor's overriding concerns was to strike the balance between spending as little as possible on existing types and as much as possible on the infrastructure of the RAF. He was prepared to lavish as much expenditure as necessary on the next generation of jet aircraft.[17] The question therefore arises: was the shift in emphasis towards the strategic bomber force when the defence budget was once more strictly limited in late 1951 merely the result of these long-term intentions or were there new factors at work?

The main historical debate on this issue has centred around the radicalism or otherwise of the 1952 Global Strategy Paper.[18] It is useful to disentangle bureaucratic innovation from strategic innovation. The Global Strategy papers of 1950 and 1952 were produced because of John Slessor. The approach of the three Chiefs of Staff secluding themselves and presenting an agreed strategy to the government was his idea. It stemmed from the belief that the Chiefs of Staff should make policy within the financial guidelines set by politicians and a desire to avoid another Harwood Report which allowed civil servants and staff officers to usurp this role.[19] Slessor had a taste for thinking about strategy in less strictly applied terms than most of his fellow senior officers and his skill at these exercises allowed him to push the RAF's case most effectively.[20] The procedure fell out of use when he retired and was replaced largely by the committees of civil servants, staff officers and politicians he so despised. Although such papers involved a certain amount of extempore writing they obviously drew on ideas developed by the participants and their staffs over a much longer period. The 1952 Global Strategy Paper was very important since as a statement drawn up by the chiefs and approved by the Cabinet it set the parameters of strategic debate. During the defence reviews of the next five years the RAF constantly referred back to it to bolster their arguments.

How strategically innovative and important was the paper? It put the bomber at the centre of British strategy which at the time was seen as a triumph for the RAF. Although the paper, like its 1950 forerunner, did not formally overemphasise nuclear weapons and deterrence it did unambiguously state that it was the 'first essential ... to establish and maintain ... a really effective deterrent against war',[21] that this deterrent was a nuclear force and that Britain should contribute part of such a force to hedge against American unilateralism in foreign policy and unreliability in targeting. It partially established the proposition that nuclear airpower could substitute for conventional land and sea forces but the roles given to the Cold War and 'broken-backed' warfare at the insistence of Field Marshal Slim, the CIGS, and Sir Rhoderick McGrigor, the First Sea Lord, ensured that no inevitable decisions about the size of forces flowed from it. It established counter-military targeting as the main role of the British bomber force within an Anglo-American deterrent but this had been generally agreed beforehand. The formal balance of defence policy was thus significantly shifted towards nuclear airpower. For the rest of the 1950s the most important assumption of British defence policy was that the deterrent would be provided for first and conventional forces financed by the residue of money in the defence budget. This concept was regularly and vigorously attacked by the Royal Navy, the Army and various government ministers but it was reaffirmed by both the Eden and Macmillan governments and held good to the end of the decade and beyond. The development of strategy in 1952 should be seen mainly in the light of ideas developed in 1949-50 but several other factors were operating to accentuate the shift away from conventional forces.

First, there was a growing awareness of the logic of the short war strategy. The strategic conception written into Global Strategy 1952 was a compromise between short war and long war strategies envisaging a violent nuclear exchange lasting, at most, a month followed by a period of 'broken-backed' warfare. Such a war 'may last only a few weeks: but at the end of that period it seems certain that both sides, particularly Russia and the United Kingdom, will have suffered terrible damage' but this could leave room for an 'intermittent struggle gradually spreading world-wide'.[22] The internal contradictions involved in this compromise were apparent in the paper itself. It argued that NATO should not plan 'exclusively for a short war' but that 'a guiding principle of the rearmament programme should be to ensure survival in the short opening phase.'[23] Slessor considered the concept of 'broken-backed' warfare or 'intermittent struggle' a nonsense and government economic difficulties enabled him to argue in the autumn of 1952 that whatever the formal strategic conception there should be more rigour in ascribing priority to the short war part of it. The atomic deterrent should be further increased and Britain would have to take more risks in its defence policy by simply assuming there would be no war or that it would be very short.[24]

Second, doubts increased about the viability of air defence as offensive and defensive weaponry improved. The limitation of Soviet nuclear blackmail seemed to be less achievable with the prospect of Russian development of a modern bomber force to replace their B-29 copies and there seemed to be no limits to the demands for an air defence force. As Slessor told the Secretary of State for Air 'in face of the atomic threat and the consequent need to achieve what is, in fact, a virtually impossible rate of kills for conventional fighters, one must arrive at some reasonable compromise ... we must look to the new weapons, not the conventional fighter to give us security against atomic attack.'[25]

Third, concentration on the bomber force was a matter of inter-departmental politics. Korean rearmament had resulted in a large build up of conventional forces.[26] There were worries that the Lisbon force goals would lead to the War Office and Admiralty placing too much concentration on conventional forces and not enough on the role of the strategic bomber offensive.[27] Indeed, given the RAF's success in arguing that its primary role should be to provide a deterrent, it was criticised over the size of the conventional forces it had constructed over the Korean period.[28] Any attempt by the Air Ministry to stress defence as well as deterrence left it in an exposed bureaucratic position and was, therefore, avoided.

Lastly, the development of tactical nuclear weapons by the Americans seemed to offer the prospect of putting less emphasis on conventional forces in the future. Although the Chiefs of Staff position as set out in the Global Strategy Paper did not emphasise tactical nuclear weapons, they could agree on the proposition that American possession of a 'substantial and increasing number of the smaller atomic bomb ... can add materially to the strength of the tactical defence' and that , in consequence, NATO force levels should be adjusted.[29] As early as 1947 the Air and General Staffs had agreed that 'it may be necessary to use atomic bombs in direct support of the Army, in which case they will have to be dropped with the greatest possible accuracy of position and timing'[30] but Tedder had dismissed the idea of using atomic weapons on the territory of Germany or Russia's satellites.[31] By the end of 1952, however, Slessor had concluded that developments in tactical atomic weapons were potentially of the greatest importance. He assumed that the Soviet Union was planning to use nuclear weapons on the battlefield and that NATO would have to be prepared to respond accordingly.[32] Alternative uses for tactical nuclear weapons, such as attacks on Russian cruisers by the Royal Navy, muted opposition to planning for their use.[33]

There is, however, little evidence that the detonation of the hydrogen bomb by the Americans had an important influence on strategy during 1952. In subsequent years this weapon significantly strengthened the deterrent and short war arguments advanced by the RAF but the policies of 1952 were constructed around atomic weapons. Despite possible technical developments in tactical atomic and in thermonuclear weapons the shift towards reliance on nuclear weapons looked back rather than forwards. As Sir Frank Cooper has said of Global Strategy: '.... there was still this pervasive belief that if you had a small number of nuclear weapons of which you could guarantee the air delivery you would not merely not have a war but also you needed very much smaller naval and air forces and he [Slessor] believed in that passionately.'[34]

Documents accompanying the Global Strategy Paper proposed a British Medium Bomber Force of 304, 'ultimately carrying atomic weapons', with further V-bombers dedicated to radar counter-measures (RCM) and photographic reconnaissance. The doctrine of substitution was clearly stated. 'We should be exploiting more fully the flexibility and mobility of air power. In particular, we should be using what is the most efficient and cheapest means of preventing war, or of giving us hope of survival if war came, the long-range high performance bomber.' The RAF proposed that the force be mobile, with bases in the Middle and Far East as well as Britain. It planned to start rearming Bomber Command with the new bombers in late 1955.[35] There was obviously heavy criticism of these proposals since the size of the target force was reduced to 240 during the negotiations on the defence budget in late 1952 or early 1953. Since the 304 strong force closely mirrored the proposal for 320 medium bombers made in 1949, when it had been stated that there would not be enough to carry out all the roles suggested for them, it became increasingly important for the Air Staff to articulate a clearly defined role for it if large-scale expenditure was to remain politically credible.

It was possible to argue that nuclear deterrence was central to NATO strategy and that conventional forces could be greatly reduced as a result without believing that Britain needed a bomber force. Sir Henry Tizard was the most vocal proponent of this view between 1949 and 1951 but he was not without support from civil servants in the Ministry of Defence[36] and from junior but articulate ministers such as Aidan Crawley. Most importantly Churchill's views sometimes seemed to be inclining in the same direction. As Slessor recognised in early 1950 although no-one liked leaving the strategic air offensive to the USAF that would, in reality, be the case for at least five years because of the inadequate equipment of Bomber Command. He also acknowledged that because of the economic weakness of Britain the main offensive would be left to the USAF throughout the age of the bomber. He only foresaw a more equal relationship when nations developed 'unmanned bombers'.[37] It was obvious to the Air Ministry that the small British bomber force would be politically vulnerable. Even the Air Staff's own civil servants were moved to comment 'CAS suggests we may not be able to afford more than 40 B9/48s [Valiants] (its not so very long ago that the Air Staff target was 528 4-engined jets!) The question arises: is it worth having any long range bombing force at all, if we can't afford more than 40? Should we not frankly admit that that role must be left to the USAF?'[38]

The Air Staff was thus under pressure to find a role, or roles, for the British bomber which would be bureaucratically as well as militarily useful. The three missions for the V-bombers it evolved between 1950 and 1952 were, therefore, all counter-military: an attack on Soviet air bases to lessen the damage done by atomic attack to Britain, the use of the bombers in support of NATO land forces and attacks on Soviet submarine pens as a contribution to the defence of sea communications. The political rather than military function of these roles is clearly demonstrated by the fact that although the first was the most important in terms of actual planning each was given prominence at different times in order to increase support for the bomber force.

The decision that the V-bombers would concentrate on a counterforce offensive against Soviet bases seems to have been taken in the first six months of 1950. Slessor's draft Global Strategy paper of March 1950 suggested that the only chance of survival lay in the bomber but much more emphasis was laid on its deterrent role.[39] In May the Air Staff were still uncertain about the exact size of bomber force it should suggest[40] and was looking at Moscow as a possible target for the British.[41] By July, however, it was quite clear about the justification for a British force. In its submission of RAF force plans it argued that the RAF should not be limited to defensive equipment since air defence needed air striking power to reduce the enemy effort by attacking air bases. It was unsound to surrender permanently a part in the strategic air offensive against 'the more distant sources of enemy air power'.[42] The language of this statement is much more definite than suggestions about a war fighting as well as a deterrent role for the bomber force mooted in the 1940s. Given the analysis of 1940s presented above it is apparent that the role of the British bomber force crystallised under Slessor's leadership.

This did not mean that other arguments were not used to bolster the position of the bomber. In the autumn of 1950, for instance, Slessor circulated the idea of an 'effective modern bomber force' able to attack the airfields, guided weapon sites, rail centres and lines of communication of Soviet armies invading Western Europe. He argued that to do this the RAF needed aircraft capable of carrying more destructive weapons, at a greater range, including into Russia, than the Canberra. Yet as he later noted: 'This was tactical. I thought it was not time to come into the open at this stage about a British share of the main air offensive'.[43]

The Air Staff feared that the new prime minister, Winston Churchill, would not support an independent bomber force of the the magnitude of the 200 Valiants it proposed during the 1951 rearmament programme and that, as a result of the Temporary Council Committee report on NATO force levels which served as the basis for the Lisbon force goals, the Americans would suggest the cessation of medium bomber development by Britain.[44] Slessor pointed out to Churchill that the Valiant force would be used in a wide range of roles; as part of the counter-offensive against Soviet air bases, to attack submarine pens and to assist in land warfare.[45] It was not until some months later that he officially stated that the counterforce mission was the most important of the three.[46]

Even though Slessor had pushed the importance of the bomber force in direct support of NATO mainly as a political manoeuvre there was, nevertheless, a real intention that it should have a role substituting for land forces. He envisaged the medium bomber carrying out an offensive counter-air mission for SHAPE or being called in as a last throw to prevent the total destruction of NATO land forces. These scenarios remained, however, predicated on the scarcity of nuclear weapons for use in Europe. Slessor believed that 'our limited stock of fissionable material must be used where it is most effective and that includes consideration of what sort of targets it is most effective against, effect on troops over-estimated, moral effect imponderable, but killing effect not decisive, especially against an enemy with Russia's supreme disregard of human life. The A-bomb is extremely effective against aircraft in the open: far the best counter-air weapon in existence. This is where it may have a decisive effect on the outcome of the opening battle.' He suggested the creation of a single Air Commander-in-Chief operating closely with SACEUR at all times. SHAPE would be responsible for pre-planned operations, such as counter-air and interdiction, in the event of an attack, shifting the bomber effort between subordinate land commanders. SACEUR would have the authority to take a final decision whether the bombers needed to be called in direct support of his forces in an extreme emergency.[47]

The role of the attack on submarine pens remained more nebulous in Air Staff thinking. It provided a useful stick with which to beat the Royal Navy,[48] and it was a role in which Slessor had shown an early interest. Its main importance, however, was the personal interest Churchill took in the issue. Slessor tried to get talks going with the Americans, pointing out that 'we have some extremely highly trained crews in Bomber Command who could do this job if they gave us the bombs'[49] but although he aroused some interest from General Ridgway there was little enthusiasm in the United States Navy.[50] The RAF continued to accord prominence to this mission in the carriers versus bombers controversy of 1953-4 but the primary motivation for doing so may well have been a distaste for the carrier's proposed strike fleet role and the threat that major expenditure on naval air forces presented to the whole RAF.

Slessor's last months as CAS saw a concentrated effort to ensure that the need for the medium bomber force was unchallengeable. Throughout 1952 he still saw the threat to the force as considerable. In February he noted 'the Prime Minister does not deny the need for a bomber force, he says leave all that to the Americans.' Later in the year these worries had not diminished and this was the genesis of Slessor's well known paper 'The Place of the Bomber in British Policy' which he published in considerably revised form soon after his retirement. The thrust of the internal government paper of the title was aimed primarily towards Churchill[51] and to a lesser extent Lord Alexander.[52] As Slessor told Lord Trenchard:

> I don't trust our masters about the Bomber force. So far all is pretty well, but Alexander ... said something about leaving the long range bomber business to the Americans and the PM frequently refers to that. I'm afraid if the Treasury push really hard, the eyes of the Cabinet will turn, not to teeth and spectacles and housing and Welfare generally, but to the Bomber force as a means of saving money. ... I think even Churchill may find it difficult to laugh off the quotations from himself.[53]

Slessor also wanted the RAF to be completely committed to the V-bombers since he feared 'that by no means all RAF officers, even senior ones, fully recognise the vital importance of the Bomber force.' He ordered his paper to be widely circulated within the service.[54]

In 'The Place of the Bomber in British Policy' Slessor pulled together all the arguments for the British bomber force. He started with Churchill's own public statement from a speech in Boston in 1949: 'For good or ill, air mastery is today the supreme expression of military power and Fleets and Armies, however necessary, must accept a subordinate rank'. He then went on argue that the bomber was the main weapon of 'air mastery'. Above all it was the 'Great Deterrent' to war. It alone could put direct pressure on the enemy, overcoming the vast spaces that were Russia's main defence. The bomber offensive had been the great 'unseen campaign' of the Second World War since the winning of air superiority had enabled the armies and navies to win their victories. He described the bomber as vital to the support of the land campaign, the most efficient, economical and accurate weapon available. Thus far he had dealt with an Anglo-American force preserving the 'Pax Atlantica'. He went on to make the case for a British force. He cited the practical argument that although Britain could never match American numbers it had a unique contribution to make in terms of fighting value, battle experience, training, design and invention. His main case, however, revolved around the bomber and great power status. The RAF in the 1950s without bombers would be like the Royal Navy in the eighteenth century without ships of the line. Ground support, maritime and fighter aircraft were like gunboats, frigates and seaward defences of the fleet. Without the bomber Britain would be a '3rd Class' power comparable with France or even Turkey and unable to influence the USA. 'In war, we should have no more influence on the direction of Allied strategy or on the determination of the terms of peace than did Canada last time. In peace, we should lose what influence we have, and it is still important, upon American policy.'[55]

It would be misleading to suggest that the advocacy of Slessor and the RAF kept the bomber project alive. Indeed Slessor complained that Churchill did not acknowledge his final paper on the role of the bomber; a snub which ensured that Slessor would publish his views so that they could not be ignored.[56] The independent atomic programme had other, equally important, allies such as Lord Cherwell who shared some of Slessor's opinions. Cherwell told Churchill that: 'If we are unable to make bombs ourselves and have to rely entirely on the United States army for this vital weapon we shall sink to the rank of a second-class nation, only permitted to supply auxiliary troops, like native levies were allowed small arms but not artillery.'[57]

The other Chiefs of Staff still felt that Britain should have an independent deterrent hence their agreement to the main part of Global Strategy. The Army and Navy envisaged a basic deterrent which would be as small as possible in order to allow resources to be allocated to their own services but the bitter inter-service battles over the size of forces were just getting under way in 1952.[58]

The way in which Slessor chose to argue his case to Churchill suggests that the practicalities of military strategy were of secondary importance in maintaining political support for the V-bombers. Nevertheless, military thought was also important since a role which could not be militarily justified had little political utility. Britain would probably have begun construction of a nuclear force even without the advocacy of John Slessor and others in the Air Ministry and RAF but their activities between 1950 and 1952 shaped the way in which its eventual role was conceived and hence its subsequent position in political and defence debates. The need to protect the bomber force in the defence programme ensured that its role, as a counterforce element of a larger Anglo-American offensive, was closely defined. The attractions of the counterforce mission stemmed from the assumptions of nuclear scarcity around which Global Strategy was based. Its main usefulness, however, was that it provided a distinct role for a British bomber force.

The proselytizing effort of the early 1950s was successful both within and to a certain extent outside the RAF. To quote Sir Frank Cooper's summary:

> you can date from about 1952 the fact the Air Staff was actually fighting for the deterrent very much by itself but with heavy political support and, indeed, heavy economic support because it was proven to be much cheaper than spending money on conventional forces. But from then on ... there was really Parliamentary disagreement with the Navy and Army as to how much should be spent. ... That fight was, I think, well carried by the Air Staff but they were fortunate in the sense that things were running their way; nobody had any better ideas. ... But the Air Staff was remarkably cohesive, remarkably coherent and remarkably consistent in the sense that it said that we were going to build up the V-force and that was what its policy was.[59]

RAF-USAF Nuclear Relations

The central element of British nuclear strategy was the reliance on American atomic air power and in the longer term a desire to achieve a co-ordinated Anglo-American nuclear policy. Yet RAF-USAF relations went through a difficult time in early 1950. At the root of the problem was the explosion of the first Soviet atomic bomb in August 1949. For several years to come Britain would be under the threat of nuclear devastation whilst the United States was relatively secure. The immediate problem was confusion over the 'Galloper'/'Offtackle' plan and provision of airfields for the USAF. 'Galloper' seems to have been negotiated by the Air Ministry on its own initiative since on taking office Slessor insisted to the senior USAF officer in the United Kingdom that the Chiefs of Staff and ministers would have to be informed of the plan to receive six USAF heavy bomber groups in Britain in time of war. He explained that only a few people outside the Air Ministry knew about 'Offtackle' and officially no plan existed. He felt the RAF were already in the wrong for agreeing to even a paper plan for the reception of Allied forces in Britain and that permission would have to be sought for money to be spent on new facilities. In reply to the argument advanced by General Vandenberg that the United States had not yet agreed on its own strategy so was unable to become involved in government to government negotiations he pointed out that the JCS seemed to be completely in agreement about the need to deploy in Britain. Slessor stressed the necessity of informing the Defence Committee that plans were in existence for the use of atomic weapons from British bases very early in any war.[60] When pressed by the USAF, who wanted to start exercises to practice the movement of forces over the Atlantic, he was forced to admit that although the the RAF wanted to continue joint planning it needed political authority to do so and to go any further on its own would have very embarrassing repercussions.[61]

The picture in 1950 shows much less certainty in air atomic relations than two years previously. Slessor blamed the confusion on Bevin's preoccupation with other issues especially the January 1950 Colombo Conference. It could be added that by 1949, unlike in 1946-7, there were regular meetings between British and American planners so planning tended to take on its own momentum. Slessor saw a real danger that if the United States was told that it was welcome as a wartime ally but not necessarily in peacetime the anglophobe Secretary of Defense, Louis Johnson, could be goaded into withdrawing American forces at once.[62] He told the Chiefs of Staff that the Americans had developed a fixation over the airfields, believing not only that Britain should pay for them but also that they had agreed to do so. He warned that they could become difficult over the whole field of military co-operation.[63]

Formal negotiations with the United States were begun in February 1950 when Slessor wrote to Vandenberg stating that although the USAF were welcome in Britain the United Kingdom could not afford to pay the £7 million for its airfields since the money would come out of the RAF budget and seriously affect its usefulness as an ally.[64] The outcome of this approach was the 'Ambassadors' Agreement' negotiated in April 1950 by the Under-Secretary of State for Air, Aidan Crawley. This agreement provided funding for the four heavy bomber airfields in Oxfordshire and welcomed the USAF in peacetime whilst assuring Britain of the right to terminate its stay.[65] Discussions about the ensuing Special Construction Programme, which significantly enlarged American facilities, went on into 1951. The final agreement stipulated that each country would meet half the costs.[66] These financial arrangements rapidly grew beyond Britain's ability to pay; the 1950-1 arrangements were effectively the last major cash contribution made by the British towards the American bases; from then on expansion was funded almost exclusively by the USAF[67] and there were fears that a change in relations would follow. As Slessor himself wrote:

> I think in many rather imponderable ways it would pay us to make some contribution - make it a partnership instead of us being vis-a-vis the Americans in the position the Egyptians and Iraqis have been in vis-a-vis us in the past - we paying the whole cost of our stations in their countries. ... I do know the Americans pretty well and I have a very strong hunch this is the right thing to do.[68]

Yet there was no fundamental change in British attitudes to match such fears, inasmuch that increased financial dependence did not alter the policy of remaining an ally supplying the whole range of military capabilities including an independent nuclear force.

The long-term future of the USAF in Britain, as it was formalised in the early months of 1950, was integral to British strategy since it coincided with the reappraisal of that strategy started by Slessor himself.[69] The Chiefs of Staff's 1950 Defence Policy and Global Strategy paper called for global unity with the United States. The first aim would be the stabilisation of the European front followed by agreement on political and military strategy in the Middle East and Asia. Atomic air power was to be the key to this strategy both as a deterrent and as the main offensive weapon in war.[70]

The RAF was completely committed to an independent force but always saw it in the context of an Anglo-American joint bomber effort.[71] Whilst the British lacked the atomic bomb, and even after they gained atomic capability, knowledge of American atomic strategy was therefore vital for British strategy. If the USA proved unwilling to provide information and refused to admit any British influence on its thinking British reliance on the American atomic deterrent would be demonstrably hollow. From 1951 onwards there was a persistent and determined attempt to gain information on and influence over United States strategy. These efforts were linked with the repeated and futile attempts, starting with Attlee's flight to Washington in December 1950, to gain some measure of joint control over SAC bombers based in Britain.[72] The concept of a joint Anglo-American atomic strategy was constantly reiterated. Adherence to this theme can be explained by a mixture of British wishful thinking, the realisation that there were few other options and the success of contacts at an air force level.

In 1949 Slessor had felt that it was vital to have joint planning on the British bomber force but he was highly critical of American policy. First, because the United States military establishment seemed paralysed by inter-service disputes. Second, because, although it seemed very likely that the United States would be willing to use A-bombs against Russia in the event of war, it lacked any concept of using heavy bombers and atomic bombs for an 'Overlord' style offensive in Europe rather than long-distance flights from the Western Hemisphere.[73] These views were reinforced in June 1950 when the Commander-in-Chief of Bomber Command met SAC's commanding general Curtis LeMay to discuss deployment plans in the United Kingdom and the use of B-29s. It became clear that LeMay was thinking purely in terms of the threat to the United States and an air atomic offensive against Russia itself. Nevertheless Slessor took some comfort from statements made by Louis Johnson and the Army Chief of Staff Omar Bradley that showed some American thinking in terms of committing nuclear weapons to Europe.[74]

There was not much encouragement to be drawn from talks during and after Attlee's visit to Washington. Tedder asked Bradley for details of the strategic air plan but the latter refused to divulge anything of importance. The JCS did meet Slessor but little progress was made.[75] In the light of these exchanges Slessor did not alter his view that the main air offensive would have to be left to the United States. He did, however, insist on the importance of creating an atomic armed Valiant force as quickly as as possible since without it the Americans would simply continue to brush off Britain's views on the grounds that it had no significant military nuclear capability.[76] Slessor's conviction was based on a sound understanding of his counterparts in the American military. The JCS did not want Britain to develop atomic weapons or a bomber force and were thus unlikely to offer any encouragement or technical assistance. At the same time they recognised that Britain could probably not be prevented from developing a nuclear force and if it did some bilateral links would become desirable.[77]

In February 1951, dissatisfied with bilateral contacts up to that point, Slessor wrote to Paul Nitze, the Director of the State Department's Policy Planning Staff that 'it was a matter of vital importance and extreme urgency that the United States should agree to immediate joint study of the strategic use of the bomb, and to a disclosure to Britain of plans for its use.'[78] These efforts to elicit information were in some ways counterproductive. Vandenberg was angered by what he saw as British attempts to trick Truman into restoring Britain's right to take part in a joint decision over the use of atomic weapons and Slessor's effort to circumvent the American military by taking his case to the State Department.[79] The hard line taken by the JCS ensured that talks conducted by Herbert Morrison in September 1951 were fruitless.[80]

The British do, however, seem to have made some progress at a less exalted level by the end of 1951.[81] Churchill's visit to Washington in January 1952 achieved some further advance. The demonstration of the strategic air plan he was given on 18 January was important mainly in establishing a good atmosphere. It does not seem to have revealed anything that the British did not know already[82] but it did enable British military representatives to persuade the Americans to agree to strategic and tactical discussions at a professional level.[83]

Slessor's summary of the situation in January 1952 was:

> We do in fact know quite a lot but not yet enough to enable us to make an assessment of the plan adequate to enable us to advise HMG in a period of tension when the possibility of having to put the plan into effect may be imminent.[84]

Air Chief Marshal Sir Ralph Cochrane, who was accompanying Churchill's party to advise Lord Cherwell on nuclear negotiations, and Sir Kenneth Strong, the head of the JIB, went on to SAC headquarters at Omaha in order to discuss operational plans with LeMay.[85] They took with them detailed requests for information which give some idea of the state of British knowledge about American plans. They wanted to know about American nuclear capability, the provision made for targets of special interest to Britain, and in more general terms other target systems the Americans were considering.

The nature of the questions would suggest that the British military were not particularly well informed about detailed American plans. They requested information on the number of American bombers available for strategic and tactical missions from 1952 to 1955, the operational sorties they were capable of over a six month period, the estimated casualty rate and bombing error. They asked about target objectives, the target systems and individual targets within these systems selected for attack, the arguments underlying target selection, the effect an attack would have on a target and its general influence on a war, and the extent to which the initial attack would be limited by the need for prior reconnaissance.[86]

Cochrane and Strong then identified the targets of special interest to the United Kingdom and asked what allocations had been made to them and at what stage in the offensive. The British wanted a guarantee that the USAF would attack Russian medium bomber airfields in order to reduce the threat Britain. They wanted to know how the United States planned to tackle the Russian tactical air force, with which aircraft and weapons and to what planned effect. The representatives of the Chiefs of Staff made it clear that it was this counter-air offensive which had a vital bearing on Britain and the employment of Bomber Command. They also wanted to know the scale of attack to be devoted to Russian submarine and mining bases and the retardation of Soviet land forces. Finally they inquired about other possible targets, the consequential effects of attacks on primary targets and the allowance made for re-attack. In each case the British felt they had enough technical information on atomic weapons to perform an independent analysis on American plans.[87]

Slessor himself travelled to the United States in July in order to present the 1952 Global Strategy Paper to the JCS. Global Strategy was written partly with the aim of convincing the Americans that the planned NATO build up of ninety-eight divisions and ten thousand aircraft was 'an economic impossibility, a logistic nightmare and a strategic nonsense' and that an increase in atomic air power coupled with a reduction in conventional forces was sound strategy, economically possible and best way of preventing war. Slessor met with rebuff. Bradley told him that Allied bombing had not defeated Germany and that a new strategy was premature since no tactical atomic weapons would be available until 1955.[88] The British side did, however, conclude that the USAF was more amenable to their ideas.[89]

On Churchill's instructions Slessor took a particular interest in possible American atomic attacks on Soviet submarine bases and was just as disappointed with the results. He found that they were not included in United States air plans except for carrier strikes on Black Sea bases. He held inconclusive discussions with LeMay and SACLANT, Admiral McCormick, on missions in the Arctic and Baltic. The USAF said this was a USN problem but SACLANT claimed he did not have the resources to attack these bases. Slessor complained that USAF/USN co-operation was woeful[90] and found that SACLANT was particularly uncommunicative on atomic matters.[91]

Despite these setbacks by the autumn of 1952 there was a perceptible increase in confidence about American atomic planning. Slessor told Lord Trenchard: 'I do not think our influence is negligible in their thinking; anyway we did give them some useful moral support by bringing the views of the British Chiefs of Staff (all three) to the support of the USAF case'.[92] He wrote to Sir William Elliot:

As you know, we have made valuable progress in combined planning for the Strategic Air Offensive since Ralph Cochrane's visit in March and I am most anxious to maintain and nourish that co-operation. Ken Strong thinks it very important, and I agree, that it shall receive periodical boosts from high level visits ... he [Sir William Dickson, CAS-designate] should have a briefing on the Strategic Air Plan. He is not really in that picture at all and obviously should be; the fact of the Americans having taken me so much into their confidence on it paid off in a big way in the Global Strategy negotiations here.[93]

Slessor was able to dismiss the worries of the Canadian CAS about the lack of a coherent air policy. He did, however, agree that a meeting with Vandenberg would be useful[94] in order to get USAF/RCAF approval for Global Strategy and to work out a system of air command in NATO with reference to the British-based bomber force.[95] At this meeting in late November 1952 it was agreed that urgent action was necessary to co-ordinate the air operations and targeting plans of SAC, RAF Bomber Command, SHAPE and USN carrier task forces for both the air offensive against Russia and the land and counter-air campaign in Europe. Slessor and Vandenberg agreed that RAF and USAF staffs should examine the problem and exchange papers.[96] Yet looking back on the period between 1952 and 1956 Sir Dermot Boyle was to comment 'the UK ... had been denied information on the planned targets for SAC forces based in this country'.[97]

In 1950 to 1952 the United States gave very little away. An increased flow of information and vague statements that co-operation in air operations would be desirable, balanced by a refusal to accept British strategic prescriptions and attempts to limit the United States' freedom of action. Exactly what the British were told must be open to doubt since there were serious disputes within the American defence establishment over targeting. As a result of this, and the USAF's attempts to achieve the biggest and most powerful Strategic Air Command possible, five to six thousand targets - covering all possible systems ranging from Soviet nuclear capability through ground forces to industry - were under consideration.[98] Nevertheless, there was a considerable impact on British thinking. This was partly due to the influence of Sir John Slessor who, like Churchill, had a tendency to overestimate his own importance to the Americans.[99] More importantly, it seemed that USAF/RAF contacts were producing worthwhile results, that Britain had some impact on United States thinking and that superior knowledge of American plans was useful for the RAF in British strategic and budgetary debates. On the other hand obvious differences with the United States and the realisation that Britain was not going to achieve any worthwhile co-operation until it had something concrete to offer in return strengthened the existing belief in an independent British nuclear force and increased the emphasis on counterforce operations in its justification.[100]

Slessor and NATO Strategy

Sir John Slessor firmly believed European security was vital to the defence of the United Kingdom. In July 1945 he had written:

> England's frontier is on the Oder ... Norway, Denmark, Holland, Belgium, even France, make no strategic sense except as part of a Western European security bloc ... and that bloc could not ultimately survive without the support of America, any more than America could survive, in the long run, the loss of her outpost in Europe.[101]

When he became Chief of the Air Staff in January 1950 Slessor felt that British planning was drifting aimlessly and that the Chiefs of Staff should take a firm personal hold of it.[102] He placed the question of European defence at the heart of his 1950 Defence Policy and Global Strategy Paper. The aim of British strategy was described as the confinement of Russian communism within the borders of the Soviet Union without resort to a 'shooting' war: a policy requiring worldwide unity between Britain and the United States. According to the paper the first aim of this alliance should be to stabilise the European front but this was only to be the first step. In the long-run the aim was agreement on political and military strategy in the Middle East and Asia.

Slessor argued that the defence of the Rhine was vital to the defence of the United Kingdom and that this defence was, at present, impossible even with an atomic offensive launched against Russia itself. The key to any change in strategy was the remilitarisation of Germany. He dismissed fears of Germany as a threat to European security on the grounds that atomic airpower offered a final sanction against revanchism. His ultimate aim was the formation of a German army as a land component, lacking tanks and aircraft, in the unified forces of Western Europe. His preferred strategy in the event of a Russian attack would be to hold a bastion in Germany whilst sacrificing Scandinavia and Italy. The paper outlined Slessor's belief that the Middle East was important but not as important as Europe to the survival of the United Kingdom.[103]

As forcefully expressed by Slessor the reordering of strategic priorities towards Europe seemed quite clear. Yet although there was a significant shift in British policy before the outbreak of the Korean War it was highly conditional and once more looked primarily to the influence Britain could have on America. Europe was identified as the first stage in a global framework not as an area to which British power could be limited.

Although there is no available record of the private discussions between the Chiefs of Staff which produced the agreed text of the Global

Strategy Paper the general course of these negotiations can be gleaned from papers exchanged within the regular Chiefs of Staff framework. The Joint Planners reported in March 1950 that Europe would have to become more important to British strategy since the early development of the A-bomb by the Russians would mean the loss of the deterrent effect of the American nuclear stockpile. Britain had survived the loss of Europe in 1940 but with the offence so much stronger the two now had to be regarded as one defensive unit. The threat to the Middle East was also reassessed to discount any major Soviet offensive in the first six months of a war. The planners acknowledged that although much had been achieved between 1948 and 1950 it was mainly in the realm of planning and consultation and a real defence effort had to be built on it.[104]

Reviewing American intentions the planners gave weight to the statements of the JCS that no American forces would be available to reinforce the Rhine until three months after the outbreak of any war and, if European defence had collapsed already, these forces would be sent to North Africa instead. They advocated a British promise to send two divisions to Europe immediately on the outbreak of any war.[105] One reason cited for such a guarantee was the lack of French faith in British support which would hinder any attempt to develop NATO. Both the planners and Slessor made clear, however, that the main justification for the reinforcement of BAOR was an attempt to persuade the Americans to put forces on the Rhine. Sir Gladwyn Jebb, representing Bevin and the Foreign Office, observed that whatever Britain did the French would not be satisfied but it was nevertheless in Britain's best interests to make the commitment to Europe. He quoted Bevin's view that assistance for the French could be used as a lever to get American forces involved in the Middle East as well as Europe.[106]

When the chiefs came to present their conclusions to ministers they minimised the the radicalism of the shift, arguing that the three 'pillars' of British strategy remained the same but needed two important modifications. First, the acceptance that the defence of the Rhine was vital to the defence of the United Kingdom and, second, the realisation that despite the Middle East's importance its defence could not be allowed to compromise the first 'pillar'. Yet they only suggested a very limited continental commitment, the promise of two divisions in the event of war, on the grounds that these divisions were not intended to be decisive militarily: they would, in fact, take three months to mobilise; if France fell they could easily be deployed elsewhere, something of which the allies were not to be informed. The chiefs stressed that Britain must resist any pressure to agree to a full continental army.[107]

Before these proposals were presented to the Defence Committee the chiefs met with the Minister of Defence, Shinwell, who believed that the defence of Western Europe was the most pressing concern for British strategy.[108] Shinwell set himself up as 'devil's advocate' and asked the military to meet the charges that the French would regard a two division contribution as farcical and that it was unwise to enter into any commitments without knowledge of American policy. The primary reason the chiefs cited for agreeing to the commitment was the hope of ensuing American involvement. Both Tedder, now the Chiefs of Staff representative in the United States, and Slim had been told by members of the JCS that American forces would be switched from North Africa to Europe if the Rhine could be held and the British detected encouraging signs in the NATO planning machinery about the build-up of American divisions outside the United States.[109]

The chief's ideas went to the Defence Committee fully supported by Shinwell but some, unnamed, ministers did indeed argue that the size of the force was militarily unrealistic and that France had no chance of resisting a Russian attack which would be heavier than the invasion of 1940. It was also stressed in committee that, given the emphasis previously placed on the Middle East, the commitment involved a major change in British strategy. With Attlee's support the proposals were finally accepted.[110]

Slessor had a pivotal role in the reorientation of British strategy around the propositions that the defence of Europe was integral to the defence of the United Kingdom and that this defence was only practicable with major German and American contributions, which the British would have to take the lead in obtaining. This shift in British strategy towards Europe in the first half of 1950 was obviously political in nature. Yet Slessor also explicitly stated that the defence of the Rhine was vital to the United Kingdom; if the Soviets ever occupied Western Europe they could destroy Britain with ease. The dual nature of Slessor's strategic thinking in early 1950 raises an important question about British policy: were armed forces in Europe meant to deter the Soviet Union and head off defeatism and neutralism in the Western nations or was there a real belief that in the long-term a conventional defence of the Rhine was possible?

The answer to this question lies in the actual defence planning which went on around the high-level political decision. Of particular interest for a study of the RAF's role is the fact that, although the short-term debate about a contribution revolved mainly around land forces, there were important airpower issues involved in this planning. For the RAF the continental commitment could have meant the build-up of a tactical air force to support the army on the continent. Although there had been little enthusiasm for a tactical air force before 1950 the period between 1950 and 1952, especially after the invasion of Korea, is usually seen as the high point of the attempt to construct a conventional defence strategy for NATO. For the RAF, however, this was always a short-term expedient and, despite the fact some thought was put into the role of tactical airpower, well before the agreement of the Lisbon force goals in February 1952 thinking within the air force was concentrated on the substitution of nuclear armed bombers for conventional forces. Thus military thought predated the Radical Review of the mid-1950s. Economic restraints certainly made alternative strategies more politically desirable but did not create them.

On becoming CAS Slessor had already made clear his view that in the long-run the nuclear armed bomber was the best weapon system not only to attack Russia but also to contribute to the European land campaign.[111] He was equally insistent that Britain needed to build up its land and tactical air force commitment to the continent in order to help preserve the European alliance and to convince the United States to commit forces to it.

He ordered RAF plans to be changed to commit all British heavy bomber squadrons to the European land campaign rather than being split between Europe and the Middle East, as envisaged under Plan 'Galloper'.[112] He then sedulously expounded this proposal, linking it with the two division continental commitment, despite Foreign Office doubts that such a change would be politically useful.[113] The change was announced in March to a meeting of Western Union senior officers.[114] The senior RAF officer in NATO reported that it had had a positive effect in convincing Europeans of Britain's commitment but he acknowledged that it was a relatively minor gesture compared with the tasks faced by the alliance.[115]

Although Slessor had opposed Tedder's neglect of the tactical air force much less emphasis was put on this force in the first half of 1950 than the commitment of Bomber Command. The RAF argued that the commitment of two divisions did not mean that they had to strengthen BAFO accordingly; a position which was attacked by Lord Fraser, who pointed out that it was ridiculous to contemplate sending an army to Europe bereft of air support.[116] The Ministry of Defence under Shinwell also urgently requested that consideration be given to the formation of a more impressive tactical air force. It was not until June 1950 that Slessor ordered an Air Staff study on the need for a British commitment to the Western Union tactical air force beyond BAFO and Bomber Command.[117] This study showed that in July 1950 BAFO would consist of 48 fighter-bombers, 32 obsolete light bombers and 26 reconnaissance aircraft. It was planned that this should increase in 1954 to 32 Canberra jet bombers, 26 reconnaissance aircraft and 96 Vampire or Venom jet fighter-bombers. Referring back to the 1949 Air Advisory Committee report, which had set the target strength of the WUTAF at 1800 plus 200 light bombers by 1954, with the RAF providing 45% of the total, the most the Air Staff could envisage providing was 276 front-line aircraft, some 28 squadrons short of the target.[118] When considering the aircraft the air force had a prospect of receiving, the Hunter, the Vampire and the Canberra they did not recommend the build-up of a tactical air force but of a Canberra force operating from outside the battle area.[119]

This lukewarm attitude to tactical airpower can be explained in three ways. First, the independence of the air force was best guaranteed by bombers rather than fighter-bombers which had to operate in concert with land forces. Second, many officers interpreted the experience of the Second World War as showing fighter-bombers to be only of limited military effectiveness. As Tedder put it 'in the latter stages of the Overlord campaign thousands of fighter-bomber sorties were spent on shooting up railways and roads; the moral effect was undoubtedly considerable but the material effect was slight'.[120] Finally, there was no real confidence that even with a major American contribution NATO could build up an air force to match the Soviets. A 1949 intelligence report estimated that in April 1950 Soviet front-line air strength would amount to 20,480 aircraft as opposed to a total of 6,361 for the USA, Britain, the rest of NATO and the Commonwealth and that the Soviets had a similar advantage in aircraft production.[121]

In examining the development of strategy it is important to realise that there was never a deep commitment in the RAF to the build up of tactical air forces. The major programme initiated after the outbreak of the Korean war was a response to the perceived political fragility of the Western European countries. As Slessor put it a month before the Korean invasion:

> I don't think it will necessarily be a question of military defeat, because there may not be a hot war at all, it is no good blinding ourselves to the fact that, on present form, an ultimatum by Russia within the next two to three years, especially if backed by the threat of atomic attack on London, Paris, Brussels and the Hague, would result in the Western Union folding up like a pack of cards. I would hope, even then, we (the UK) would reject the ultimatum and stand up to it. But I do not even feel absolutely sure of that unless we can make ourselves far less defenceless than we are now.[122]

In responding to the Korean War he did not fear an impending Soviet attack on Europe but called on the government to strengthen its defensive posture.

> It may not be too much to hope that the events of the last week will convince the Government that, if we are to prevent a Third World War, we can no longer go on as we are at present on the assumption that we shall get 18 months 'warning', which is the basis of our present defence preparations. ... I do not myself believe that shooting war has been

brought nearer by Korea - rather the reverse provided we take advantage of the object lesson. But the simple fact is that we are taking fantastic risks, and the way to make reasonably sure the fire will not spread is to put ourselves in a position of strength without delay.[123]

His immediate response was to order the formation of new fighter-bomber squadrons on the grounds that 'in the present situation we cannot afford to do nothing about strengthening Western Union.'[124]

The Attlee government produced three year defence expenditure programmes of £3400 million in August 1950, £3600 million in September and £4700 million in January 1951 which effectively removed financial constraints from military planning.[125] Over the summer a Western Union plan for a 6000 strong tactical air force was drawn up and the Western Union chiefs of air staff agreed on an initial total of 2200. In August 1950 the RAF agreed to start transforming BAFO from a static occupation force into a mobile tactical air force.[126]

Looking back from 1952 Slessor offered two reasons for this immediate build-up of forces. First, the risk that if no real and visible effort was made the United States would withdraw its support from Europe and the European nations would lapse into neutralism and defeatism leading to Communist domination. Second, the general conception of World War Three as a Red Army offensive through Germany which it would be vital to hold on the Rhine since England would be unable to survive the prolonged occupation of the Channel coast. Slessor claimed that he had never believed in this latter view of strategy, although it was the one put forward in his own Global Strategy paper as a justification for a shift of forces from the Middle East.[127] It seems that he feared the shock of the Soviet Union attaining a nuclear capability could create despondency and required plans, the defence of the Rhine, a counterforce targeting policy for British bombers, improved air defence, which showed that Britain could be defended. As he commented in January 1950: 'We must never overlook the danger that, if we put the case [that Britain's defences were inadequate] too strongly, we may induce in some quarters the attitude of mind that as nothing we can do ... can give us security why spend even what we are now spending on defence'.[128]

Despite Slessor's private reservations, British strategy actually proceeded along the lines set out in the 1950 Global Strategy paper with its emphasis on maximum American and German involvement in the conventional defence of Europe. It became clear in early September 1950, before Bevin left for the North Atlantic Council meetings in New York, that the Americans were willing to consider the creation of unified military force in Europe involving both themselves and the Germans.[129] The American proposals, which envisaged a German Army under an

American Supreme Commander, were actually more in line with those contained in Global Strategy than the *Gendarmerie* under Federal government control proposed by Adenauer and accepted by the British government under Bevin's guidance. The key Chiefs of Staff recommendation, however, was that Britain should show maximum flexibility. At this stage it was the fact rather than the exact nature of American and German involvement that mattered to the British military.[130]

Against this background Britain's own continental commitment rapidly took shape. On 15 September 1950 Shinwell formally announced that Britain would send one armoured division to France in 1951 and earmark two further divisions to be sent in the event of war. In response to the NATO force goal discussions of October 1950 the Defence Committee approved the dispatch of a further armoured division[131] and it was accepted that these land forces would be given full air support with a planned forty RAF squadrons to be stationed in Germany.[132]

The traditional view of British strategy is that it was only seriously reconsidered when the strains on the British economy caused by rearmament became insupportable from late 1951. In 1950 these commitments were not seen as a decisive shift of ground forces from other theatres to Europe since they were entered into in the context of army plans to expand to ten regular and twelve territorial divisions by 1954 under the £3600 million programme.[133] Slessor's 1952 comments suggest serious strategic doubts emerged whilst money still seemed to be available for ambitious force programmes. This leaves the question of whether the emergence of the belief that the defence of Europe should rest primarily on nuclear airpower was inevitable or whether it needs to be explained with reference to the events of 1951-2. As already demonstrated the support for tactical air forces in Europe was never particularly strong within the RAF and long-term planning always concentrated on the light and medium bomber force but there was, nevertheless, an important process of change at work.

Despite Air Staff scepticism about the continental commitment there were attempts in the air force to work out some kind of balance between conventional and atomic air power. Various views on this theme were put forward by Aidan Crawley, the Under-Secretary of State for Air in the Labour government,[134] Sir Hugh Saunders, Eisenhower's Air Deputy who warned: 'we must not expect to find an easy solution to our problems by the prodigal and ineffective use of the atomic bomb'[135] and Sir Robert Foster the commander of 2nd TAF.[136] Probably the most cogent case, however, was put forward in 1951 by Air Vice-Marshal Sir George Mills. Starting from the position that the classical means of conducting an air/land campaign was to disrupt essential enemy bases and lines of communication he pointed out that the Western European front was huge and had an advanced transport system with few bottlenecks. He believed conventional or atomic attacks against this system would be of only limited efficacy citing the Ardennes offensive and the Chinese and North Korean invasions of South Korea. He then suggested that since airpower could not stop a land offensive on its own the West needed strong ground forces. He argued that the experience of the early campaigns of the Second World War, Poland, France, Burma and the Pacific had shown that if the enemy had overwhelming air superiority land forces would be brushed aside so these armies needed supporting air forces. He further argued that once Russia had achieved a large nuclear stockpile there would be doubts whether the allies would use atomic bombs against it thus strengthening the case for the conventional defence of Europe.[137]

Such proposals were undermined by the experience of trying to set up air forces in 1951. This experience suggested to British officers that whatever Britain did the continental countries were not going to build up sufficient conventional forces. In addition not only were none of the officers who favoured a balanced continental commitment in positions of major influence but, as Sir Hugh Saunders complained, there was little contact between senior officers serving in NATO posts and the Air Staff.[138]

As early as February 1951 Slessor had conceived grave doubts that the continental air forces would meet the contributions agreed by NATO in late 1950 in a document known as DC.28. The DC.28 plan called for a front line of 9212 aircraft by the end of 1954.[139] Both the British and the American air leaders agreed that the most pressing need was to get the maximum build-up possible in the short-term and Slessor proposed that NATO chiefs of air staff should meet to co-ordinate their expansion programmes. At American insistence only the United States, Britain, France and Canada were to be initially involved in these discussions.[140]

Meetings were held in Washington in May and Paris in June. At the Washington meeting the United States produced the 'Pentagon Plan', a scheme of allocations for the DC.28 force goals, which Slessor criticised as unachievable by France and the other continental countries. At Paris he was shocked to find that all the European countries accepted the Pentagon figures. France claimed it could produce an air force twice the size of its DC.28 contribution and five times its present size in five years. When Belgium, Denmark, Italy, the Netherlands and Norway were consulted at the end of the meeting only Denmark and Holland claimed they could not meet their targets. Slessor came away from the conference convinced that the Europeans were not to be relied upon. Although acknowledging that useful work was being done in such areas as infrastructure he believed that all that was being produced were unrealistic paper plans.[141] Slessor was also highly critical of the USAF for launching an air expansion programme which would produce a huge air defence establishment for the continental United States but relatively little for Europe.[142] Despite his belief that only a large increase in USAF deployment in Europe could make sense of NATO plans, however, he advocated the diversion of resources to Strategic Air Command rather than tactical air forces.[143] By the summer of 1951 Slessor's belief that the build-up of conventional forces in Europe was strategically wrongheaded had been confirmed.

Military reasoning, such as Slessor's, economic pressure and pessimistic assessments of Russian military capabilities all had an impact on British strategy in period up to the acceptance of the Lisbon force goals in February 1952. Once more there was a tension between that which was considered politically necessary in order to maintain the cohesion of NATO and that which was believed to be militarily desirable.[144] As a result Britain was in favour of the American proposal, made at the December 1951 Ottawa NATO Council meeting, to set up the Temporary Council Committee (TCC) in order to produce some realistic planning to bridge the recognised gap between between military needs and 'politico-military capability'.[145] Averell Harriman, Sir Edwin Plowden and Jean Monnet, more colloquially known as 'the three wise men', were appointed to lead the committee.

Central to the reconsideration of strategy which shaped their endeavours was a SHAPE report, MC.33, endorsed by the Standing Group in November 1951, on NATO and Soviet capabilities and strategy. MC.33 was to be the basis for the assessment of Soviet strength until the early 1960s. It described Soviet military manpower rising from between 5.4 and 6.6 million in 1952 to between 5.9 and 7.2 million in 1954. It was estimated that by 1954 NATO would face 175-180 Soviet divisions, 65-70 satellite divisions and rapidly modernising air forces of over 20,000 front-line aircraft. The intelligence specialists argued that although Soviet industry was vulnerable to air atomic attack such an attack would not halt the land offensive. To achieve victory on the European battle front NATO would need 96 divisions and 9141 front-line aircraft by the end of 1954.[146]

The report was not accepted at its face value by the British government. Lord Cherwell questioned the figures as merely an average of estimates by various NATO intelligence agencies.[147] Churchill only accepted the 'working hypothesis' that the Soviet threat amounted to about 80 divisions.[148] Nevertheless, both men regarded the report as 'sombre reading' which demonstrated that the West would find it almost impossible to match Soviet conventional strength.[149]

The TCC accepted the recommendations of MC.33 but there was considerable disagreement between its three members. Monnet forced discussion on immediate defence needs and pressed the Americans for more aid whilst the British tried to shift discussion on to longer-term strategy 'in order to get a moral commitment from the United States to give adequate support to Europe'.[150] When Churchill met Harriman he did acknowledge that interim readiness of conventional forces was an important deterrent and pressed for greatly expanded economic and military aid for both Britain and France but he also urged that the nature of the Russian threat and the potential of nuclear weapons to combat it should be reassessed.[151]

The key political figures in the British government, Churchill, Eden and Butler, and their professional military advisers all agreed in late January 1952 that the TCC report should be accepted[152] but there was considerable disappointment about its results. Eden reported to the Cabinet that Britain had had two aims, to use the report to extract more aid from Congress and to improve the readiness and efficiency of existing forces. The United States government had maintained that its effort was so large that it could not be increased. The possibility of better conventional forces seemed to be vitiated by the French contention that they would have to decrease their forces without more aid and the refusal of Italy and Belgium to increase their expenditure as required. Eden therefore labelled the exercise a failure but admitted that it was politically impossible make this view public because of the enthusiasm of the Americans, particularly Eisenhower, for the report.[153]

The Chiefs of Staff accepted the report although they too doubted its practicability. Their views on strategy were moving towards Slessor's position and they argued that the risk of extending the period of conventional inferiority was greatly reduced by growing atomic superiority which was 'unlikely to be offset by a corresponding increase in Russian ability to defend themselves against it'. They also made clear the view that 'we must give the closest attention and priority to the development of atomic warfare to offset these deficiencies by the tactical use of atomic weapons in the field and for the attack of enemy airfields and submarine bases'.[154]

At the NATO Lisbon summit in February 1952 the British government endorsed the TCC plan on the grounds that defensive strength was the best deterrent to aggression.[155] This was, however, merely a holding exercise whilst a new strategy was worked out. In the first few months of 1952 there was agreement within the defence establishment that British policy towards Europe would involve a greater reliance on nuclear weapons but no consensus on the exact nature of this reliance.

Slessor was important in the formation of this new strategy not only because of his role in the writing of the 1952 Global Strategy Paper but also because he was recognised as the leading military adviser on NATO policy. Churchill insisted that he represent Britain at the December 1951 Rome NATO Council meeting which prepared the way for the Lisbon

Summit,[156] he was appointed as the representative of the Chiefs of Staff for Lisbon[157] and was the senior military figure at the informal meeting Churchill held at Chartwell, also attended by Eden and Lord Ismay, to discuss Britain's stance at the summit.[158]

Slessor was by this stage clear on what he thought strategy should be but was very aware of the political constraints placed upon it. As he wrote in March 1952:

> Supposing we and the United States were to say, in effect, 'Right, we are not going to go on wasting all this money and effort on conventional arms, divisions and Tactical Air Forces and carrier task forces, to defend Western Europe in a conventional way; which is impossible anyway. We are going to set ourselves (a) to make war impossible or (b) if we fail, making certain of eliminating the aggressor country from the face of the map in a week'. ... I think personally that makes sense. But how are you going to sell it (i) to the Western European countries, none of whom understand air power and (ii) to the Armies and Navies of the United Kingdom and United States. Eisenhower would never buy it; and he has established this extraordinary position as a sort of military demigod. I'm not sure the United States Navy will not buy it, if we accept they will provide the mobile A-bomb bases. But I wonder what the French and Benelux and the Germans would say![159]

His emphasis was very much on the deterrent effect of nuclear weapons and not on the defence of Europe as demonstrated by his response to the Stalin Note on Germany:

> I believe the only practicable safeguard ... would be an Anglo-American guarantee, given equally to Russia, Germany and France, that an attack by one against the other would automatically involve immediate and overwhelming atomic attack. That would mean retaining US bomber bases in East Anglia and building up the Valiant force. But it would not involve retaining US and British forces indefinitely on the Continent, and it might enable us to release forces for use in Asia where the real crunch in the Cold War may well come.[160]

Slessor wrote this idea into the 1952 Global Strategy Paper only to have it rejected by a Cabinet committee in July 1952.[161] Despite the opposition to his actual prescription for Germany it was within the context of such thinking that he also addressed the role of air power in support of SACEUR and concluded that the key to any European land battle was air superiority to be won by the use of nuclear weapons. Slessor argued that the most effective military force for NATO after 1954 would be 600-700 long-range fighter-bombers armed with atomic bombs.[162]

The role of tactical nuclear weapons within a massive retaliation strategy was not altogether clear but MC.33 had contended that the Red

Army would not be immediately halted by an attack on its homeland and Churchill believed:

> After the first phase the war may go forward in a broken-backed condition in various theatres apart from Europe, which would be overrun. The position of the Russian armies in Europe after their central government had been broken down and their communications with their homeland were severed, would indeed be peculiar. It might be that an arrangement could be come to on a non-Communist basis with the Russian Generals.[163]

Lord De L'Isle, the Secretary of State for Air, also accepted that 'if it does prove possible to hold the Russians in the West ... it will be due to the atom bomb used tactically as well as strategically to overcome Russian superior air power'.[164]

This is not to suggest that the British approach to continental defence was cut and dried by early 1952 but that RAF commitment to nuclear defence for Europe emerged early and strongly under Slessor's leadership. There was certainly an economic element to this development of ideas since Slessor believed that the Red Army could not be opposed by the conventional forces 'which NATO can ... build up without busting Europe and the UK economically; which may well be the Russian game'[165] and there were clear doubts emerging about the economic feasibility of the £4700 million rearmament programme by the end of 1951.[166] The conviction that Britain's role was as a world rather than a European power and that the threat was not a Soviet invasion of Europe but Communist subversion worldwide[167] meshed with the genuine attempt to think about the role of nuclear weapons. As cuts in defence spending became unavoidable the room for pluralism in strategy and procurement was correspondingly reduced and the Air Ministry as an important bureaucratic player became determined proponents for this approach to European defence.

To some extent RAF radicalism was masked by important practical considerations: the first British A-bomb was only exploded in October 1952, strategy had to be 'sold' to Britain's allies and there did not seem to be much prospect for an actual change in defence posture until 1955-6 at the earliest. Thus the RAF was much more advanced than the other services in proposals for co-operating, and to some extent integrating, with the EDC[168] Slessor was highly critical of announcements about the cutback of the British defence programme by Butler and Churchill because they were unilateral and not submitted through NATO machinery[169] and he made determined efforts to allay French fears that Britain was about to abandon its continental commitment.[170]

Yet in reality the Air Ministry had already abandoned the military objective of a conventional defence of Western Europe. The main role of forces in Europe was seen as 'the need to sustain the interest and faith of the US in an organisation which so largely stems from their initiative and relies on their support'.[171] In September 1952 the Air Ministry proposed a cut in the RAF contribution to SACEUR's forces so deep that it would equal the loss of the entire air forces of France, Belgium, Holland and Norway.[172]

Notes

1. Gowing, *Independence and Deterrence*, pp. 406-7.

2. 'The Role of the RAF', 25 July 1949, London, Ministry of Defence (Air Historical Branch), Slessor Papers, XIIF.

3. CAS to VCAS/DCAS, 1 March 1950, London, Public Record Office (P.R.O.), AIR8/1590.

4. CAS to VCAS, 13 Jan. 1950, London, Public Record Office (P.R.O.), AIR8/1590.

5. CAS to Air Staff, 3 Jan. 1950, London, Public Record Office (P.R.O.), AIR8/1590.

6. CAS to VCAS/DCAS, 1 March 1950, London, Public Record Office (P.R.O.), AIR8/1590.

7. 'Size and Shape of the RAF' Note by CAS to COS, July 1950, London, Public Record Office (P.R.O.), AIR8/1590.

8. DO(50)3rd, 31 Jan. 1950, London, Public Record Office (P.R.O.), AIR8/1590

9. AMSO Minute on CAS 186, 10 Feb. 1950, London, Public Record Office (P.R.O.), AIR8/1590.

10. 'Draft Paper on Defence Policy and Global Strategy' Slessor to Secretary of COS, 20 March 1950, London, Ministry of Defence (Air Historical Branch), Slessor Papers, XIVA.

11. DO(50)45, 7 June 1950, CAB131/9 printed in *DBPO*, Series 2, IV, pp. 411-431 and CAS to VCAS, 8 May 1950, London, Ministry of Defence (Air Historical Branch), Slessor Papers, XIVA. The paper was approved by the Chiefs of Staff on 11 May and by the Defence Committee on 25 May. Instructions were given to prepare a slightly amended version suitable for transmission to the US JCS and the governments of Canada, Australia and New Zealand. It is the slightly later version which has been declassified and is cited here.

12. *DBPO*, Series 2, IV, p. 411.

13. 'Draft Paper on Defence Policy and Global Strategy' Slessor to Secretary of COS, 20 March 1950, London, Ministry of Defence (Air Historical Branch), Slessor Papers, XIVA.

14. CAS to Secretary of State for Air, 10 March 1952, London, Public Record Office (P.R.O.), AIR20/8711.

15. 'Detailed Report by a Working Party set up to prepare revised Squadron Patterns and a revised Production Plan (CAS 1318), Sept. 1950, London, Public Record Office (P.R.O.), AIR8/1462.

16. 'Size and Shape of the RAF' Note by CAS to COS, undated, London, Public Record Office (P.R.O.), AIR8/1462.

17. CAS to VCAS, 8 May 1950, London, Ministry of Defence (Air Historical Branch), Slessor Papers, XIVA.

18. This debate is usefully summarised in Clark and Wheeler, *The British Origins of Nuclear Strategy*, pp. 160-1, 170. A detailed account of the paper itself can be found in Baylis and Macmillan, 'The British Global Strategy Paper of 1952', pp. 200-226.

19. Slessor to Slim, 3 April 1950, London, Ministry of Defence (Air Historical Branch), Slessor Papers, XIVA.

20. Cooper, 'The Origins and Development of the British Strategic Nuclear Deterrent Forces, 1945-1960', p. 28.

21. Baylis and Macmillan, 'The British Global Strategy Paper of 1952', p. 206.

22. Ibid., p. 212.

23. Ibid., p. 213.

24. 'Defence Policy in Economic Crisis' Paper by Sir John Slessor, 20 Oct. 1952, London, Ministry of Defence (Air Historical Branch), Slessor Papers, XIVD.

25. CAS to Secretary of State for Air, 10 March 1952, London, Public Record Office (P.R.O.), AIR20/8711.

26. CAS to Secretary of State for Air, 10 March 1952, London, Public Record Office (P.R.O.), AIR20/8711.

27. Slessor to Vandenberg, 1 March 1952, London, Ministry of Defence (Air Historical Branch), Slessor Papers, XXVC.

28. Secretary of State for Air to Slessor, 15 March 1952, London, Public Record Office (P.R.O.), AIR20/8711; Humphreys-Davies to Bancroft, 11 Dec. 1953, London, Public Record Office (P.R.O.), T225/350.

29. Clark and Wheeler, *British Origins of Nuclear Strategy*, pp. 147-8 and Baylis and Macmillan, 'The British Global Strategy Paper of 1952', p. 215.

30. LAWC/P(47)9, 18 Sept. 1947, London, Public Record Office (P.R.O.), AIR2/9881.

31. Tedder to Slessor, 6 April 1949, London, Ministry of Defence (Air Historical Branch), Slessor Papers, XIVA.

32. CAS to VCAS, 18 Dec. 1952, London, Ministry of Defence (Air Historical Branch), Slessor Papers, XIVD.

33. Clark and Wheeler, *British Origins of Nuclear Strategy*, pp. 149-50.

34. Cooper, 'The Origins and Development of the British Strategic Nuclear Deterrent Forces, 1945-1960', p. 28.

35. Brief for VCAS for meeting of Powell Working Party, 11 Aug. 1952, London, Public Record Office (P.R.O.), AIR8/1689.

36. Gowing, *Independence and Deterrence*, p. 230.

37. CAS to VCAS/DCAS, 1 March 1952, London, Public Record Office (P.R.O.), AIR8/1590.

38. Head of S.6 to AUS(G), 6 June 1950, London, Public Record Office (P.R.O.), AIR20/7086.

39. 'Draft Paper on Defence Policy and Global Strategy' Slessor to Secretary of COS, 20 March 1950, London, Ministry of Defence (Air Historical Branch), Slessor Papers, XIVA.

40. Slessor to VCAS, 8 May 1950, London, Ministry of Defence (Air Historical Branch), Slessor Papers, XIVA.

41. CAS to ACAS(I), 8 May 1950, London, Ministry of Defence (Air Historical Branch), Slessor Papers, XIVA.

42. 'Size and Shape of the RAF' Note by CAS, July 1950, London, Public Record Office (P.R.O.), AIR8/1462.

43. Slessor to Sir Frederick Brundrett, Sept. 1950, London, Ministry of Defence (Air Historical Branch), Slessor Papers, IIIE.

44. Chief Staff Officer to Minister of Defence to Prime Minister, December 1950, London, Ministry of Defence (Air Historical Branch), Slessor Papers, IIIE.

45. 'The Place of the Valiant in the Re-equipment of Bomber Command' CAS to Prime Minister, 23 Dec. 1951, London, Ministry of Defence (Air Historical Branch), Slessor Papers, IIIE.

46. 'British Bomber Policy' Note by CAS, 1 March 1952, London, Ministry of Defence (Air Historical Branch), Slessor Papers, XIIF.

47. 'Note on Control of Air Striking Forces in support of SHAPE, 31 March 1952, London, Ministry of Defence (Air Historical Branch), Slessor Papers, XIVD.

48. Clark and Wheeler, *British Origins of Nuclear Strategy*, pp. 154-5.

49. Slessor to Prime Minister, 9 July 1952, London, Ministry of Defence (Air Historical Branch), Slessor Papers, XIVD.

50. Slessor to Admiral Fechteler (CNO), 5 Aug. 1952, London, Ministry of Defence (Air Historical Branch), Slessor Papers, XIVD.

51. Slessor to Churchill, 30 December 1952, London, Ministry of Defence (Air Historical Branch), Slessor Papers, XXVC.

52. Slessor to Minister of Defence, 3 Oct. 1952, London, Ministry of Defence (Air Historical Branch), Slessor Papers, XXVC.

53. Slessor to Viscount Trenchard, 3 Oct. 1952, London, Ministry of Defence (Air Historical Branch), Slessor Papers, XXVC.

54. Slessor to VCAS/DCAS, 5 Dec. 1952, London, Ministry of Defence (Air Historical Branch), Slessor Papers, XXVC.

55. 'The Place of the Bomber in British Policy' Note by CAS, 3 Oct. 1952, London, Public Record Office (P.R.O.), AIR20/8711.

56. 'The Place of the Bomber in British Policy' Draft with later pencil notes by Slessor, undated, London, Ministry of Defence (Air Historical Branch), Slessor Papers, XXVC.

57. Gowing, *Independence and Deterrence*, pp. 407-8.

58. Cooper, 'The Origins and Development of the British Strategic Nuclear Deterrent Forces, 1945-1960', pp. 28-9.

59. Ibid., pp. 29-30.

60. Slessor to Maj-Gen. Leon Johnson (HQ, 3rd Air Division), 6 Jan. 1950, London, Ministry of Defence (Air Historical Branch), Slessor Papers, XIVA.

61. Slessor to Johnson, 7 Jan. 1950, London, Ministry of Defence (Air Historical Branch), Slessor Papers, XIVA.

62. Notes on the US Airfields in the UK, undated, London, Ministry of Defence (Air Historical Branch), Slessor Papers, XIVA.

63. 'Facilities for the USAF' Memorandum by CAS, undated, London, Ministry of Defence (Air Historical Branch), Slessor Papers, XIVA.

64. Slessor to General Vandenberg, 3 Feb. 1950, London, Ministry of Defence (Air Historical Branch), Slessor Papers, XIVA.

65. Duke, *US Defence Bases in the UK*, pp. 50-56.

66. Ibid., pp. 86-90.

67. Ibid., p. 91.

68. Slessor to PUS, 16 Nov. 1951, London, Ministry of Defence (Air Historical Branch), Slessor Papers, XLIIIH.

69. Slessor to Field Marshal Slim, 3 April 1950, London, Ministry of Defence (Air Historical Branch), Slessor Papers, XIVA.

70. 'Draft Paper on Defence Policy and Global Strategy' Slessor to Secretary, COS Committee, 20 March 1950, London, Ministry of Defence (Air Historical Branch), Slessor Papers, XIVA and DO(50)45, 7 June 1950, CAB131/9 printed in *DBPO*, Series 2, IV, pp. 411-431.

71. 'British Bomber Policy' Note by CAS, 1 March 1952, London, Ministry of Defence (Air Historical Branch), Slessor Papers, XIIF.

72. Botti, *The Long Wait*, pp. 80-86, 90, 93, 101, 115, 204.

73. Slessor to Tedder, 7 April 1949, London, Ministry of Defence (Air Historical Branch), Slessor Papers, XIVA.

74. Slessor to Air Marshal Sir Hugh Lloyd (C-in-C Bomber Command), 22 June 1950, London, Ministry of Defence (Air Historical Branch), Slessor Papers, XIVA.

75. Botti, *The Long Wait*, p. 81.

76. 'The Place of the Valiant in the Re-equipment of Bomber Command' Note by CAS, 23 Dec. 1951, London, Ministry of Defence (Air Historical Branch), Slessor Papers, IIIF.

77. JCS 2208/3 Hoyt Vandenberg (chief of staff, USAF on behalf of JCS) to Secretary of Defense, 20 Nov. 1951.

78. Duke, *US Defence Bases in the UK*, p. 69; Botti, *The Long Wait*, p 82.

79. Botti, *The Long Wait*, pp. 82-83.

80. Botti, *The Long Wait*, pp. 83-86; Duke, *US Defence Bases in the UK*, pp. 70-71

81. Slessor to Sir William Elliot, 15 Jan. 1952, London, Ministry of Defence (Air Historical Branch), Slessor Papers, XIVD.

82. Slessor to COS (Draft Minute to Churchill), 5 Feb. 1952, London, Ministry of Defence (Air Historical Branch), Slessor Papers, XIVD.

83. Ibid.

84. Ibid.

85. Slessor to Sir William Elliot, 15 Jan. 1952, London, Ministry of Defence (Air Historical Branch), Slessor Papers, XIVD.

86. This last request was presumably an attempt to discover how important the spy plane flights flown from the United Kingdom since 1950 were to the Americans. Campbell, *Unsinkable Aircraft Carrier*, pp. 127-8.

87. Slessor to Sir William Elliot, undated, London, Ministry of Defence (Air Historical Branch), Slessor Papers, XIVD.

88. Botti, *The Long Wait*, p. 107.

89. Clark and Wheeler, *British Origins of Nuclear Strategy*, p. 174.

90. Slessor to Prime Minister, 9 July 1952, London, Ministry of Defence (Air Historical Branch), Slessor Papers, XIVD.

91. Slessor to Admiral Fechteler (CNO), 5 Aug. 1952, London, Ministry of Defence (Air Historical Branch), Slessor Papers, XIVD.

92. Slessor to Lord Trenchard, 16 Oct. 1952, London, Ministry of Defence (Air Historical Branch), Slessor Papers, XIVD.

93. Slessor to Sir William Elliot, 27 Oct. 1952, London, Ministry of Defence (Air Historical Branch), Slessor Papers, XIVD.

94. CAS to VCAS, 8 Sept. 1952, London, Public Record Office (P.R.O.), AIR20/7567.

95. CAS Agenda for Meeting with USAF/RCAF, 28 October 1952, London, Public Record Office (P.R.O.), AIR20/7567.

96. Notes on Meeting with General Vandenberg, undated, London, Ministry of Defence (Air Historical Branch), Slessor Papers, XXVC.

97. COS(58)7th Confidential Annex, 21 Jan. 1958, London, Public Record Office (P.R.O.), DEFE4/103.

98. Ball and Richelson (eds.), *Strategic Nuclear Targeting*, pp. 40-2. For further details on United States nuclear planning see: Rosenberg, "'A smoking radiating ruin at the end of two hours'", pp. 3-38; idem., 'The origins of overkill', pp. 3-71; idem., 'Reality and responsibility: power and process in the making of United States nuclear strategy', pp. 35-52; Friedberg, 'A history of US strategic "doctrine", 1945-80', pp. 37-71; Pringle and Arkin, *SIOP*, pp. 20-92.

99. This impression is increased because Slessor's papers are much fuller than the available official records.

100. 'British Bomber Policy' Note by CAS, 1 March 1952, London, Ministry of Defence (Air Historical Branch), Slessor Papers, XIIF.

101. Sir John Slessor to VCAS, 16 July 1945, London, Ministry of Defence (Air Historical Branch), Slessor Papers, XIVA.

102. COS(50)39th Confidential Annex, 13 March 1950, London, Public Record Office (P.R.O.), AIR20/10613; Slessor to Slim, 3 April 1950, London, Ministry of Defence (Air Historical Branch), Slessor Papers, XIVA.

103. 'Draft Paper on Defence Policy and Global Strategy', Slessor to Secretary, COS Committee, 20 March 1950, London, Ministry of Defence (Air Historical Branch), Slessor Papers, XIVA.

104. JP(50)22(Final), 10 March 1950, London, Public Record Office (P.R.O.), AIR20/10613.

105. Ibid.

106. COS(50)39th Confidential Annex, 13 March 1950, London, Public Record Office (P.R.O.), AIR20/10613.

107. COS(50)93, 16 March 1950, London, Public Record Office (P.R.O.), AIR20/10613.

108. COS(50)74th, 11 May 1950, London, Public Record Office (P.R.O.), AIR8/1588.

109. COS(50)46th, 21 March 1950, London, Public Record Office (P.R.O.), AIR20/10613.

110. DO(50)5th, 23 March 1950, London, Public Record Office (P.R.O.), AIR20/10613.

111. Slessor to Tedder, 7 April 1949, London, Ministry of Defence (Air Historical Branch), Slessor Papers, XIVA.

112. CAS to VCAS, 3 Feb. 1950, London, Ministry of Defence (Air Historical Branch), Slessor Papers, XIVA.

113. COS(50)39th Confidential Annex, 13 March 1950; COS(50)93, 16 March 1950; COS(50)62nd, 21 April 1950, London, Public Record Office (P.R.O.), AIR20/10613.

114. Slessor, *The Great Deterrent*, pp. 102-117.

115. Air Chief Marshal Sir James Robb to Slessor, 21 June 1950, London, Public Record Office (P.R.O.), AIR20/10612.

116. COS(50)39th Confidential Annex, 13 March 1950, London, Public Record Office (P.R.O.), AIR20/10613.

117. CAS to DCAS, 1 June 1950, London, Public Record Office (P.R.O.), AIR8/7086.

118. ACAS(P) to DCAS, 8 June 1950, London, Public Record Office (P.R.O.), AIR8/7086.

119. VCAS to Air Marshal Sir Thomas Williams (C-in-C BAFO), 3 Aug. 1950, London, Public Record Office (P.R.O.), AIR20/10612.

120. Lord Tedder to Slessor, 6 April 1949, London, Ministry of Defence (Air Historical Branch), Slessor Papers, XIVA.

121. AUS(G) to ACAS(P), 14 October 1949, London, Public Record Office (P.R.O.), AIR20/9135.

122. Slessor to Air Marshal Sir William Elliot, 8 May 1950, London, Ministry of Defence (Air Historical Branch), Slessor Papers, XIVA.

123. CAS to Members of Air Council/Staff, 3 July 1950, London, Public Record Office (P.R.O.), AIR8/1610.

124. CAS Minute 'Reaction to Korean War', 17 July 1950, London, Public Record Office (P.R.O.), AIR20/7086.

125. CAS to Secretary of State for Air, 10 March 1952, London, Public Record Office (P.R.O.), AIR20/8711.

126. CAS1567 Record of Meeting, 15 August 1950, London, Public Record Office (P.R.O.), AIR20/7086.

127. CAS to Secretary of State for Air, 10 March 1952, London, Public Record Office (P.R.O.), AIR20/8711.

128. Note from CAS, 25 January 1950, London, Public Record Office (P.R.O.), AIR20/10612.

129. COS to Lord Tedder, 5 Sept. 1950, London, Public Record Office (P.R.O.), AIR20/10612.

130. COS(50)144th, 8 Sept. 1950, London, Public Record Office (P.R.O.), AIR20/10612.

131. AUS(G) to Secretary of State for Air, 16 Oct. 1950, London, Public Record Office (P.R.O.), AIR20/10612.

132. AUS(G) to Secretary of State for Air, 16 Oct. 1950, London, Public Record Office (P.R.O.), AIR20/10612.

133. Bullock, *Ernest Bevin, Foreign Secretary*, p. 818.

134. Under-Secretary of State for Air to Secretary of State for Air, 19 July 1950, London, Public Record Office (P.R.O.), DEFE11/101.

135. 'Unicorn' Conference, 24-28 March 1952: 'Progress of the build-up of Allied Air Forces in SHAPE' Air Chief Marshal Sir Hugh Saunders, London, Public Record Office (P.R.O.), AIR8/1805.

136. 'Unicorn' Conference, 24-28 March 1952: '2nd Allied Tactical Air Force' Sir Robert Foster (C-in-C 2nd TAF), London, Public Record Office (P.R.O.), AIR8/1805.

137. 'The Employment of Air Power in the Defence of Western Europe' Lecture to US Air War College by Air Vice-Marshal G.H. Mills, 4 June 1951, London, Public Record Office (P.R.O.), AIR8/1740.

138. Slessor to Chief Staff Officer, Ministry of Defence, 8 February 1952, London, Ministry of Defence (Air Historical Branch), Slessor Papers, XXVC.

139. Slessor to Lieut-Gen. A. M. Gruenther (SHAPE Planning Group), 14 Feb. 1951, London, Ministry of Defence (Air Historical Branch), Slessor Papers, XXVB; CAS to Pirie (BJSM (AFS)), 26 Feb. 1951, London, Ministry of Defence (Air Historical Branch), Slessor Papers, XXVB.

140. COS(51)384, 22 June 1951, London, Public Record Office (P.R.O.), AIR8/1811.

141. Ibid.

142. Slessor to CS(A) (Controller, Aircraft, Ministry of Supply), 12 March 1951, London, Ministry of Defence (Air Historical Branch), Slessor Papers, XXVB.

143. Slessor to Sir Hugh Saunders, 8 Aug. 1951, London, Ministry of Defence (Air Historical Branch), Slessor Papers, XXVB.

144. 'The Next Stage in the Development of the Western Democratic Alliance' CAS to Sir Pierson Dixon, 27 Aug. 1951, London, Public Record Office (P.R.O.), AIR8/1806; Sir Pierson Dixon to CAS, 29 August 1951, London, Public Record Office (P.R.O.), AIR8/1806; 'Atlantic Treaty Organisation' Memorandum by First Sea Lord, 6 Sept. 1951, London, Public Record Office (P.R.O.), AIR8/1806.

145. Minister of Defence to Sir William Strang, undated, London, Public Record Office (P.R.O.), AIR8/1806; COS(52)25, 8 Jan. 1952, London, Public Record Office (P.R.O.), PREM11/155.

146. MC.33 'Estimate of the Relative Strength and Capabilities of NATO and Soviet Bloc Forces at Present and in the Immediate Future' Report by Standing Group, 10 Nov. 1951, London, Public Record Office (P.R.O.), PREM11/369.

147. Lord Cherwell to Prime Minister, 28 Feb. 1952, London, Public Record Office (P.R.O.), PREM11/369.

148. Prime Minister to Minister of Defence, 13 March 1952, London, Public Record Office (P.R.O.), PREM11/369.

149. Lord Cherwell to Prime Minister, 28 Feb. 1952, London, Public Record Office (P.R.O.), PREM11/369.

150. FO Telegram No.916, Sir Edwin Plowden to Foreign Office, London, Public Record Office (P.R.O.), PREM11/160.

151. Sir Norman Brook to Prime Minister, 4 Dec. 1951, London, Public Record Office (P.R.O.), PREM11/160.

152. 'United Kingdom Comments on Parts I-V of the TCC Report' Paper by Officials - Approved by Foreign Secretary, Chancellor of the Exchequer, Chiefs of Staff and Prime Minister, 29 Jan. 1952, London, Public Record Office (P.R.O.), PREM11/155.

153. C(52)49 'The Report of the Temporary Council Committee of the North Atlantic Council' Memorandum by Secretary of State for Foreign Affairs, 19 Feb. 1952, London, Public Record Office (P.R.O.), PREM11/155.

154. COS(W)191 COS to Air Chief Marshal William Elliot (Standing Group), 11 Jan. 1952, London, Public Record Office (P.R.O.), PREM11/155.

155. FO Telegram No.11 UK Delegation to NATO, Lisbon to Foreign Office, 26 Feb. 1952, London, Public Record Office (P.R.O.), PREM11/369.

156. Prime Minister to Chief Staff Officer, Minister of Defence, 16 Nov. 1951, London, Public Record Office (P.R.O.), PREM11/369.

157. Chief Staff Officer, Minister of Defence to Minister of Defence (Churchill), 8 February 1952, London, Public Record Office (P.R.O.), PREM11/369.

158. Lord Ismay to Churchill, 16 Feb. 1952, London, Public Record Office (P.R.O.), PREM11/369.

159. Slessor to SAAM (Scientific Adviser Air Ministry), 14 March 1952, London, Ministry of Defence (Air Historical Branch), Slessor Papers, XIVD.

160. Slessor to Sir Pierson Dixon, 13 March 1952, London, Ministry of Defence (Air Historical Branch), Slessor Papers, XIVD.

161. Baylis and Macmillan, 'The British Global Strategy Paper of 1952', p. 216.

162. Note on Control of Air Striking Forces in Support of SHAPE, 31 March 1952, London, Ministry of Defence (Air Historical Branch), Slessor Papers, XIVD.

163. Prime Minister to Minister of Defence, 13 March 1952, London, Public Record Office (P.R.O.), PREM11/369.

164. Secretary of State for Air to CAS, 5 March 1952, London, Public Record Office (P.R.O.), AIR20/8711.

165. CAS to Secretary of State for Air, 10 March 1952, London, Public Record Office (P.R.O.), AIR20/8711.

166. Grove, *Vanguard to Trident*, pp. 78-9.

167. 'The Next Stage in the Development of the Western Democratic Alliance' CAS to Sir Pierson Dixon, 27 Aug. 1951, London, Public Record Office (P.R.O.), AIR8/1806.

168. CAS to ACAS(P), 2 Jan. 1952; 'Association of the Royal Air Force with a European Air Force within the European Defence Community (EDC)', 29 Jan. 1952; CAS to Sir Pierson Dixon, 31 Jan. 1952, London, Public Record Office (P.R.O.), AIR8/2000; S. Dockrill, 'The evolution of Britain's policy towards a European Army, 1950-54', pp. 53-56.

169. Slessor to Lieut-Gen. Brownjohn, 28 Nov. 1952, London, Ministry of Defence (Air Historical Branch), Slessor Papers, XXVC.

170. JCS.2 Slessor to COS, 8 Dec. 1952, London, Ministry of Defence (Air Historical Branch), Slessor Papers, XIVD.

171. 'Draft of General Reply to Defence Budget at Either Level of Cuts', 8 Sept. 1952, London, Public Record Office (P.R.O.), AIR8/1689.

172. RDP(52)46(Final) Ministry of Defence Committee on the Defence Programme 2nd Report, 19 Sept. 1952, London, Public Record Office (P.R.O.), AIR8/1689.

4

Defence Reviews and Nuclear Strategy: 1953-1955

The 1953 Radical Review

Under Slessor, and with Global Strategy, the RAF had won a considerable victory in placing the bomber at the centre of British strategy. The shift from defence to nuclear deterrence was a radical move. It is no coincidence that most innovative thought about nuclear weapons after 1952 did not emanate from the RAF but from other parts of the defence establishment, especially the Royal Navy. The other two services and their supporters had to challenge the new status quo in order to protect old, or gain new, roles.[1] This change in the balance between the three services did not, however, lessen the role of the RAF in the formulation of strategy. The service was increasingly on the defensive but effectively repulsed attacks on its strategic prescriptions until the end of the decade and beyond.

Three main issues faced British defence planners in the mid-1950s: how to remain a world power; how to do it on a limited defence budget; and how to respond to the hydrogen bomb. In response to each of these issues the logic of nuclear substitution could be pushed further. It was not always the Air Staff which pursued this logic: Duncan Sandys, Minister of Supply in 1953 and 1954, was often the most radical figure in the defence establishment. Nevertheless, the Air Ministry played a major part in the proliferation of the suggested roles for the nuclear and conventionally armed bomber.

The most significant military development affecting strategy was the H-bomb. This weapon could either be portrayed as a revolutionary new development in warfare, requiring a fundamental reconsideration of British defence policy, or as an incremental improvement to existing

weapons which confirmed the correctness of policies adopted in 1952. The Air Ministry chose to argue a case based on the latter assumption. According to its representatives the increased destructive power of thermonuclear weapons enhanced their deterrent effect since the risk of thermonuclear war deterred all forms of warfare, at least in Europe, by rendering controllable escalation an impossibility.

These propositions were accepted as the basis of British strategy but within a system which was itself strategically incoherent. The 1953 Radical Review, the 1954 Radical Review, the 1955 Long Term Defence Review were all concerned with setting defence priorities and then adhering to them; none was particularly successful. The frequency of challenge produced repeated defences of the bomber and thus emphasised its importance even more, sometimes at the expense of the RAF's other roles.

The Air Staff have sometimes been criticised for becoming too enamoured of the V-bombers, too committed to a policy of massive retaliation. In some ways this was a stance forced on them by their bureaucratic position. Whilst Duncan Sandys and the Treasury pressed for economy by stricter adherence to a short war strategy and sought to enhance the role of land-based airpower at the expense of the carrier, the Army and Navy criticised the V-bombers in order to protect their own roles. It is important, therefore, to separate the ideas that were integral to RAF thinking from some of the views it expressed as part of the short-term political battle.

Slessor had left the Air Staff firmly committed to three general propositions. First, nuclear deterrence was central to British strategy and Britain should contribute to that deterrent not only because she was an independent great power but also because such a contribution would ensure that the United States would treat her as one. Second, in order to be credible as a deterrent, as a diplomatic tool and as a defensible part of the British defence budget the bomber force had to be militarily effective. Third, although the concept of 'broken-backed' warfare championed by the Navy was nonsensical this did not preclude an attempt to compromise with the other services. Looking back at the period between 1953 and 1956 the former Air Ministry official Sir Frank Cooper has commented:

> It was ... a very straightforward policy, in that we were going to build up the V-force and were going to have as many aircraft as we could possibly get with a maximum of 240. The Air Staff stayed on a figure of 240 V-bombers. ... They then came down to 200 and eventually ended up with ... 184, but that really was, in those days, a very good target to hit. My own view is that the Air Staff themselves came to be much happier about 180 because the priority given to the V-force meant other parts of the Air Force had to suffer.[2]

According to Cecil James, another 1950s Air Ministry official, this was still the case when the V-bomber front-line was reduced to 144 in 1957. 'The Air Staff were not too disappointed. The [102] Mark 2 V-bombers were the crucial element ... a credible airborne deterrent could be poised until well into the nineteen sixties.'[3]

In 1953 the mood of the Air Staff was conciliatory. As the new CAS, Sir William Dickson, told Sir Norman Brook who was heading the first stage of the Radical Review: 'I can say at once that I am not suggesting that air power, still less one particular element of air power, is the only answer';[4] the conduct of the Cold War and the maintenance of allied confidence by conventional forces was integral to the policy of deterrence. The Secretary of State for Air, Lord De L'Isle, was also concerned that in the coming defence reviews the RAF should defend its effectiveness over a whole range of operational roles.[5]

In part this caution was due to an awareness of the potential technical limitations of the V-bombers. According to the Vice-Chief of the Air Staff the proposed medium bomber force would not constitute a credible counter-offensive force. Its only conceivable military role was an attack on Soviet bomber bases to prevent a second wave of Soviet nuclear attacks on the United Kingdom. There was no possibility of pre-empting or preventing a 'bolt from the blue' attack since not enough resources could be dedicated to reconnaissance. Yet even if the force was assigned this limited second-strike role it would only be of any use in preventing a second wave of Soviet attacks if atomic bombs could be dropped sufficiently accurately to make airfields worthwhile targets. Disquietingly, however, senior RAF technical officers simply did not believe that the bombing aids which they could foresee would be accurate enough for this task. According to their best estimates, to be fully effective, the medium bomber force would have to await the guided bomb, however many atomic weapons it was provided with.[6]

This did not mean that the Air Staff presented anything but a vigorous case for the bomber in 1953. It certainly did not make its doubts about the credibility of counterforce targeting known outside the RAF. Dickson argued that since financial limits were so strict and the strategic environment so threatening lower defence priorities, such as 'broken-backed' warfare, would have to be abandoned altogether. In 1954-55 the Russian long-range bomber force would be capable of forcing the capitulation of the United Kingdom within a month. If there was a counter-attack against its bases and air defence forces were equipped with guided weapons on a large scale there was some chance of defeating this threat; but this chance would be removed once the Russians had operational thermonuclear weapons. He suggested that the Soviets would have hydrogen bombs in service in 1958, before the V-force was expected to be equipped with the guided atomic bomb, and concluded that if Britain was hit by either an atomic or thermonuclear offensive it would be 'finished for generations as a worthwhile country' even if the United States went on to win any war. His recommendation was that absolute priority would have to be given to measures to deter war and to stop Russia inflicting mortal damage on the United Kingdom. He acknowledged that deterrence was infinitely more important than damage limitation except inasmuch 'the knowledge [of such a capability] ... is a deterrent.'[7]

The Air Staff nevertheless continued to stress the importance of the medium bomber force's counterforce mission. Although it acknowledged that the main threat came from a surprise, 'bolt from the blue', attack against which there was no defence it argued that there was no certainty that Russia would pursue such a strategy. The Soviets might attempt to 'blast a way across Europe' for their armies or delay the atomic offensive in the hope of avoiding atomic warfare. There was, therefore, the possibility that an immediate nuclear counteroffensive would be effective. If this was so the first few days would be vital. The offensive would have to be launched immediately by forces under British control. The United States could not be relied on because there was no threat to its national existence. The British attack would be on 30-40 Russian bomber airfields within 1200 nautical miles of the United Kingdom. One atomic bomb would be used for each airfield with each nuclear-armed aircraft being accompanied by five radar counter-measures (RCM) and decoy aircraft. Apart from their bomber offensive the Russians would pose a threat by air mining and submarine attacks and the V-bombers would also have missions to attack the submarine pens and in counter-mining. Finally, the bombers would replace the 560 light bombers promised to SACEUR under the Lisbon force goals using high explosive in support of the land battle.[8]

Although the counterforce mission was firmly established as the bomber's primary role the Air Staff certainly kept other target systems under review. Apart from medium bomber airfields and factories, fleet and submarine bases and factories these consisted of oil refineries, 31 'main administrative centres' and 100 power stations. It was calculated that 85% of all possible targets were within 2500 nautical miles of the United Kingdom and, with few exceptions, those that were further away could be attacked more effectively from other bases. A Victor bomber with a maximum internal fuel load would have an operational radius of 1500 nautical miles allowing it to attack 52% of all targets or 61% of those within 2500 nautical miles. A flight refuelled Victor would have an operational radius of 2150 nautical miles, in range of 99% of targets less than 2500 nautical miles distant from the United Kingdom.[9]

The Air Staff was always aware that the medium bomber did not have to be planned solely of the basis of a counter-military mission. Indeed it acknowledged that its primary purpose was as a deterrent and that as hydrogen bombs became available the conditions to be met to create a deterrent would change.[10] In addition, it was felt that the estimate given in the Global Strategy Paper and the report of the Chiefs of Staff Air Defence Committee that a prompt counterforce offensive might reduce the scale of the Russian attack by 50% was over optimistic.[11] Although the Air Staff sedulously used the logic of the counterforce mission to justify a 240 strong V-bomber force it had its own doubts whether such a force could carry out the task before the advent of better navigation equipment and the guided bomb, whether it was possible to achieve the degree of success originally claimed, even with improved bombing accuracy, or even if the mission was relevant when H-bombs became available. The RAF were thus wedded to the counterforce mission more as a bureaucratic position rather than as an inescapable strategic role.

Against this background the Radical Review moved into a more adversarial phase in June and July 1953. At a ministerial meeting on 18 June Duncan Sandys proposed that the short war strategy should be much more strictly adhered to in the future and that only forces useful in peacetime or in the first six weeks of a global war should be maintained.[12] This led Lord Alexander to issue a directive calling for Britain to maintain only a 'basic force'. Defence forces were to be divided into three categories: Commonwealth commitments; forces essential to survive the six week opening phase of a major war; and forces for 'broken backed' war. Forces in the third category were to be omitted from the 'basic force'.[13] In late June Churchill was incapacitated by a stroke and the acting prime minister Butler reconvened the ad hoc Radical Review group as the Defence Policy Committee on 17 July, allowing Sandys to renew his attack on naval forces intended for 'broken backed' warfare.[14] These developments have some claim to originality in the way defence policy was made, being the first occasion in the post-war period when senior ministers had initiated major changes in strategy without first consulting the Chiefs of Staff.[15] Although Sandys seems to have been developing his own strategic approach, Lord Alexander's directive adopted ideas consistently put forward by the RAF. Both Sandys and the Air Ministry made the case that the nation could not afford both a strategic bomber and a large carrier force. The vast cost of fleet carriers and the high proportion of strike aircraft they were planned to carry was excessive when viewed against the relative unimportance of the Russian naval threat and the strength of the USN.[16]

Nevertheless, the RAF also had to undergo a review of the bomber force by the Defence Policy Committee, which was concerned that the planned size of the bomber force would run ahead of the British nuclear stockpile by 1958.[17] The Air Staff's response was to argue that the role of the V-force was to destroy 45 Soviet long-range air force bases in 1958 in one wave of attacks and that since, by this date Soviet air defence was expected to be so formidable, the medium bombers would need formations of at least six aircraft per target.

The Air Staff also claimed that conventionally armed V-bombers were a cheaper and more effective way of meeting NATO commitments and that USAF bombers lacked conventional capability and were not versatile enough to take on such a role. The V-bombers were supposedly more accurate, less vulnerable and carried a greater bomb load than fighter or light bombers. Many targets in a land battle were not suitable for atomic attack and there might be a political problem in using nuclear weapons in some areas. High explosive was very effective against tactical air fields, communications, military supply dumps and bridges, all targets that 175 Soviet divisions would provide in abundance. The committee were called upon to remember that 300,000 people were killed in one night raid on Dresden whereas only 80,000 were killed at Hiroshima.[18]

In addressing the issue of nuclear substitution the most controversial question tackled by the Defence Policy Committee was how far, in the long-term, could land based air power replace carriers.[19] The submarine was identified as by far the biggest naval threat to Great Britain. Although the RAF claimed that the V-bombers could attack Soviet submarine pens it was expected that ocean going vessels would be already deployed on the lines of sea communication when war came.[20] By the end of November the Air Ministry and Admiralty had reached an uneasy compromise about a theoretical division of labour between shore-based and carrier-based aircraft.[21] Neither side felt particularly bound by this compromise and they started falling away from it almost immediately. Yet its existence indicates that the RAF saw definite limits to how far it could go with substitution.

This reluctance had a number of causes. The Air Staff was aware that the Admiralty could launch a damaging counterattack on its own plans. In June Dickson had warned that that the Navy could use the short war rationale to call for cuts in Transport Command.[22] The Navy did indeed strike back at RAF criticism by reopening the issue of the transfer of Coastal Command[23] and by questioning the V-bomber's flexibility and ability to penetrate enemy defences.[24] More fundamentally, however, there was a recognition that there was a limit to the tasks a force of 240 V-bombers could tackle. The Air Staff had identified six fleet and submarine bases of the Soviet Northern Fleet and ten of the Baltic Fleet, all in range of shore-based bombers as well as twelve submarine factories which were mostly out of range.[25] Yet as they noted in analysing the threat of Russian surface vessels although Bomber Command could attack enemy fleet bases they had a lower priority than airfields and any attack could not be carried out concurrently with the main strategic offensive.[26] Indeed they concluded that: 'to undertake, concurrently during the first week of war, a bomber offensive against the land and sea threat as well [as against bomber airfields] using atomic and conventional bombs would ... require a force of about 630 V-class bombers.'[27] This was simply not a credible proposition.

The 1954 Radical Review

From April to June 1954 a special Cabinet Committee considered whether Britain should develop the hydrogen bomb. The decision to do so was taken on 16 June and endorsed by the Cabinet in July. At the same time a new Defence Policy Committee set about finding new reductions in defence expenditure, the second Radical Review, and the Chiefs of Staff drew up a new strategic appreciation based around thermonuclear weapons.[28]

Until the end of 1954 there was relatively little direct pressure on the V-bombers. The main defence battle surrounded the Swinton Committee's proposal that the strike role for fleet aircraft carriers should be abandoned and that the Fleet Air Arm should only be equipped for convoy protection duties.[29] Yet as the Air Ministry was well aware the fates of the fleet carrier and the medium bomber were intertwined and the role of the latter was far from settled.[30] During the Radical Review process the Treasury expressed the view that although the V-bomber force was obviously important it could see no real justification for a front-line of 240.[31] The Royal Navy and its supporters argued that as guided weapons and ballistic missiles were developed the need for the carrier would grow rather than diminish.[32] They also pointed out that the RAF would be incapable of playing a major part in securing sea communications since its attention was to be fully occupied with strategic land targets.[33]

At the end of 1954 and beginning of 1955 the new Minister of Defence, Harold Macmillan, decided that there were wider considerations than strategy governing the place of the carrier. The financial savings of doing away with strike aircraft could not be justified because of the deleterious effect on relations within NATO, with the USN and on the efficiency and morale of the fleet. His case was accepted by the Defence Committee[34] as was the conclusion reached by the Ministry of Defence[35] that the Navy's proposed new strike aircraft, the NA.39, should be developed and brought into service.[36] These decisions about the Royal Navy had three important implications for the bomber force. First, the possible shift in the balance of the defence budget between strike carriers and medium bombers was limited. Second, the usefulness of the argument, used by the RAF since 1949, that the land based bomber could substitute for naval power by the targeting of ports and submarine bases was reduced. Third, the way was opened to the Navy's ambitions for a nuclear role, at least complementary to the V-force and potentially a replacement for it.

Despite these setbacks, and although it was obviously a compromise still based on a two-phase war, the Chiefs of Staff's 'thermonuclear' strategic review reflected RAF views.[37] The review was based on the present nuclear superiority of the United States but its future vulnerability. It surmised that the Americans had a large advantage over the Russians because of their advance bases in allied countries including the United Kingdom. As a result the United States would be able to effectively launch a nuclear attack with aircraft at any time from 1954. By 1965 they would be able to do the same with ballistic missiles. The USSR could launch an effective attack on the United Kingdom with aircraft from 1955 and with missiles from 1960. America would become vulnerable to air attack in 1958 and missile attack in 1970.[38]

Given these predictions the review argued that there was a very low risk of nuclear war for the next three to four years since Russia was vulnerable to nuclear attack but had no means of striking back. Thereafter the deterrent would remain 'since global war would probably result in mutual annihilation.'[39] A number of conclusions about the future nature of international relations were drawn from this proposition. First, the Cold War would continue for a very long time. Second, careful judgement would be needed to prevent a local war developing into a global war, with the American attitude to China presenting particular dangers. Third, the best policy was still one of deterrence and the more deterrent power the West possessed the less the threat. The primary deterrent was the hydrogen bomb and the accumulation of nuclear and thermonuclear weapons in both the strategic and tactical role deployed in Allied bases around the periphery of the Communist bloc. The complementary deterrent was holding forces in key positions with dispersed and immediately available supplies. Lastly, in Europe NATO would maintain sufficient forces to prevent easy territorial gains from an attack on Western Europe and and in the rest of the world the United States, Britain and the Commonwealth would station forces to fight the Cold War.

Nuclear weapons were seen as the primary instrument of military power. Due to Russian conventional superiority the West would use them from the outset of a major war leading inevitably to all out global war. Employment of nuclear weapons would at once become general and Allied strategic and tactical air forces would have to strike at once without limitation on targets or weapons. The United Kingdom would be a primary target and would be subject to devastating attack. No air defence would be possible and despite a nuclear air offensive to decrease

Soviet nuclear capability Britain would rapidly cease to function as a military base. Major population centres in Britain, Western Europe and North Africa would be devastated in the first few days of any war. British defence policy would be threefold: to possess all up to date weapons especially atomic and thermonuclear ones; to stop the spread of Communism in concert with allies; and to preserve the security and stable government of Britain's colonial territories.[40]

It is obvious that in the short-term critiques of British nuclear strategy such as those advanced by Rear Admiral Buzzard had little impact on policy-making, whatever their place in the history of thought about nuclear strategy. British nuclear strategy as formulated by the Air Ministry and accepted by the government was based on the proposition that an Anglo-American bomber force armed with the hydrogen bomb would serve as a deterrent to all major wars. It was a strategy of mutually assured destruction that assumed the Soviet government shared the belief that controllable escalation was impossible. Although British plans were explicitly based on the reliability of SAC as a tool of massive retaliation the RAF themselves had expressed doubts that the United States would react immediately to a Soviet attack with a full thermonuclear offensive. It became part of the rationale for the British bomber force that it would act as a 'trigger', under British government control, for all the nuclear forces arrayed against the Soviet Union. On the other hand, although the counterforce mission as part of a joint SAC-Bomber Command offensive was still the proposed role for the V-bombers, from 1954 onwards doubts were increasingly cast on their military usefulness.

The Nuclear Debate in 1955

Although the 1954 Radical Review had seemingly endorsed RAF policy of concentrating on nuclear deterrence rather than nuclear war-fighting the concept of continued military operations following an initial nuclear exchange still remained part of strategic debate. The Chiefs of Staff's strategic review denied that it was possible to predict accurately the nature or duration of a global war[41] and claimed that such a war was likely to continue beyond the initial phase with loss of centralised control.[42] It was acknowledged that plans needed a major overhaul as a result of the increased nuclear threat but as the Army's Quartermaster-General remarked 'it was clear that [although] less than at present planned could move in conditions of atomic attack and far less in conditions of H-bomb attack, it did not mean we cannot move anything.' Plans were put in hand to prepare alternative centres of government, ensure an early resumption of movement, use small ports and beaches to bring in supplies and to control civil manpower and material. The aim of these plans was to assist the survival of the United Kingdom and to enable forces in North-West Europe to fight an intensive land battle.[43]

Potentially as important was the argument put forward by the Royal Navy to justify fleet carriers with advanced fighters and strike aircraft. The policy of deterrence contained in the review, it suggested, should be adopted but with the caveat that large allied nuclear forces deterred nuclear war, not all war. Since pressure would increase to carry on struggles by other means local wars and crises worldwide would become more likely, demanding the mobility and flexibility of carrier air power.[44]

Thus, at the beginning of 1955 there were still three major areas of uncertainty in British nuclear strategy: could Britain rely on American thermonuclear weapons to deter war? Was Britain planning to deter a nuclear war or to both deter and fight it? Did thermonuclear weapons deter all major wars or only thermonuclear war? Within this context the role of the V-bombers was re-examined. In December 1954 Macmillan made clear that fundamental decisions about the force needed to be taken in the near furure and implied its strength could be anywhere between 180 and 240 aircraft.[45]

In 1955 a complex combination of political, strategic, financial and diplomatic issues came to bear on what, in some respects, was a relatively simple procurement decision: what should be the front-line strength of the V-bomber force? Although the final decision was postponed until the summer of 1957 the key issues in the debate emerged at the highest governmental level in 1955. With the capability to deliver nuclear weapons finally in its grasp the British government had to try and define what such weapons actually meant for Britain in its relations with other states, particularly America, and as an independent great power. These attempts at strategic definition can be broken down into four main areas. First, the aspects of the relationship with the USA which led the British to seek Anglo-American co-operation. Second, aspects of the relationship with the USA which led to an emphasis on independent nuclear power. Third, the ways in which nuclear weapons seemed to enhance British power globally. Lastly, the ways in which nuclear weapons seemed to both enhance British power in Europe and enable fewer resources to be committed to continental defence.

Anglo-American Nuclear Relations and British Strategy

The rapidly increasing physical presence of American forces in Britain was almost bound to enhance their role in British planning. Yet this build-up also had the effect of convincing the British that whilst American forces should be central to their own strategy a significant independent capability, both in terms of nuclear and conventional forces, was necessary.

In July 1948 there had been three American bases in Britain, in August 1950 there were ten and by October 1953 there were twenty-seven Third Air Force bases and fifteen SAC Seventh Air Division bases and other facilities; a total of forty-two American installations.[46] Increased American deployment was initially a reaction at times of crisis: the Cabinet accepted a United States offer to deploy two more bomber groups and a fighter group to the United Kingdom on 10 July 1950 in response to the invasion of South Korea.[47] It then became more routine: the arrival of one hundred long-range fighter-bombers and thirty-five medium bombers as part of NATO commitments was approved in April 1952[48] at which time Slessor commented that the 'planned deployment of American air forces in this country, roughly equivalent to 50% of the planned total first line numbers of the whole RAF, ... represents an enormous accretion of defensive strength to the UK out of all proportion to the cost involved.'[49] He further noted that the USAF and RCAF squadrons were the only element of Britain's fighter defences which could deal with the most modern Soviet aircraft.[50]

Yet the importance of American forces rested on the political commitment implied by a physical presence rather than on any real military role. There were no nuclear weapons stored in Britain until sometime after the summer of 1952.[51] In 1953 when the USAF contribution to the defence of the United Kingdom was examined it amounted to seventy-five fighters based in Britain and the intention under Plan 'Galloper' to bring over seventy-five per month in three months until the total reached 300. Global Strategy, however, described the crucial period of any war as the first thirty days: the very period in which no reinforcements would arrive. USAF fighter aircraft actually in Britain amounted to about 12% of the planned fighter force[52] but the Air Staff concluded that United States support for air defence was purely political. The all-weather fighters which were in very short supply were kept back in the USA and although part of the role of American units was to conduct air defence operations under the control of the RAF[53] the USAF had no real commitment apart from the defence of its own bases. As one senior RAF officer put it: 'I am sure that if Russian air attacks against American strategic air bases in this country were at all successful, particularly in daylight, then the Americans would demand that their fighter squadrons be employed in close defence of those airfields, however detrimental that might be to the overall defence of the UK.'[54]

Such scepticism about American reliability persisted throughout the 1950s. The Secretary of State for Air, Nigel Birch, told Eden that the value of the bases should not be overestimated. Birch pointed out that not only did the Americans have bases in Spain, North Africa and Arabia but Strategic Air Command also routinely carried out flight refuelled missions from the United States. He argued that the bases gave Britain little influence if they were the main contribution to joint military efforts.[55] This view was endorsed by a 1959 Joint Planners study for Macmillan which pointed to 17 major overseas SAC bases and American access to 107 other airfields capable of handling B-47 bombers besides those in Britain along with IRBM sites in Italy and Turkey.[56]

Linked to the increasing presence of the USAF in Britain was the increasing importance of American aid to the RAF. During his visit to Washington in January 1952 Churchill pressed the Americans on military assistance for the British defence programme. At a meeting between an American team led by the Secretary of Defense and Averell Harriman and a British one led by Lord Cherwell the Americans proposed that since the British had decided to spread their £4700 million rearmament programme over four rather than three years they should produce equipment for the United States to supply to European countries under dollar earning off-shore contracts. The British instead proposed that the Americans take over orders for jet aircraft, Venoms and Canberras, already placed by the British government for the RAF. The Americans were reluctant to acquiesce to this since they feared that France would ask for the same facility leading to mass default on the force goals proposed by the Temporary Council Committee. The Americans were, however, jolted by the revelation of British economic weakness and agreed to speed up the delivery of $300 million already promised under the Mutual Security Act,[57] which from 1949 to 1955 funded 88 B-29 bombers, 52 Lockheed Neptune maritime patrol aircraft and 430 Sabre fighters for the RAF.[58] By June 1952 there had been a radical change of American policy to 'picking up the check' for domestic production programmes because many countries, again France in particular, could not meet their obligations.[59]

Relations were also shaped by the advent of the the Eisenhower administration and its own rethink of strategy. New members of the JCS appointed in May 1953, especially the chairman Admiral Arthur Radford and new USAF Chief of Staff General Nathan Twining, advocated a more aggressive foreign policy backed by closer co-operation with allies and exchanges on the use of atomic weapons.[60] The strategic conclusions of this review, set out in NSC 162/2, which was approved on 30 October 1953, placed emphasis on the importance of allies to provide forces, accommodate bases and to conduct the Cold War. The aim was to build up the strength and cohesion of the free world through collective security systems and it was thought necessary that allies understood the purposes and assumptions of American strategy. European allies had to be convinced of both 'the manifest determination of the United States to use its atomic capability and massive retaliatory striking power if the area is attacked' and its will to keep military forces in Europe.[61] Radford presented the new policy to the British Chiefs of Staff in November 1953 as an American Global Strategy paper addressing the same essential problem, the impact of the H-bomb on policy within budgetary constraints, as the Radical Review .[62]

Thus for both the Americans and the British the nuclear issue and the military aid issue coalesced. The Americans wanted to use military aid and increased openess about reliance on nuclear weapons to strengthen the North Atlantic alliance; the British wanted to take advantage of new American policies to increase the flow of aid and to achieve a degree of nuclear co-operation.

Thus, in December 1953 the Chief of the Air Staff approached the Department of Defense and proposed that Britain would put its V-bomber force (when it became operational) at the disposal of SACEUR if the United States made a large financial contribution to re-equipping Britain with modern fighter aircraft.[63] The exact timing of the approach, at the North Atlantic Council meeting in Paris, was determined by the desire of the Air Staff to divert attention away from a SHAPE proposal for enhanced tactical air forces in Europe.[64] Once the Department of Defense made it clear that it approved of this idea[65] Lord Alexander, the British Minister of Defence, put the proposal to his American opposite number Charles Wilson.[66] In their initial approaches the British appeared to be suggesting that they would compromise the independence of their nuclear force by putting it under the operational command of SACEUR and committing it to a main mission of attacking Soviet land and air forces in Europe.[67] This was, of course, directly counter to actual British nuclear planning which stressed the complete independence of the British force and which toyed with counterforce targeting to prevent a Soviet nuclear strike against Britain. As a result the final Wilson/Alexander agreement reached on 12 March 1954 acknowledged that Britain's main role for its nuclear force would be independent and strategic rather than NATO-oriented and tactical. In return for a limited commitment of the British nuclear force to SACEUR the Department of Defense promised, in the face of Congressional opposition to subsidising the British aircraft industry,[68] to allocate an extra $210 million of military aid in hard currency to Britain from the FY1955 budget. On the other hand it completely refused to discuss joint strategic nuclear targeting or the establishment of formal links between SAC and Bomber Command.[69] The last thing the British actually wanted was for their independent nuclear force, which was in sight of realisation, to be tied to the United States by anything other than paper guarantees.[70] There certainly was no actual plan for the deployment of the V-bombers in the tactical role in Europe during the mid-1950s.[71] The Americans were unwilling to countenance closer co-operation unless the British would effectively place their nuclear force under the command of an American military officer. The Wilson/Alexander agreement was, therefore, strictly limited;

its nuclear clauses were only fulfilled in January 1960 when three squadrons of Valiant bombers, judged ineffective against the air defences of the Soviet Union, were assigned to SACEUR. It was, nevertheless, important as the first step to the much closer military collaboration in two main areas, British access to American nuclear technology and joint targeting, which developed over the next four years.

American interest in the Wilson/Alexander agreement can be explained in terms of their new strategy. Collective security meant that military forces in Europe had become an index of commitment for allies and it was psychologically valuable that Britain should also be making a large visible effort. The RAF also needed to be of sufficient strength and properly equipped in order to make a useful contribution to the defence of American bomber bases in Britain. NSC 162/2 had stated that 'in the event of hostilities, the United States will consider nuclear weapons to be as available for use as other munitions'.[72] Since it was obvious that the British would press ahead with their independent nuclear force even in the face of American disapproval it was preferable to have it tied into American strategy for NATO. The Americans in no way limited their own freedom of action by this agreement but they were willing to pay $210 million to obtain some influence over the British nuclear force.

The most immediate outcome of the agreement was an offer from the USAF to supply the RAF with B-47 bombers, which had started to enter large scale service with the USAF in 1953, as stop-gap V-bombers. The British response to this offer clearly demonstrated their fear of becoming too enmeshed by the Americans. Although the Air Ministry put forward a number of detailed objections to adopting the B-47, the impossibility of cross-training aircrew for the B-47 and the Valiant, the political difficulties in cancelling Valiant and Canberra contracts in favour of American aircraft, experiences with the B-29 which had shown that it was very difficult to keep complex American aircraft serviceable, and the extra infrastructure spending involved in providing longer and stronger runways, it was clear that the objections were political rather than practical. The Foreign Office spoke of 'this generous but somewhat delicate offer' and the the Defence Committee agreed to thank the United States but refuse the offer.[73]

Indeed in the short-term it seemed that the American financial stake in British defence policy could be accepted without necessarily acceding to their wishes. The 1954 Radical Review approved by the Cabinet reduced the RAF front-line planned for 1958 from about 1800 to 1600 aircraft. The whole cut fell on Fighter Command with a cut in plans from 792 to 576 aircraft, although with an increase in all-weather fighters. This ran directly counter to Britain's undertakings to the United States. The Americans had been promised that two extra squadrons would be added to Fighter Command and that the size of 2nd TAF would be substantially increased. As part of the aid package it had also been agreed that the RAF would exchange the Sabre fighters already received in aid from the United States and Canada for 345 Hunters bought under an American off-shore contract. Once Britain had reneged on its promises officials began to worry that if the exchange did not go ahead the Sabre force would waste away leading to a substantial reduction in the strength of 2nd TAF. Ministry of Defence officials believed that because of their cuts and American reconsideration of their policy on aid towards Europe aid to the RAF was under serious threat.[74]

In order to avert this threat the Minister of Defence, Macmillan, and Dickson met with with Secretary of the Air Force Anderson and Admiral Radford in December 1954 and made clear to them that the size of 2nd TAF depended entirely on the continuance of the Hunter/Sabre exchange and the receipt of full Plan 'K' aid. They argued that any change in arrangements would lead to a drastic cut in the British contribution to SACEUR.[75] The American position was that aid could be maintained if there was 'no change in plans for 2nd TAF and the medium bomber force, of which, (in the terms of Mr. Secretary Wilson's letter to Lord Alexander of 17th February, 1954) a primary task in the event of war will be to assist SACEUR in retardation operations'.[76] Ministry of Defence officials privately admitted that Britain was on very shaky ground. British statements in February 1954 were 'tantamount' to promises that the purpose of the MBF was to support SACEUR yet in reality there was no intention of using it for retardation operations and therefore a very bad ethical case for continuing to accept aid.[77]

Unsurprisingly, aid negotiations, which resumed in April 1955, proved very difficult due to the announcement of a £400 million United Kingdom budget surplus for 1954. The American negotiators asked forcefully why Britain could not afford the RAF.[78] The United States became less accommodating over how aid was spent. The RAF was forced to accept 115 Hunter F.4s worth $35 million, originally intended for a rearmed Luftwaffe, as part of the second instalment of Plan 'K' aid. This meant an increased proportion of F.4s to the superior Hunter F.6 in the RAF front-line. The RAF was not, however, completely dissatisfied by this development since it meant it could accelerate the re-equipment of its obsolete Venom squadrons in 2nd TAF and Meteor squadrons in Fighter Command and guarantee the full amount of Plan 'K' aid.[79]

Further cuts in the planned RAF front-line in 1955 soon renewed fears, however, of a loss of aid. These fears were peculiar to the RAF since the Army and Navy relied far less on United States money and what they did receive was not tied to any specific undertakings about the size and deployment of forces. Hunters were supplied under the Special Aircraft Program with the specific understanding that the United States could demand repayment if they were deployed or sold outside the NATO area without being replaced by new types and Plan 'K' aid rested on agreements about Fighter Command, 2nd TAF and the MBF that had largely been abrogated. Ministry of Defence officials believed that further reductions could be legitimately be regarded as invalidating previous agreements.[80]

This was a view shared by the the United States government officials. At a meeting in February 1956 they pointed out that the original plan had been for £75 million of aid over three years to cover the gap between RAF plans and what the United Kingdom could afford. Now that British plans had been substantially reduced Plan 'K' aid would not be needed because the problem it had been designed to solve did not arise. Sir Richard Powell agreed that the United Kingdom had failed to meet its commitments but asked the United States to reconsider any decision to withdraw aid on the grounds of the Britain's contribution to the Western Alliance. Powell argued that Britain had kept up defence spending despite economic problems and therefore deserved the balance of $30.5 million. Interest in securing the balance of aid became even more pressing when American refusal to pay for the unsatisfactory Gloster Javelin all-weather fighter pushed it up to $108 million.[81]

Negotiations over Plan 'K' aid subsequently got caught up in those surrounding the deployment of American IRBMs in Britain. At Bermuda Macmillan and Eisenhower confirmed a proposal, first suggested by the United States in late 1955, that $30.5 million should be diverted from Plan 'K' aid for the purchase of Corporal missiles for the British Army but the United Kingdom would spend the sterling equivalent on mutually agreed projects for the RAF. The remaining balance went towards paying for Thor missiles.[82]

The development of aid negotiations between 1953 and 1956 shows increasing dependence on the United States. The RAF was a leader in this development because close contacts and convergence of interest with the American defence establishment enabled it to gain favoured access to funds. By 1956 the British were no longer basing their aid requests on the offer of a specific quid pro quo but on the general grounds of worthiness as an ally. Despite this it could be argued that American aid had very little effect on British strategy: it did not prevent changes of policy over fighters, tactical air forces or bombers. It did, however, pave the way for the deployment of Thor and British involvement in the Skybolt project. The amount of money involved in Plan 'K' aid was admittedly relatively small and was only part of substantial military aid received by Britain since 1949.[83] By September 1957 the RAF had received not only the B-29s, Neptunes and Sabres but 70% of the cost of 173 Canberras, 240 Hunters and 34 Valiants. 390 Hunters had then been paid for as replacements for the Sabres originally supplied. Under Plan 'K' itself $80 million had been spent on 117 Hunters, 120 Sapphire engines and 50,000 1000lb bombs. A contract for 177 Javelins had been cancelled.[84] Plan 'K' aid had been agreed at £75 million over three years when planned overall expenditure on the RAF was expected to rise from £550 million in 1955 to £560 million in 1957.[85] It was, nevertheless, important not only because the aid was in dollars but because it tied a part of the defence establishment close to the Americans. Uneasiness about the role of aid did exist but never pushed itself to the forefront of British thinking. There was a general belief that Britain deserved favoured treatment for her major rearmament efforts. Yet in the long-term, as Sir Ian Jacob noted as early as 1952, although Britain was America's most powerful and reliable ally she remained a client for military and economic aid and this was bound to have a cumulative effect on decision-making.[86] Such arrangements tended to increase the stress on Anglo-American co-operation. They also short-circuited worries about placing too much reliance on the United States.

The use of Bomber Command as a means of achieving closer co-operation with the United States was only partially successful. The RAF received financial assistance and its influence over NATO strategy was, arguably, increased but there was no agreement on joint planning with SAC. Yet the exercise did seem to indicate that if the British had something to offer the Americans were willing to negotiate without putting unacceptable demands on Britain's freedom of action.

In this context, according to the Air Ministry in 1955, the mission of Bomber Command was to act within this Anglo-American framework as part of a joint deterrent along with SAC. The deterrent consisted of the ability of allied air striking power to destroy the 'vitals' of Russia twinned with a clear appreciation by the Soviets that there was no defence against such an action.[87] The tasks for an Anglo-American operation would be to strike immediately at Russian centres of government, production and communication, to limit the Russian nuclear offensive by destroying airfields and nuclear potential, to reduce Russian sea power at source, to act in support of the war at sea and to support Allied forces in the Middle East and Europe. The primary objective of Bomber Command was to attack Soviet air bases on their first sortie in order to prevent, at the very least, a second wave of nuclear strikes against the United Kingdom. Yet it was acknowledged that each task of the bomber force had different possible target systems which would alter with changing circumstances. For instance, once ballistic missiles were developed the only effective counter to attack would be the destruction of Russia's internal organisation.[88]

The Air Ministry estimated that by 1960 Russia would have enough nuclear forces to simultaneously attack the United States and the United Kingdom, with about 450 bombers allocated to each. There were thought to be 150 airfields from which such attacks could be launched and that this number would rapidly increase in the future. Although it was argued that all these bases would have to be destroyed within a few hours[89] it was obvious that such a mission was already beyond Bomber Command which would be unable to mount the necessary number of missions in one strike. Thus the counterforce mission was a vital part of a joint rather than an independent deterrent. Yet the counterforce mission envisaged a second-strike when 450 Soviet bombers were more that enough to drop ten hydrogen bombs on British cities in their first sortie with the disastrous consequences envisaged by the Strath Report.

A counter-city offensive was also seen as part of the joint mission but the Air Ministry viewed the destruction of centres of government, administration, production and communications as a formidable undertaking. It argued that it was not reasonable to assume that dropping hydrogen bombs on Moscow, Leningrad, Stalingrad and other major cities would necessarily terminate a war because of the shock to morale. The Soviet army and air forces would still be operating and industry could still function with effective decentralisation. The effect of fall-out from thermonuclear weapons would greatly increase the risk to the ordinary Russian population but the Soviet Union was a vast country. 'Thus whether thermo-nuclear or atomic bombs were dropped, a large number would have to be used to achieve an effective concentration'. A counter-city strategy would only be effective if a large number of targets, over a wide area, were destroyed in a very short time.[90]

As to other missions, Britain was bound by the Wilson/Alexander agreement to assist SACEUR. The Air Ministry continued to argue for the importance of this mission on two grounds. First, that it was useful if the Russians believed that the V-bombers would be used in this way and, second, that even with the increasing atomic capability of the tactical air forces the medium bombers were important for their all-weather potential. Attacks on the bases of the Baltic and Northern Fleets and on sea targets were still cited as possible missions.[91]

In order for the V-bomber force to carry out a mission of any description it was obvious that it would have to be operationally viable. This meant that the force would have to be able to survive a surprise attack and then penetrate Soviet defences. The Air Ministry pinned hopes of survival on dispersal and readiness. Such preparations would make necessary the building of a large number of the 2000 yard runways, needed to cope with the bombers, in the United Kingdom and frequent overseas deployments so the Russians would not know where the bombers were at any one time. It was hoped that in periods of tension forces could be brought to readiness in one hour.

A problem created by such tactics would be the difficulty of maintaining the aircraft at a level beyond 75% serviceability. Given also that the bombers would have to fly through a fully alerted Russian air defence system, including all-weather fighters, guided missiles and improved radar, some would have to be diverted to electronic counter-measures (ECM) duty. Yet the suggested figure of two supporting aircraft for every bomb carrier was a considerable reduction on the original 5:1 ratio proposed in 1953.[92] The necessity of getting the maximum number of bombs into the first sortie was a reflection of the rapidly increasing number of targets which were not to be matched by increasing resources. This constraint led the Air Staff to make the 'favourable and possibly unreasonable assumption' that after losses to lack of serviceability, Russian air defences and diversions to ECM duties 50% of the force would deliver their bombs on 120 targets on the first sortie. The size of the British nuclear stockpile was not deemed to be a limiting factor since it was believed that 1960 there would be sufficient bombs to equip the first mission and it was also hoped that American bombs would be available.[93]

Operational viability was an important factor in the bomber debate. It was universally accepted that for the force to be a deterrent it had to be able to carry out its mission. The RAF had to create and retain confidence in the V-force's capability or it would have been nearly impossible to justify its existence. The capabilities of the force also had great importance for its targeting. Yet the the original calculations which were produced to justify a force of 240 based on the need for forty Soviet airfields to be attacked, each by a force of six bombers, had already been invalidated by 1955.

As a result each of the proposed missions for Bomber Command only made sense if planned and carried out in conjunction with SAC. This left the old problem of why British involvement in the strategic air offensive was important, given the imbalance of forces involved. Compared to a proposed V-force front-line of 240 in 1959 the British estimated that the total front-line of SAC in 1955 was already 2,691 aircraft. This included a nuclear bomber strength of 1099 mainly consisting of 916 B-47s and 174 B-36s. According to information provided by the USAF this bomber strength would rise to 1500 by 1960 with 1170 B-47s and 330 new B-52s.[94] It was in this context that three types of justification, operational concerns, the reliability of the United Kingdom as an ally and the unreliability of the United States as an ally, were offered for the independent V-bomber force.

The Air Ministry argued that one of the most important operational factors governing the validity of the deterrent was the ability to penetrate Russian air defences and attack the target systems of choice. It claimed that the Valiant had superior performance to the B-47 and that, in some respects, the Victor and Vulcan were superior to the B-52 and thus the British would make a significant contribution to any joint effort. The Air Ministry maintained that 'these factors are of the greatest significance to the capability of Anglo-American offensive power and consequently to the validity of the Deterrent'.[95] This claim was, however, rejected by the Ministry of Defence.[96] The elite nature of the V-force nevertheless remained an important strand in RAF thinking although the emphasis was shifted to the elan of Bomber Command crews.[97]

Second, the Air Ministry pointed out that in the negotiations over the Wilson/Alexander agreement the American government had been told that Britain intended to have a 240 strong bomber force. The RAF had used this force to divert criticism from plans to run down the planned Canberra force to be allocated to SACEUR from 240 to 100. The Americans had agreed to give financial aid to the RAF on the basis that Fighter Command and 2nd TAF would be maintained but both had been reduced on the grounds that priority was being given to Bomber Command.[98] According to the Air Ministry, therefore, a reduction in the front-line V-bomber strength would weaken is political role.[99]

The aim of inextricably linking British and American nuclear forces was vital because, in the Air Ministry's view, the United States was a potentially unreliable ally on two counts. The United States itself was inevitably coming under the threat of nuclear attack. As the Russians developed ballistic missiles the Americans could decide that Britain was no longer valuable as a major base because of its vulnerability to surprise attack. The situation could develop in which America withdrew nuclear forces from Britain and, fearing the possibility of nuclear attack on its own cities, could no longer be relied upon to deliver an immediate massive retaliatory attack on Russia in the event of war. In this disastrous political situation it would be vital to have a force that could inflict significant damage on Russia.[100] It does not seem that anyone connected with the RAF believed in 1955 that an independent British nuclear force could actually destroy Russia but its role in preventing America from decoupling itself from Europe was regarded very seriously.

The Air Ministry also maintained that although Britain had no precise knowledge of American nuclear plans it had enough general information to know that the USAF's main objectives would be the air bases from which Soviet nuclear strikes on America could be launched and the destruction of Soviet industrial potential. The preservation of the United Kingdom was not of the same importance to the United States as it was to the British and its importance was decreasing as the Americans both achieved the capability to launch a major offensive from their own continent and themselves became vulnerable. They were likely to become less interested in the destruction of bases from which it was impossible to reach the United States. Conversely, the Americans would consider bases in Asia and the eastern Soviet Union, which presented no threat to Britain, as vital. In addition, Britain could not expect an early strike against other targets such as Baltic naval bases. The Air Ministry highlighted the stark fact that since the Russian's were improving their air defences at the same time as they were building more bomber bases British resources would already be impossibly stretched by the time the V-force was fully operational. If there was to be any future for counter-military targeting it had to be co-ordinated with SAC.[101]

Although the Ministry of Defence challenged the Air Ministry's contention that the United States was a potentially unreliable ally it was obviously an important and controversial issue in 1955.[102] The more general conclusion that Britain needed to have a formal link to American nuclear forces was more readily accepted. As a result the overt emphasis of the policy debate in 1955-6 was on a joint Anglo-American deterrent. The justifications for an independent force were, however, clearly understood. These issues were also raised by the Chiefs of Staff's Air Defence sub-committee, particularly by one of its members a Ministry of Supply scientist, Dr. Robert Cockburn,[103] but it is misleading to suggest that the sub-committee was unrepresentative and isolated. Whilst it is correct, in the sense that there was no agreed government policy, to say 'there is no evidence that the Government was drawing the conclusion that, when United States cities were vulnerable to Soviet nuclear attack, American willingness to come to the defence of Europe would be more problematic'[104] this matter had been directly raised at ministerial level.

The Independent Nuclear Force

Although the formal policy debate in the mid-1950s tended to be couched in terms of influence over the Americans the remarkable consistency with which Air Ministry representatives used the argument that nuclear air power could be equated with great power status strongly suggests that it was an influential belief.

Their simplest argument was that thermonuclear weapons and their delivery systems were the primary measure of military power. Therefore policy for them should be decided first and the rest of the defence budget moulded around them. As the Air Ministry put it: 'The long-range bomber with nuclear weapons is the most important weapon in war today. ... If risks are to be taken, they must be taken in conventional weapons and warfare; not in nuclear bombs and the force to carry them.' The Air Ministry maintained that this aspect of British power would not cost an unreasonable amount. It projected a V-force building up from 32 in 1956 to 240 in 1959 with expenditure rising from £21.5 million in 1955/6 to a peak of £74 million in 1959. Along with works services, maintenance costs and the costs of the nuclear weapons programme it was claimed that the nuclear force would take up 6-7% of a defence budget of £1500 million over the following four years.[105]

Closely linked with the idea that an independent nuclear force played a part in Britain's great power status was a new doctrine of limited nuclear war. During 1955 all three services agreed that, although it was impossible to envisage nuclear war limited by a division between thermonuclear and atomic weapons in Europe, they would plan for a nuclear war which was limited in the sense that it occurred outside Europe. This conclusion enabled Lord De L'Isle, the Secretary of State for Air, to argue that the nuclear bomber force had great value in political and military situations short of global war. According to De L'Isle not only did the Anglo-Iraqi-Turkish Agreement signed in April 1955 rest primarily upon British ability to use nuclear weapons against a Russian invasion of the Near East but the knowledge that Britain could base a nuclear force in Malaya affected China's foreign policy and Britain's whole position in South-East Asia.[106]

In order to understand the emergence of this set of ideas in 1955, and in the context of both alliances and limited nuclear war, one has to look back to the late 1940s and early 1950s. The role of nuclear weapons overseas had been part of British strategy since 1946. By 1949 two main propositions about 'peripheral' nuclear strategy had been agreed. First, that it was necessary to threaten the Soviet Union from a number of directions. Initially, the military justification for this policy had been the belief that since the United Kingdom was likely to be destroyed as a base British forces needed to deployed overseas to guarantee retaliation. Later it was maintained that the threat of nuclear attack from multiple directions would overload Soviet air defences, increasing the chances of successful penetration and forcing the USSR to put resources into defence rather offence. The second proposition was that British bases, and potentially atomic weapons overseas, would give Britain global influence with the United States.[107]

In the 1950s three further propositions were considered. First, that nuclear weapons could be used for 'tactical' purposes, for instance to deter or destroy a Soviet attack on the Middle East. The second proposition was that nuclear weapons had a 'symbolic' importance in cementing alliances. The last proposition was that threat of nuclear attack could be used against non-nuclear weapon states in the Middle and Far East. No deep military thought seems to have gone into any of these propositions. They were primarily a spin-off from debates about the role of nuclear weapons in the European context. They gained in prominence for two main reasons. First, because of the failure of conventional strategy overseas; to get any agreement on a Middle East Defence Organisation with the regional powers or to elicit promises of substantial force deployments from the United States or the Dominions. Second, because overseas nuclear strategy was less rigorously fought since it seldom challenged the force levels or preferred roles of the Army and Navy.[108]

These new propositions started to enter strategic thought, especially about the Middle East, between 1950 and 1952. The full ramifications in policy terms did not emerge until 1954-55 with the decision to withdraw from Egypt and the formation of the Baghdad Pact. The two main internal motors of change were the growing tendency to think purely in Cold War terms and the realisation that nuclear weapons had to be factored into strategy. Potentially, both of these stimuli could have prompted a radical rethink of strategy. Indeed the vulnerability of the Canal Base to thermonuclear weapons made its retention in the face of vast political difficulties seem pointless. In the main, however, the recasting of military strategy had a conservative effect; making it seem sensible for Britain to hold on where possible.

The strategic review which had taken place, at the prompting of Sir John Slessor, in the first six months of 1950 had stressed the close interaction between Cold and potentially real war. In Slessor's view security rested primarily on the combination of deterrent atomic air forces and a strong Cold War policy. In the 1940s he had shown himself to be an ardent 'Cold Warrior'. His firm belief was that 'the way to avert a hot war is to win the cold one'. He was also convinced of the centrality of Western Europe to British security and the short- to medium-term importance of concentrating armed forces there. The result, expressed in the 1950 Global Strategy Paper, was that British policy overseas ceased to be based primarily on the need to meet a large-scale conventional attack. Such a change had little real significance in the Far East where a threat of this kind was merely a gloss on policy. It was much more important for the Middle East. Slessor had come to believe that although this region was important as an area in which Western and Soviet interests would clash it would not be the most important theatre in any major war between the Western world and the Soviet Union. Indeed Slessor echoed Attlee's 1946 judgement that the Mediterranean was indefensible against shore-based airpower.[109]

The 1950 Defence Policy and Global Strategy paper had, however, contained an implicit contradiction over policy in the Middle East. On one hand it argued that the key area was Turkey and on the other that the retention of the Canal Zone was vital.[110] In part this was because the RAF still saw Egypt as an important base for nuclear air forces[111] but this approach had also rested on a fundamental misunderstanding of Egyptian attitudes. At the time Slessor believed that: 'In their heart of hearts the Egyptians don't really want to be left on their own to defend Egypt.' He had therefore felt that the main political problem was with the British Army rather than with Britain per se and that an RAF base would remain after 1956 as long as the Egyptians were offered enough 'sops and rake-offs'.[112] The uncertainties of the Global Strategy Paper had persisted in British thinking for some time. In August 1951 Slessor was still advocating the same policy.[113] Four trends were, however, already at work altering British policy. First, America was interested in the 'outer ring', especially Turkey, rather than Egypt. Second, the RAF was embarking on a fundamental rethink about the role of nuclear weapons in the defence of Europe which inevitably influenced thinking about other regions. Third, Turkey formally joined NATO in 1952. Fourth, the Egyptians continued to express an unremitting hostility to the presence of the British in their country, denounced the Anglo-Egyptian treaty in October 1951 and sabotaged every attempt by Britain to construct any kind of Middle East Command or Defence Organisation.

Thus by 1952 Slessor had altered his views about British strategy in the region. He now argued that the 'Northern Tier' was of primary importance and that the Egyptian base was not indispensable.[114] As he told the Chief of the Imperial General Staff: 'a base [in Egypt] is no earthly use unless one can operate effectively from it with some hope of success, and I cannot see what we hope to gain by this Lebanon strategy. I think we must really re-examine Middle East defence on new lines; imagine the effect on the Turks and Iraqis ... if we up and say our strategy is to secure a position in the Lebanon'.[115]

Slessor's new strategic prescription was to deny the Dardanelles to the Russians and, in the event of a war, to destroy their forces with nuclear airpower. As with the debate about the use of nuclear weapons in the defence of Europe no settled policy was agreed in 1951-2 but ideas were formulated that served as the basis of defence arrangements in the mid-1950s. Indeed, although the arguments about the Egyptian base continued at Cabinet level into July 1954[116] at a practical level, such as approving building works, it was acknowledged within the Air Ministry during the course of 1952 that Britain had little military future in the Canal Zone.[117] In December 1952 Eden told the Cabinet that the intention was to move British military headquarters from Egypt to Cyprus.[118] No clearcut decision about complete withdrawal was taken because of Churchill's opposition to 'appeasement on the Nile'. It took eighteen months to convince him of the Air Staff view that not only did the defence of the region rest on the use of nuclear weapons on the mountain passes in north-east Iraq, through which Russian forces had to advance, but that the base itself was hopelessly vulnerable to nuclear weapons.[119]

Plans for the deployment of air forces in the Middle and Far East drawn up between 1952 and 1956 amounted to a whittling down of numbers in response to the financial demands of the yearly defence reviews rather than any fundamental rethink of strategy. Nevertheless, over this period the ideas adumbrated in the early 1950s started to work through into military planning. Initially, the Air Ministry attempted to find an overseas role for the V-bombers with conventional weapons. Lord De L'Isle wished to strengthen his hand in budgetary debates by demonstrating that the bombers could have a large Cold War role. He pointed out that the V-bombers had ranges of 3000 to 4000 miles, an operational radius of 800 miles in the conventional role and could carry at least 30,000lbs of bombs which could be dropped from 20,000 feet with a bombing accuracy of 500 yards. Although he acknowledged that in many situations such striking power could not be used for political reasons he felt that the V-bomber force's quick deployment and destructive capabilities could be of great use and he cited the need to resist attacks across the Songhkla position between Thailand and Malaya. He also saw a more symbolic role for the bomber.

> One of the most significant advantages we shall gain will be the moral effects our air force can produce. There is a feeling in some parts of the world that our position as a great power came to an end a generation ago. The medium bomber is part of our hot war preparations which, unlike so many of these preparations, can be used to show our strength in peace-time ... units of Bomber Command will carry out flights to the Middle East and elsewhere. I think that these will serve to remind other countries that we are very much a modern power, and that in fact in the most modern weapon we are in advance of any other country.[120]

Air Staff officers certainly believed that support for forces in overseas theatres should be provided by a centrally based bomber force[121] but after lengthy deliberation they found: 'we have been able to produce no new ideas as to how the Air Force could take over any of the Cold War duties of the Navy or Army ... the general theme should [therefore] be ... a greater economy of naval and military forces for overseas operations resulting from the planned re-equipment of Transport Command and Bomber Command.'[122]

In South-East Asia planning was concentrated almost wholly on Malaya. In 1953, responding to the likelihood of French defeat in Indochina, two plans were produced. 'Ringlet' to meet Chinese inspired infiltration and 'Irony' to fight a Chinese invasion of Malaya. Both assumed that British land forces, with air support, would be sent forward to occupy the Songhkla position on the narrow Kra Isthmus which joins Malaya and Thailand (Siam).[123] Although the French defeat in Indochina the following year brought a spate of new planning activity little was actually changed. It was felt that the need for a purely British operation in the area was unlikely and the signing of the Manila Treaty brought expectations of an increased contribution from the Commonwealth. The RAF made some infrastructure improvements to its facilities in Malaya but refused to countenance major upgrading. The British military believed that if the Chinese moved south through Siam this would signal the start of a nuclear war since the Americans would refuse to commit ground forces to another Korean style operation. In this scenario the actions of British land forces seemed fairly irrelevant. This still left the possibility of limited Chinese aggression by irregular and proxy forces against which it was unlikely nuclear weapons would be used. Under Plan 'Warrior' the seizure of the Songhkla position in Siam was still seen as central. 'Warrior' set out the intention to seize the position if Chinese subversion threatened to destabilise Malaya, if they mounted a proxy invasion or in the event of a full-scale attack as part of a global war.[124]

Military planners recognised, however, that such plans rested on forces inadequate to take on anything other than the most unsophisticated opposition.[125] Some senior officers such as Admiral Sir Charles Lambe, Commander-in-Chief of the Far East Station, also criticised British plans for looking entirely in the wrong direction and saw Indonesia presenting a more likely threat than China.[126] Nevertheless, following consultations in ANZAM a revised 'Warrior' renamed 'Hermes' was produced in October 1955. It assumed that British and Commonwealth troops would seize the position within twenty-eight days against light Siamese opposition. To some, however, such plans were becoming increasingly unrealistic. Although the Australian Prime Minister, Robert Menzies, had approved planning in January 1955 there was no guarantee of Australian support. It was also assumed that the Americans would insist on using nuclear weapons in a SEATO defence of Siam north of Bangkok. At this stage a split opened up in British opinion with the Chiefs of Staff maintaining that a 'Hermes' type plan was pointless whilst the British Defence Co-ordinating Committee (Far East) argued for its continued relevance on the grounds that there were no wider plans for the defence of the region and that it was inadvisable to rely on the success of SEATO.[127] All the military planners involved realised, however, that British policy was shackled by American dominance in the area and Britain's own lack of military resources. They also argued that since global nuclear deterrence rested on a Soviet belief that their nuclear forces could not fatally damage the United States it would be possible for western powers to use nuclear weapons in the Far East without precipitating a global nuclear war. As a result the attention of military planners began to shift away from conventional defence to providing British forces with nuclear weapons.[128/]

The combination of the Cold War conceptions and thinking about nuclear weapons also underlay the military response to the Baghdad Pact. As part of the campaign to maintain the bomber force under the Long Term Defence Review it was proposed to allocate part of the V-bomber force to the Middle East. In the event of war its mission would be to prevent the advance of the Russians through the Zagros and Caucasus passes by mounting nuclear attacks on the mountain passes themselves, lines of communication and airfields in southern Russia. In all there were over 100 targets linked to the defence of the Middle East.[129]

Britain acceded to the Pact in April 1955 and its Military Committee first met in October of that year. Although the aims of the Pact were as much political as military, it was designed to encourage American involvement in the defence of the Northern Tier and to secure British facilities in Iraq,[130] the British military authorities did regard it as a proper military alliance. They ascribed three, not particularly coherent, objectives to British policy. First, to 'bolster up resistance to Communism in the cold war.' Second, to 'build up an effective defence organisation in the Middle East under British Command' and, third, to 'achieve [these objectives] with the minimum financial expenditure and without incurring any increased military commitment in the theatre, but at the same time to maintain the momentum of the Pact.'[131]

The problems of constructing a military alliance in the Middle East were considerable as shown by the earlier failure of the Middle East Command and the Middle East Defence Organisation but these earlier attempts had at least been built around Egypt when Britain had large armed forces based there. Now Britain proposed to construct an alliance with minimal forces of its own. The solution offered to this challenge was found in the ideas Slessor had propounded in 1952. The British offered the Pact a nuclear air force, made up of Canberra light bombers rather than the V-bombers, targeted against Soviet airfields, mountain passes, ports and communication centres.[132]

Given developments in nuclear strategy in the European theatre and, increasingly, the Far East it can be surmised that such a plan was regarded as a genuine contribution to the strength and stability of the alliance. The Air Staff certainly clung to the concept of a nuclear strike force in the Middle East. Even before the Suez crisis the RAF had shown scepticism about large-scale conventional forces in the region. It blamed the Army for preventing any radical review of British military commitments in order to maintain their own force levels.[133] Following the Suez operation some senior airmen expressed the opinion that it would much more sensible to deploy the maximum number of fighter-bombers, which had proved more useful than either Canberras or Valiants in combat operations,[134] but such views were disregarded because of the supposed supremacy of the global war role and support for the Pact.[135]

Whilst there was little latitude for a policy of planning for a limited nuclear war in Europe there seemed to be in the fight against 'worldwide communism'. In February 1955 a joint Air Ministry/War Office working party was cautious about the use of nuclear weapons in anything but all-out war, on the grounds that limited wars might not provide suitable targets for atomic bombs[136] and in April the Minister of Defence ruled that 'tactical nuclear weapons ... must take their place amongst the items of second importance' in the British research and development programme.[137] By June, however, the Chiefs of Staff had concluded that the rapid development of tactical nuclear weapons would make their use conventional by 1962 and that 'small tactical weapons would almost certainly be used in a limited war but not thermo-nuclear megaton weapons with their consequent fall-out effect' on the grounds that the greater the primary deterrent the less likely it would be that the use of atomic weapons would lead to global war.[138]

This shift in policy was of considerable importance over the next five years since it provided the missing link between the RAF's assertion that an independent nuclear force made Britain a world power and a way such power could be used. It suggested a practical method by which the United Kingdom could both provide independent local deterrents against aggression in the Middle and Far East and replace conventional forces with much smaller nuclear forces for war-fighting. This is why the growing tide of criticism of such a limited war policy was so damaging to Britain's pretensions as a world power in the 1960s.

The rapid adoption of this strategy, which had been so long in gestation, in mid-1955 suggests a complex set of motives. Indeed, these motives were based in interpretations of military power, international relations and technological development. The military believed that the Soviet Union had changed its political tactics in 1955 following the overthrow of Malenkov in February, particularly in agreeing to the July Geneva Summit, because its new leaders realised that a Soviet/NATO war would destroy human civilisation and were thus determined to avoid such a conflict. They continued to interpret the Soviet Union's aim as communist world domination by means of the Cold War and expected exploitation of nationalist and racial disturbances to lead to local and limited wars in the Middle and Far East.[139]

At the same time they did not believe that the Russians were in control of the communist regimes in the Far East, China and North Vietnam, so, although they would stir up trouble, the Soviets would be unable to control the level of aggression these countries showed; possibly resulting in major wars. This lack of direct Soviet control also meant that the use of nuclear weapons against these countries would not necessarily escalate into a global war against Russia.[140] China was held, probably because of Mao's description of the atomic bomb as a 'paper tiger',[141] to be a destabilising influence which did not show an appreciation of the risks of nuclear war.[142] The British were also aware that the Americans, with whom they were allied in the Far East under the Manila Treaty, intended in any case to deter war in the region with nuclear weapons, attack China with such weapons if it started a major war and to use tactical nuclear weapons to reduce the scale of Chinese attack so that it was not necessary to commit ground forces on a large scale.[143]

It also seemed in mid-1955 that a British tactical nuclear weapon would be available for deployment overseas within three years and indeed the 'Red Beard' type atomic bomb was probably deployed in this way in 1958.[144] This type of weapon could be used by both the RAF and the Royal Navy[145] and the Army could also see a role for itself with tactical nuclear weapons overseas[146] so there was little resistance to such ideas in the defence establishment. The RAF had already proposed that plans to defend Malaya with ground forces should be replaced by ones envisaging the interdiction of the Kra Isthmus between Thailand and Malaya by high density attacks with conventional weapons dropped from V-bombers.[147] The replacement of conventional with tactical nuclear weapons seemed to be a relatively small step to better achieve the desired effect. Finally, it was believed that in future Britain would have to face countries in the Middle and Far East which would have armed forces capable of presenting a significant military challenge rather than those which could be defeated in a police action or brushfire war.[148] It was, therefore, implicit that British air and land forces might need tactical nuclear weapons to overcome them.

The British Bomber Force and NATO Strategy

Despite the increased attention given to nuclear weapons outside Europe the most important role for such weapons in maintaining British power remained indirect. If it was possible to extend the logic of deterrence to NATO as a whole and to shift the burden of European defence from conventional to much smaller nuclear forces a return to the policy of 'limited liability' envisaged by the Chiefs of Staff when the North Atlantic Treaty was signed in 1949 seemed feasible. There was general agreement within the British defence establishment that the Lisbon force goals had no future as the basis of European defence. Little consensus existed, however, about the nature of the continental commitment which was to replace the attempt at full-scale conventional defence. Under Slessor's leadership the RAF had outlined a radical case for the reliance on nuclear weapons. Towards the end of his tenure as CAS Slessor had argued that financial constraints meant that new policies in this regard would have to be more thoroughgoing than even the Global Strategy Paper. It was his view that defence planning should proceed on the assumption that the the deterrent would either work or, if it did not, that there would be a very short and utterly devastating nuclear war to which the armed forces would have to be tailored.[149]

As a result of such thinking the reduction of the RAF contribution to NATO from 1953 onwards was much larger than that proposed by the other two services. The 27% shortfall from the 1953 Lisbon goal was set at 749 aircraft, the bulk of which, 576 aircraft, was made up from the forces directly assigned to SACEUR. This cut was not simply a reflection of the slow-down of the defence budget since it was acknowledged that if the RAF could get more funds they would be directed towards air defence and forces outside Europe.[150] Looking ahead to 1957 RAF planners saw that new interceptor and ground attack types, to replace Sabres and Venoms, could only be funded by cutting other RAF commands. This option was rejected on the grounds that MEAF and FEAF had already been cut to their minimum strength and it was more desirable to have light and medium jet bombers than a tactical air force. In addition there was some hope that German forces would begin to come into existence in 1957. 2nd TAF was seen, therefore, as having no role except encouraging allies. It was concluded that although 'undoubtedly it would be desirable to maintain the strength of 2nd TAF indefinitely and to re-equip it' it was less critical than other parts of the RAF and should be run down.[151]

The Air Staff approach had harsh critics within the RAF, most notably, from his post at SHAPE, Air Chief Marshal Saunders who commented 'that we should (except for France) be the biggest defaulter on our NATO commitments is regrettable; but that we should even contemplate the expediency of inventing a military justification to cover up our inability to meet our commitments, displays, ethical considerations apart, a dangerous tendency to under-rate the capacity of our allies to distinguish between truth and fiction.'[152]

Saunders argued that it was impossible to simply replace a military policy of defence with a political one of deterrence. 'How can any build up of conventional forces, which is insufficient to conduct a holding action successfully during the period required for strategic air operations to take effect, be regarded as an adequate deterrent to war?'[153] It was around this question that the debate about British strategy in Europe took place during 1953. Virtually all parties agreed that nuclear weapons would have an enhanced role but whereas some wished to see them twinned with relatively large conventional forces others wanted to replace such forces almost entirely with nuclear systems.

It was the Air Staff view which proved influential in the Ministry of Defence. In March 1953 Lord Alexander presented a paper reflecting its position to the Defence Committee. Although he acknowledged that in the short-term cuts in the rearmament programme had been made for purely economic reasons he argued that the 1952 Global Strategy Paper shifted the emphasis away from light and tactical bombers towards the V-bomber force and endorsed the view of the Chiefs of Staff that to supply SACEUR with over 1500 tactical aircraft was economically impossible and strategically unsuitable. According to Alexander, Britain had held back any attempt to review NATO strategy as a result of Slessor's talks with the JCS on the Global Strategy Paper. 'The US JCS were not convinced by the new concept of global strategy, and we have hitherto refrained from launching it in NATO because we could not count on any support from other countries'. The JCS had, however, agreed to give General Ridgway information on atomic weapons; a development which the British hoped would produce lower force requirements. Despite the JCS promise of enhanced nuclear forces for SACEUR Ridgway continued to demand large conventional forces and a counter-offensive strategy. His unwillingness to reduce his force requirements meant that the British government felt it necessary to launch a new strategy in the NATO Council during 1953. Alexander concluded that this strategy should be based around the strategic air forces and relatively small conventional forces:

> the build up of armed forces which, considered in relation to the striking power to the US SAC, increasingly reinforced by the RAF medium bomber force, and the power to protect their essential bases, can be regarded as an adequate deterrent to war, though they might not actually be sufficient to conduct a successful holding action should hot war break out. A decision on the size of the forces which could be deemed adequate for this purpose would be political rather than military.[154]

This paper sparked a strong response from the Army and Navy who let it be known they believed 'that the "adequate deterrent" must include sufficient ground and air forces to withstand the initial onslaught to gain time for the strategic air offensive on Russia to take effect; and sufficient naval forces to ensure the safety of our sea communications'.[155] Apart from these internal arguments for caution there were other powerful constraints on British policy. It was generally agreed that the presentation of British views should not be rushed since the most important policy objective was to achieve German re-armament through the EDC and that nothing should be allowed to interfere with this goal.[156] It was also recognised that 'we shall not get very far with this unless we can carry the Americans with us'[157] and in late March 1953 Churchill instructed that informal approaches should once more be made to the United States to try and persuade them of British views.[158]

The other major determinant of British strategy in Europe during 1953 was the response to the death of Stalin which, despite Churchill's foreign policy initiatives, was cautious. In the run up to the April 1953 NATO Council meeting in Paris the Cabinet agreed that whilst NATO should welcome the more conciliatory attitude of the new Soviet regime the ultimate objective of Soviet policy, communist world domination, was unchanged and that it was desirable that NATO remain militarily strong.

It was also felt that prolonged Western firmness would make it harder for the Soviets to revert to aggressive methods and that in this context it was unwise to canvass immediate changes in NATO strategy.[159]

This cautious attitude towards the Soviet Union was balanced by the belief that American financial support for maintaining conventional forces would be limited. It was assumed that the Eisenhower administration's attempt to reduce defence expenditure would lead to the reduction of defence aid to Europe. Rab Butler reported from Paris that, despite public unanimity against relaxation in the face of the Soviet threat, in private the United States had informed Britain and France that there would be little American economic aid available and only a certain amount of defence aid on offer in the future.[160] Butler told the Cabinet that the obvious divisions in the Republican party on external economic and defence policy meant that America would not be able to give the full co-operation and support in Europe the United Kingdom had hoped for.[161]

Clear decisions on Europe were not taken because of Churchill's stroke in late June 1953 but the consensus in the Ministry of Defence was that NATO needed a 'New Look' and that relatively little attention should be paid to military authorities such as SHAPE or the British army and naval staffs who believed otherwise.[162] As Richard Powell, the Ministry's Deputy Secretary, put it 'the only way of tackling the problem was a new political approach. It would not be solved by asking the Standing Group to write down the existing force requirements. NATO had to be made to recognise that, while the force requirements for defending the North Atlantic area were as stated by the military authorities, smaller forces would be able to provide an effective deterrent against Russian aggression.'[163]

At the same time NATO's Deputy Supreme Commander Lord Montgomery, an important if detached figure in British defence debates, was arguing that the A-bomb was of great importance and might enable the West to redress the imbalance of conventional forces. Although Montgomery was sure that NATO needed to recast its strategy he pointed out that the exact role of nuclear weapons in the theatre was extremely uncertain since the Russians would also possess them. Montgomery described the best strategic concept as that of 'hammer and anvil', with the hammer being the strategic air offensive and the anvil tactical air and land forces holding vital areas.[164] His views received powerful support. Lord Salisbury, effectively the leader of the government with both Churchill and Eden too ill to take an active role, argued that there could be no question of criticising the forward strategy since this would weaken the resolution of Norway and Denmark and could jeopardise the German military contribution. He described the proper policy as the retention of the biggest armed forces governments' could afford as a deterrent whilst emphasising improvements in quality and the rapid integration of German forces. Atomic weapons were important but should be kept more in the background. His suggested benchmark for the size of NATO forces was the 1953 total plus a full German contribution.[165]

The views of Salisbury and Montgomery supported by Lord Ismay, Secretary-General of NATO and Churchill's confidant,[166] were accepted by Butler with the caveat that there would still have to be a reduction in defence expenditure.[167] Further pressure for this compromise approach came from the French government which proposed that military expenditure should be maintained at 1953 levels. Like Salisbury the French identified the improvement of existing forces as the first aim and remained lukewarm in their attitude to nuclear weapons. Although they called for the nuclear air offensive to be directed against the operational capabilities of Soviet forces they warned that there must be no change to the forward strategy. The French position was that atomic weapons should not be regarded as a miraculous solution to defence problems or an excuse for reduction in effort.[168]

In the final preparations for the December 1953 tripartite Bermuda summit conference a compromise between conventional and nuclear forces seemed an increasingly attractive solution to the problem of how to put a new strategy in place without discouraging the rest of NATO, especially France. The most likely prospect seemed to be a guarantee from Britain and the United States that they would maintain their forces at 1953/4 levels despite the expense.[169]

At Bermuda Lord Ismay presented a review of NATO forces. At the end of 1953 these forces amounted to amounted to 39 divisions and 25 brigade groups supported by 4,090 aircraft directly under SACEUR's control although, as Ismay acknowledged, many of these units were at a low level of combat readiness. The Secretary-General nevertheless maintained that NATO could build up impressive conventional forces with a realistic chance of defending Europe.[170] In the foreign ministers' meetings Eden, Dulles and Bidault all endorsed the view that NATO strategy should be based around both the 'long haul' and the forward strategy. Despite French reservations about the role of nuclear weapons all also agreed with Ismay's proposal that SACEUR should be requested to hold an enquiry based around the 'long haul', fighting as far east as possible and the use of atomic weapons.[171]

Although the RAF's case for almost complete reliance on nuclear weapons was considerably watered down its influence was strengthened during 1953. Its policy of putting the strategic bomber at the centre of Britain's approach to Europe was confirmed by the negotiations to commit the V-force to NATO which led to the Wilson/Alexander agreement of February 1954 even though this agreement was twinned with the attempt to maintain conventional forces with American military aid. The Chiefs of Staff agreed that the Chief of the Air Staff should be their representative to NATO during 1954 on the grounds that all future NATO planning would be related to plans for the use of strategic bombers and atomic weapons delivered from the air.[172] This belief was further strengthened by Dulles' speech to a restricted meeting of NATO ministers on the American attitude to the tactical use of atomic weapons in which he argued that:

> The US had developed atomic weapons in such quantity and variety that they could now play a role very similar to that of conventional weapons. They could be used by all three services and for tactical as well as strategic purposes. They were in many respects cheaper than conventional weapons in terms of explosive power. The great problem was on what scale to develop them. It would be financially difficult, if not impossible, to duplicate atomic and conventional weapons. We must assume that the Soviet forces would be equipped with atomic weapons and we should think very carefully about the problem of using them ourselves.[173]

Early British enthusiasm for the nuclearisation of NATO might have influenced American policy.[174] It is more likely, however, that the American approach was a result of internal debates within the United States' defence establishment. It is certainly the case that the RAF later came to regret the proliferation of tactical nuclear weapons in Europe. Slessor and his successors had been thinking in terms of relatively few nuclear weapons. They underestimated American ingenuity and productive capacity. Yet Air Ministry proposals for the support of ground forces in Europe dismissed any role for conventionally armed fighter-bombers once tactical nuclear weapons became available and called for their numbers to be drastically reduced in the interim.[175] The Air Ministry's own plans for the RAF and its strategic advice to government actually pointed to a very significant reduction in conventional forces.

In the short-term the 'hammer and anvil' was acceptable to all parts of the defence establishment since it laid the basis for British efforts to ensure that German military power would become available to NATO despite the failure of the EDC. The most important aspect of this effort was Eden's London Conference promise to maintain four British divisions and a tactical air force on the continent at their existing levels. Although John Young and Saki Dockrill have shown, in separate articles, that this offer had deeper roots than the 'spur of the moment' emergence of this idea which Eden portrayed in his memoirs and that the offer was made with the, somewhat reluctant, acquiescence of the Chiefs of Staff[176] it nevertheless caused consternation in the Air Ministry. The Air Staff feared that such a treaty commitment might undermine its strategic ideas and force structure plans.[177] The RAF did not want to stabilise the level of forces in Europe at 1954 numbers but to completely replace the tactical air force with nuclear armed Canberras based in the United Kingdom.[178] In the interim it intended to reduce the strength of 2nd TAF. NATO had already been informed that as a result of the 1953 defence review 2nd TAF was to be reduced in strength from 502 to 464 aircraft in 1957. Its strength in 1954 was actually 476 aircraft. The Air Staff planned to reduce the force even further by 1957, in particular the number of day fighters and fighter-bombers was to be reduced from 384 to 264 aircraft.[179] RAF planners immediately fastened on to the escape clauses contained in the Paris Agreements which allowed the British commitment to be altered either because of economic difficulties or if forces of 'equivalent fighting capability' were provided.[180] Indeed, bolstered by the argument that the actual rundown of the 2nd TAF from 476 was not that great, RAF representatives were able to persuade Generals Gruenther and Norstad that a cut in numbers balanced by re-equipment was acceptable.[181]

Short-term agreement, however, merely papered over the cracks. Both NATO and British statements of strategy could be read to give more or less weight to nuclear air power. The new strategic directive prepared by SHAPE following the Bermuda Conference decisions and known as MC.48 stated that superiority in nuclear weapons and the means of delivering them was the most important factor in any future war. Such a war was likely to open with an initial short atomic exchange, a second phase might follow but the result would largely be determined by the first onslaught. The best defence against Soviet atomic attack was retaliation against its sources. Stemming from these conclusions the paper argued that the avoidance of surprise was essential and that priority had to be given to NATO forces in being, largely concentrated, with a German contribution, east of the Rhine-Ijssel line, and that these forces should have the capability and war plans to use nuclear weapons from the outset.[182]

In Britain the twin propositions that emphasis should be placed on nuclear armed forces in being and that the defence of the West could only be carried out on the basis of the immediate large-scale use of nuclear weapons remained controversial but there was little dissent from the conclusion that 'with Allied conventional forces at the present size it would seem that no practical alternative to the conclusion of the report could have been reached'.[183] The American government strongly endorsed the report and MC.48 was adopted as NATO strategy in December 1954.[184]

Once MC.48 was in place the British government proceeded to clarify some of its own ideas about the exact role of nuclear weapons in Europe. In April 1955 the Cabinet accepted the proposition that no dividing line could be drawn between small and large nuclear weapons. They also acknowledged that, even if it was possible, such a division would be contrary to British interests since it would weaken deterrence by encouraging Russia to think it could resort to aggression. From this ruling the Chiefs of Staff drew the further conclusions that a policy of massive retaliation was the only possible deterrent both in 1955 and in the future and that such a policy made it pointless to distinguish tactical from strategic targets. These conclusions were not reached in ignorance of contending ideas. In the course of compiling advice to the government the Joint Planners had interviewed Rear Admiral Sir Anthony Buzzard, the main proponent of 'graduated deterrence'. Buzzard's critique of British nuclear strategy rested on the belief that as Communist nuclear strength grew the Soviet Union might become more aggressive whilst the West would not risk the nuclear destruction of their homelands over relatively minor aggression. He concluded, therefore, that massive retaliation could only deter an all-out Soviet nuclear attack on the West. It was not relevant to other forms of Soviet aggression. Buzzard's recommendation to the Chiefs of Staff was that the Western powers should publicly declare the principle of using minimum necessary force, differentiate between tactical and strategic nuclear weapons and renounce the use of the strategic weapons. The planners refuted these views on the grounds that it was in Britain's interest to concentrate on deterrence rather than the limitation of nuclear war. They argued that to succeed in global war the Soviets would have to launch an initial surprise attack strong enough to prevent any significant nuclear retaliation. The geographical advantage of the West made such a huge attack impossible as long as NATO remained united. Any declaration on limiting war would sow doubt in the minds of Russian leaders about the West's commitment to nuclear weapons. According to the joint planners if Russia did attack NATO:

> A determined Communist drive would only be stopped by nuclear attack, not only on targets close to the front-line of the ... armies but also on airfields, communication centres, bases and perhaps cities, many of them remote from the front-line. The distinction between tactical and strategic targets thus becomes impracticable. Furthermore such distinctions would be unacceptable to nations whose territory was in the 'tactical zone', whilst the cities of Russia, the UK and the US were declared strategic and thus immune, at any rate in the opening stages of a Limited War.

They therefore argued that the concept of limited nuclear war in Europe was unworkable both militarily and politically.[185]

The planners nevertheless also pointed out that existing military plans provided for a reaction to an attack by a Soviet satellite by a counter-attack against that Soviet satellite, although they advised against any declaratory policy to this end.[186] The Chiefs of Staff confirmed that the correct response in the event of aggression by a Soviet client state would be retaliation against the client state not Russia. They believed that Dulles had made this clear in his public speeches.[187]

Although the Chiefs of Staff were capable of producing agreed papers on nuclear strategy there was, under pressure of further efforts to cut defence expenditure, little practical agreement about the forces needed for Europe. The divergences between the services were once more apparent during the 1955 Long Term Defence Review. In the medium-term the RAF challenged the whole MC.48 concept. 'It must surely be extremely doubtful', the Air Staff argued, 'whether a concept which envisages a two-phase war, the second phase of which is a coherent land/air campaign in Western Europe making a decisive contribution to ultimate victory, can remain valid once both sides have achieved a nuclear potential sufficient for all practical purposes ... when this state of affairs might be reached is no doubt a matter of guesswork but can hardly be much later than 1960!'[188] The Air Staff was determined to argue for the downgrading of everything except nuclear forces.[189]

The Air Staff was restricted by Eden's August 1955 ruling in the Defence Committee that the maintenance of forces in Europe was vital to defence policy but encouraged by his acceptance that these forces were of political rather than military importance.[190] The Air Staff recognised the political sensitivity of the issue but felt that Britain could decide on the proper force reductions and then justify them to the other NATO countries without putting unbearable strain on the alliance. It hoped that a new common concept of strategy could be agreed with SACEUR and the direction of NATO and national defence planning changed over a five year period.[191]

In Air Ministry plans all-weather and day fighters would, initially, continue to be stationed in Germany. The purpose of their continued deployment was to render other force reductions more palatable to SHAPE and to provide reinforcements for any overseas emergency. As the Luftwaffe started to build-up it could take over the air defence of Germany. The plans provided for the reduction of the strength of 2nd TAF to 184 aircraft in 1958/9.[192] The final stage was to be the provision of a Canberra nuclear striking force based in Britain and the withdrawal of all but reconnaissance planes from Germany. The Germans, Dutch and Belgians were then to take over the air defence of their own countries. The exact timing of these developments was in some doubt but it was hoped to give the Canberra nuclear capability by 1958 with American help and that by 1958/9 the Germans would have about 350 operational combat aircraft.[193]

The other services refused to accept the strategic reasoning which underlay these proposals. 'The other two service departments', the Air Staff noted, 'both believe in preparation for a two phase war and they do not accept in practice the concept ... that the first phase of the war would be brief and final'. The RAF criticised the fact that '[the] Army have regarded their contribution to NATO as inviolate. There is ... no suggestion that the advent of new weapons (e.g. Corporal) might enable the Army to maintain or increase the effectiveness of its four divisions on the Continent by radically reducing their size!'[194] Yet the RAF was itself counter-attacked by the Army and the Royal Navy who called for strict adherence to the spirit of the Paris Agreements, criticised the reductions in the 2nd TAF and called into question the priority given to the V-bomber force.[195]

By the autumn of 1955 it was clear that the reductions in the British defence programme under the Long Term Defence Review would conflict with NATO's requirements for MC.48. The Foreign Office refused to allow the economic escape clauses in the Paris Agreements to be used because to do so might undermine confidence in the economic stability of the United Kingdom. Yet the chiefs were still unable to agree on an approach to strategy.[196]

Whilst the Royal Navy and the Army argued that NATO forces should be maintained for a possible two-phase war the RAF championed the view that any war would be very short and that NATO contributions could be reduced with strategic advantage and without political detriment. Whilst the Navy wanted to retain dual-role ships for limited war and a NATO role in global war and the Army wished to retain NATO land forces and British reserve forces for NATO with the dual role of supporting out of area limited wars the RAF argued that the primacy of the deterrent and the destructiveness of thermonuclear war made forces such as 2nd TAF and Coastal Command redundant in a global war role.[197]

In the short-term the RAF acquiesced to the retention of large-scale conventional forces because of fears that the smaller NATO countries might virtually give up their defence programmes. The official British position justified conventional forces on the grounds that, however effective, the strategic nuclear offensive could not guarantee the end to land and sea attacks and forces would be required to prevent the Soviets from occupying NATO territory since 'the implications of "liberating" such territory with aid of nuclear weapons are so grave as to be unthinkable'. NATO and other conventional forces were to prevent Communist subversion or the threat of satellite aggression and thus preserve the unity of the alliance.[198]

The Long Term Defence Review was suspended in November 1955 without any final decisions on future strategy being taken but it was clear that, despite immediate set backs, RAF views were gaining ground. The main purpose of the defence review was to cut expenditure and the RAF was willing and able to make major cut-backs in its own forces and suggest ways in which these cut-backs could be repeated in the other services whereas the Army and Navy offered few savings. As important, however, was the difficulty of treating seriously plans for two-phase or 'broken backed' warfare and the maintenance of large land and sea reserve forces in the light of information presented to ministers about the massive devastation which would be wrought by thermonuclear war.[199]

The Long Term Defence Programme

The first part of the detailed review of the role and size of the V-bomber force which lasted into 1957 took place under the the auspices of the 1955 Long Term Defence Programme. This defence review was mainly concerned with weapons procurement. It had become obvious that Britain was spending vast sums trying to cover the whole field of weapons research and development and that costs would rapidly increase in the future. In April 1955 Selwyn Lloyd, Macmillan's successor as Minister of Defence, established three categories of weapons research. Top priority was given to strategic nuclear weapons and ballistic missiles. In the second category were tactical nuclear weapons, missiles and aeroplanes for air defence, cold war weapons, weapons for NATO forces and for the protection of sea communications. In the lowest category were any preparations for global war.[200] Early in May he instructed Service Ministers to prepare a review of defence expenditure over the next seven years giving prominence to new weapons developments. This review was to be fully considered by the government after the general election.[201]

The Long Term Defence Review had two phases. From May to July the services put forward their own proposals. The Chiefs of Staff failed, however, to achieve any kind of uniform response,[202] frustrating Lloyd and causing the Ministry of Defence to produce its own proposals on the size and allocation of the defence budget.[203] This intervention led to a much more intensive phase of the review from August through to its suspension in November.[204] The debate over the V-bomber was at the centre of the review. It involved vigorous attacks by the other services on the concepts of a British deterrent, one-phase war and the size of the medium bomber force matched by RAF responses and counter-attacks on the obsolescence of much Army and Navy planning for the thermonuclear age.

The first meeting of the review body decreed that the review was to go ahead on the basis of existing Cabinet decisions on the Swinton and Strath reports.[205] The findings of the Strath Report were particularly important in defining the basic principles around which the review would be conducted. The report was produced by a working party headed by a senior Ministry of Supply official, William Strath, and was considered by the Defence Committee in February 1955. It analysed the implications of thermonuclear war for the United Kingdom. Although the report itself is still classified later synopses suggest it strongly supported the RAF's case for a short war strategy by detailing for ministers, in terms of destruction and casualties, the utter devastation that would be wrought if a limited number of hydrogen bombs were ever dropped on the United Kingdom. The report was based on the assumption that ten hydrogen bombs would be dropped on London and other urban centres. It estimated that the result would be 12 million deaths, including 3 million from radiation poisoning. There would be 4 million additional serious casualties and 13 million people would be trapped in their homes for at least a week because of fall-out. Half Britain's industrial capacity would be destroyed, utilities would be totally dislocated, the distributive system, including any mechanism for money transactions, would break down completely. The water and food supply would be contaminated, no imports would be possible and 40 million survivors would have to exist under siege conditions leading to widespread malnutrition exacerbated by the disproportionate survival of 'useless mouths'. All this, it was suggested, would lead to an entirely unpredictable 'chain reaction' in the social and economic structure.[206] The combination of the Strath Report, the 1954 Swinton Report, Lloyd's ruling on the primacy of strategic nuclear weapons and the delivery of the first Valiant to the RAF in January 1955 gave the case for deterrence and the V-bombers a solid basis.

Following the Defence Committee's decision in early May that it could plan to train crews for a 240 strong V-bomber force and that a final decision on the size of the force would be made as a matter of urgency[207] the RAF submitted its proposals for the service for the period 1955/6 to 1962/3. The Air Ministry envisaged bringing the 240 bombers into service by 1959 as the highest priority. At the end of the period the Mk.1 V-bombers would be replaced by improved versions and from 1960 onwards there would be a need for a powered guided bomb to ensure penetration of Soviet missile defences. The ministry argued that both a new supersonic bomber and a strategic missile would be needed to replace the V-bombers but conceded that neither would be available during the review period. The V-bombers would be supplemented by 100 Canberra light bombers to be dedicated to SACEUR and to reinforce the striking power of the RAF in the Middle East in the event of limited war. These aircraft would need to be upgraded and then replaced by a new light bomber. Both the Canberra and its replacement would be nuclear capable and it was hoped the force could use atomic bombs from the American nuclear stockpile.[208]

The first major critic of the RAF's proposals was the Chief Scientist at the Ministry of Defence, Sir Frederick Brundrett. Brundrett, originally an

Admiralty scientist, had championed the role of the carrier during the discussions over the Swinton Report.[209] He argued that the V-force should have a front-line of 180 rather than 240. Brundrett admitted that defence priorities were clearly defined, the deterrent first, Cold and limited war fighting capabilities together with minimal secondary deterrents, such as Fighter Command and NATO forces, second, and preparations for global war a very poor third. He pointed out, however, that these defence priorities had to be modified in practice by two further considerations: defence expenditure should not cause economic disruption and Britain must act as a junior partner of the USA. He argued that although the primary objective of British defence policy was the continuous maintenance of a British deterrent the medium bomber force, in fact, only constituted a deterrent in conjunction with the United States. Yet at the same time Britain had to meet its 'Cold War' commitments independently of America. Brundrett believed that the V-bomber force would need to be superseded by a supersonic bomber and then ballistic missiles and he maintained that 'it is more than conceivable that in its original form the ballistic rocket threat may be imposed by the Navy'. The V-bomber force would thus be the main deterrent for only seven or eight years. There was no alternative to it but expenditure had to be kept to the minimum. At the same time more emphasis had to be put on Cold and limited war especially in reorientating the RAF towards air support and mobility. A force of 180, if equipped with thermonuclear weapons, would be an impressive visible deterrent and would convince the Americans to take the British deterrent seriously.[210]

The second major attack on the V-bomber force in the first part of the Long Term Defence Review emanated from the War Office in July. The Secretary of State for War, Anthony Head, made the surprisingly rare criticism that the British bomber force would not have any effect on Russian decision-making. In Head's view it therefore made no extra contribution to the Western deterrent and should be afforded no priority.[211] Given Head's subsequent defence of an 184-strong force as Minister of Defence in 1956[212] it seems likely that he was arguing for a reduction in the force rather than the complete abandonment that his point logically suggested.

The RAF responded to these attacks on a number of different levels. Sir William Dickson put forward two major justifications for a 240-strong force - it would give Britain a role in making allied nuclear strategy and enable attacks on targets other than those planned by SAC. Lord De L'Isle, on the other hand, based his case on the primacy of nuclear air power and the need for Britain as a great power to possess it in full measure.[213] The Air Ministry, led by De L'Isle, also counter-attacked its critics vigorously. He fully supported Lloyd's[214] call for a more thorough strategic review[215] since he knew that it would put the deterrent as first priority and cause serious questions to be asked about the plans of the other services,[216] especially the 'unrealistic position of spending money on the means to "bring food over the beaches" after bombardment by "H" bombs'. De L'Isle was also able to make the cogent criticism that defence policy-making was descending into casuistry. 'We used to talk about the alternatives of hot and cold war', he commented acidly, 'now we have tepid and limited wars as well. So a justification can readily be found for each item of Service expenditure actual or contingent.'[217]

The Air Ministry's arguments and tactics enjoyed only limited success, however. The Ministry of Defence decided that if any kind of useful review was to take place the Service Departments would have to be given much stricter guidance on their budgets and on the way in which they could spend them. At a closed meeting on 2 August 1955 between Selwyn Lloyd and his advisers, Sir Harold Parker, Sir Richard Powell, Sir Nevil Brownjohn and Lord Carrington, it was decided that of a £1500 million defence budget the RAF would be allocated £527 million and be told to plan a V-bomber force with a front-line of 176.[218]

The attempt to impose rigid financial constraints made the second half of the Long Term Defence Review much more bruising. It was suspended in November 1955 and De L'Isle was sacked as Secretary of State for Air by Eden in December largely for his vigorous and partisan espousal of the RAF's case.[219] All the services were united against the Ministry of Defence's financial provisions but were disunited over strategy with both the Army and Navy, joined by the Minister of Supply, Reginald Maudling, attacking the RAF's bomber plans.

In June 1955 the Chiefs of Staff had produced three different scenarios for the war which Britain was supposed to be planning for. The first scenario envisaged a thermonuclear war consisting of an initial nuclear exchange, lasting for three or four days, which would lead to massive destruction and the end of all centrally directed hostilities, this would be followed by a second phase in which British forces worldwide would fight with the weapons they had to hand and finally a resuscitation phase, lasting months or years, in which the Royal Navy would have a central part, leading to the re-establishment of central control. The second scenario was escalatory with a local war leading to a limited war, eventually involving the use of tactical nuclear weapons, and, finally, to a world war in which thermonuclear weapons would be used. The third scenario foresaw an expanded Russian navy attempting to isolate Europe from America after the initial thermonuclear exchange.[220]

In October the services were no nearer to reconciling the mutually contradictory elements in these scenarios. The RAF was arguing for concentration on a one-phase war, the Army and Royal Navy on two phases. The RAF was planning to cut Fighter Command to provide only a nominal defence of the United Kingdom whilst the Royal Navy had plans to commission a reserve fleet and the Army planned to move land forces overseas in the event of a war. The RAF was cutting Coastal Command and maritime reconnaissance from Malta whilst the Navy had a large number of ships committed to anti-submarine warfare in global war. The Army planned to maintain the order of battle of Northern Army Group in Europe whilst its air support from 2nd TAF was removed. All, however, were agreed that 'if the cuts suggested by the Minister are imposed this country can no longer simultaneously remain a world power, retain her position as leader of the Commonwealth and keep faith with NATO. ... Whatever is decided to be the correct strategic policy we consider it fundamental that our world position should not be impaired.' They also agreed that an increase in the defence vote, raising the RAF's allocation to £600 million and the Royal Navy's to £370 million would yield a disproportionate increase in military power. Yet only the RAF argued that the best way to remain a world power was to have a nuclear bomber force which would be large enough to act both as a deterrent in its own right and as a means of securing significant influence in alliance nuclear planning. The Admiralty recognised the importance of air power but argued that, in both peace and Cold War, the Royal Navy offered the best means of supporting foreign and colonial policy since it was both visible and mobile. Both the Admiralty and War Office maintained that as long as the United States supplied an effective deterrent resources would be better diverted to Cold and limited war tasks, with their NATO forces being seen as dual-purpose, and the V-bomber force reduced.[21]

In fact both the Admiralty and the War Office were even more hostile to the V-force than their formal submissions show. They conducted a 'whispering campaign' in Whitehall which suggested that not only should the force be done away with altogether but that British nuclear power could be best delivered in other ways. The Air Staff had to fend off suggestions made by the Admiralty that the Royal Navy could take over part or all of the British nuclear force by arguing that 'neither carrier-borne strike aircraft, necessarily of relatively limited performance, nor the atomic powered submarine to which Admiralty representatives have referred recently ought to be regarded as serious alternatives, such as would warrant expenditure on development.'[22]

More importantly for the immediate debate at a meeting of the Directors of Plans for each of the three services the Royal Navy questioned the whole concept of a British deterrent. Indeed the Air Staff feared that it would put forward a formal submission 'that as we cannot afford the land, sea and air forces required of a great power under modern conditions, we should concentrate on land and sea forces with their supporting air forces, but should not try to carry the crippling burden of a Strategic Striking Force. They will continue to support the policy of the deterrent, but urge that its provision should be left to the US.'[223] The Army and the Navy would 'not accept the principle of a significant British contribution to the Primary Deterrent if this means large cuts in those other RAF formations committed to the support of naval and land operations and still less if it means cuts in their own services.'[224] Although the case for abandoning the deterrent does not seem to have been made formally to ministers during the 1955 review it was implicit in all Army and Navy submissions.

The argument for abandoning the British nuclear force was, however, explicitly taken up by Reginald Maudling, the Minister of Supply. He used many of the arguments put forward by Brundrett on the need for Britain to concentrate more on its worldwide conventional forces but unlike him drew the conclusion that an independent British deterrent was not worth having.[225] As Clark and Wheeler have remarked: 'Exceptionally, a Conservative Minister, and one later to rise higher in the hierarchy, was calling into question the very wisdom of Britain's retention of an independent deterrent.'[226] On this issue, however, Maudling was a maverick, seemingly not even supported by the civil servants in his own department.[227] Nevertheless, this was the most serious challenge to Air Ministry policy on the V-bombers since Tizard's attacks in the last years of the Attlee government. Accordingly the Air Ministry presented a very detailed case refuting his views. This case can only be understood in relation to the arguments put forward in favour of the V-bomber force earlier in the year. Then the Air Ministry had suggested that the British deterrent had a role both as part as an overall Anglo-American effort and also independently as a guarantee against American withdrawal. The then Minister of Defence, Harold Macmillan, who became Foreign Secretary after the Conservative election victory in April 1955, had questioned the validity of the latter role so it was not so prominently cited later in the year. Four main roles were ascribed to the bomber force. In descending order of prominence they were as an important military adjunct to SAC, a means of securing nuclear co-operation with the Americans, a way of giving Britain a worldwide nuclear capability and finally as an independent deterrent.

The military justification presented for the V-force by the Air Ministry was that even in an age of nuclear sufficiency the West should still be superior: 'we must accept a future wherein both sides possess the power to annihilate the other. The mutual fear of the exertion of this power provides the basis for our hopes for peace but an equilibrium of such power is imperative and for world safety it should be evident that the scales tip on the Allied side.'[228] The ministry claimed that SAC no longer possessed overwhelming superiority[229] and that, in private, the Americans admitted this.[230] Before the USSR acquired a thermonuclear capability, and the Soviet Union exploded its first true, multimegaton, thermonuclear bomb, as opposed to a 'layer-cake' device with large but limited explosive potential, in November 1955,[231] the United States alone had had the power to wreck Russia's administrative and industrial potential by a systematic assault on several target systems during the first thirty days of war. According to the Air Ministry 'the future requires that the Allies, for their survival, should have the power to emasculate the Soviet Union in as many hours'. It claimed that SAC would be incapable of carrying out this task since financial limits would govern its expansion and the main front-line bomber in the future would be the unproven B-52 which 'by itself may not convince the Soviets of the inevitability of the ability of our offensive to penetrate and complete its missions.' Bomber Command would be vital because its potential for 150 missions in the first wave would tip the balance in convincing the Soviets of the immediate efficacy of the allied deterrent and provide insurance for any American operational shortcomings.[232]

This line of argument was an attempt to refute Head's assertion that the British bomber force had no effect on Soviet decision-making. The argument did not get beyond assertion since policy-makers were never presented with a detailed analysis, as opposed to anecdotes, about the Russian response to the force.[233] One weakness in the RAF's case is suggested by the fact it replaced the number of first wave missions it had previously estimated could be carried out, 120, with the number the Air Staff considered to be desirable, 150. Yet, although the planned front-line of Bomber Command was less than a fifth of the planned front-line of SAC, the argument about the relationship of American and British nuclear forces was not completely unsophisticated since it prefigured genuine American concerns. The Killian Report of February 1955, which was influential with President Eisenhower, had already begun to raise doubts about the vulnerability of the United States and its nuclear striking forces and the 'bomber gap' emerged as a major American political issue in spring 1956. There was particular concern in the Eisenhower administration about the growing number of bases from which the Russians could attack the USA leading to major efforts to maintain an adequate and secure preemptive capability.[234]

The Air Staff also fully stressed the long-term aim of achieving full nuclear co-operation with the United States. 'We would agree with the Minister of Supply', it wrote, 'that there is a very urgent need to develop UK/US collaboration, not only in the development and supply of nuclear weapons but also in planning the operations of our combined air striking forces. All our experience shows that the Americans will only exchange information or give it to those who have the means of putting it to good use.'[235] It was in this Anglo-American context that the counterforce mission was portrayed as significant since, to retain American support, the United Kingdom had to show determination to defend itself against nuclear attack.[236] It is notable that, once more, the counterforce mission was only regarded as important by the Air Ministry insofar as it was politically useful.

The Air Staff also argued that the British bomber force had an important independent role linked with Britain's position as a great power.[237] According to it the determination to defend the United Kingdom against a nuclear attack helped maintain Britain's position in world affairs by showing it was not subordinate to the United States in all fields. The knowledge that the RAF was willing and able to use nuclear weapons and would thus not yield to nuclear blackmail meant that the medium bomber force had considerable political value if it was properly militarily constituted.[238]

Having presented these arguments to ministers the RAF proposed at the end of 1955 that it should receive a defence budget allocation of £600 million a year rather than the £527 million put forward by the Ministry of Defence.[239] The £527 million programme contained provision for 176 V-bombers including, by 1961, 16 Valiants, 64 Victors and 96 Vulcans.[240] The £600 million programme included 200 V-bombers made up of 32 Valiants, 64 Victors and 104 Vulcans.[241] In each case the Victors and Vulcans would be a mixture of Mark 1 and the much improved Mark 2 types. The Air Ministry's intensive campaign was influential in that ministers became more interested in the political and military than the detailed financial arguments about the V-force.[242] The Secretary of State for Air was thus able to argue that the force should not be reduced below 200 on grounds of military effectiveness.[243] Just before the review was suspended in November the Defence Committee reached general agreement that the V-bomber force should not be allowed to fall below 200 because of its exceptional importance both practically and in the eyes of other countries.[244] By the end of 1955 the Air Ministry had won a significant victory. Ministers had accepted that the V-bomber force and its weapons were the single most important item in the defence budget. Nevertheless, with the failure of the overall review of defence expenditure to produce acceptable decisions the role and size of the force was still open to question.

Notes

1. Grove, *Vanguard to Trident*, pp. 96-8 and Clark and Wheeler, *British Origins of Nuclear Strategy*, pp. 183-8, 191-5, 200-209.

2. Cooper, 'The Origins and Development of the British Strategic Nuclear Deterrent Forces 1945-1960', p. 30.

3. James, 'The Impact of the Sandys Defence Policy on the Royal Air Force', p. 20.

4. CAS to Sir Norman Brook, January 1953, London, Public Record Office (P.R.O.), AIR20/7560.

5. Secretary of State for Air to CAS, 3 Feb. 1953, London, Public Record Office (P.R.O.), AIR20/7560.

6. Report by VCAS 'Radical Review - RAF Medium Bomber Policy', 5 Feb. 1953, London, Public Record Office (P.R.O.), AIR20/7560.

7. CAS to Sir Norman Brook, Jan. 1953, London, Public Record Office (P.R.O.), AIR20/7560.

8. 'Radical Review - RAF Medium Bomber Policy' Report by VCAS, 5 Feb. 1953, London, Public Record Office (P.R.O.), AIR20/7560.

9. 'A consideration of the benefits to be obtained from flight refuelling the Victor and Vulcan' OR.16 to ACAS(OR), 23 Oct. 1953, London, Public Record Office (P.R.O.), AIR20/8575.

10. 'Radical Review - RAF Medium Bomber Policy' Report by VCAS, 5 Feb. 1953, London, Public Record Office (P.R.O.), AIR20/7560.

11. Paper for Secretary of State in connection with Radical Review, February 1953, London, Public Record Office (P.R.O.), AIR20/7560.

12. Grove, *Vanguard to Trident*, p. 91.

13. AUS(A) to Air Council Members, July 1953, London, Public Record Office (P.R.O.), AIR20/7561.

14. Grove, *Vanguard to Trident*, p. 93.

15. Clark and Wheeler, *British Origins of Nuclear Strategy*, p. 184.

16. CAS to Secretary of State for Air, 17 June 1953, London, Public Record Office (P.R.O.), AIR20/7561 and Grove, *Vanguard to Trident*, pp. 101-2.

17. PS to CAS to ACAS(Ops)/(P)/(I) and AUS(A), 24 July 1953, London, Public Record Office (P.R.O.), AIR20/7561.

18. Radical Review - Medium Bomber Force, July 1953, London, Public Record Office (P.R.O.), AIR20/7561.

19. MISC/M(53)62, 21 July 1953, London, Public Record Office (P.R.O.), AIR20/7561.

20. Radical Review paper (untitled), July 1953, London, Public Record Office (P.R.O.), AIR20/7561.

21. RDP/M(53)9, 30 Nov. 1953, London, Public Record Office (P.R.O.), AIR20/7561.

22. CAS to Secretary of State for Air, 17 June 1953, London, Public Record Office (P.R.O.), AIR20/7561.

23. Grove, *Vanguard to Trident*, p. 107.

24. Grove, *Vanguard to Trident*, p. 106; Clark and Wheeler, *British Origins of Nuclear Strategy*, p. 197.

25. Appendix 'B' to DOR/S.5025, 23 Oct. 1953, London, Public Record Office (P.R.O.), AIR20/8575.

26. Radical Review paper (untitled), July 1953, London, Public Record Office (P.R.O.), AIR20/7561.

27. Radical review - Medium Bomber Force, July 1953, London, Public Record Office (P.R.O.), AIR20/7561.

28. Grove, *Vanguard to Trident*, pp. 109-10.

29. Ibid., pp. 111-12.

30. Secretary of State for Air to CAS, 30 April 1954, London, Public Record Office (P.R.O.), AIR8/1875.

31. Sir Herbert Brittain to Sir Harold Parker, undated, London, Public Record Office (P.R.O.), T225/437.

32. Sir Frederick Brundrett to Minister of Defence, 18 Nov. 1954, London, Public Record Office (P.R.O.), DEFE13/66.

33. MISC/M(54)123, 6 Dec. 1954, London, Public Record Office (P.R.O.), DEFE13/66.

34. D(55)1st, 13 Jan. 1955, London, Public Record Office (P.R.O.), DEFE13/66.

35. Sir Richard Powell to Minister of Defence, 2 Feb. 1955, London, Public Record Office (P.R.O.), DEFE13/66.

36. D(55)3rd, 15 March, London, Public Record Office (P.R.O.), DEFE13/66.

37. JP(54)100(Final), 23 Nov. 1954, London, Public Record Office (P.R.O.), DEFE4/74. The paper presented to the Cabinet in July is still classified but a revision prepared by the Joint Planners in consultation with the JIC, the Foreign Office and the Commonwealth Relations Office and approved by the Chiefs in November 1954 is available.

38. A/ACAS(P) to CAS on General Brownjohn's Minute NCDB/2/1111 Amendments to DP(54)6, 21 July 1954, London, Public Record Office (P.R.O.), AIR8/1875.

39. JP(54)100(Final), 23 Nov. 1954, London, Public Record Office (P.R.O.), DEFE4/74.

40. D(54)43, 23 Dec. 1954, London, Public Record Office (P.R.O.), CAB131/14.

41. JP(54)100(Final), 23 Nov. 1954, London, Public Record Office (P.R.O.), DEFE4/74.

42. D(54)43, 23 Dec. 1954, London, Public Record Office (P.R.O.), CAB131/14.

43. COS(54)386, 15 Dec. 1954, London, Public Record Office (P.R.O.), DEFE5/55.

44. MISC/M(54)123, 6 Dec. 1954, London, Public Record Office (P.R.O.), DEFE13/66.

45. Minister of Defence to Secretary of State for Air, 23 Dec. 1954, London, Public Record Office (P.R.O.), DEFE7/1111; Secretary of State for Air to Minister of Defence, 23 March 1955, London, Public Record Office (P.R.O.), DEFE11/101.

46. Duke, *US Defence Bases in the UK*, p. 95.

47. Bullock, *Ernest Bevin, Foreign Secretary*, p. 796.

48. Slessor to Minister of Defence, 5 April 1952, London, Ministry of Defence (Air Historical Branch), Slessor Papers, XLIIIH.

49. Slessor to AMSO, 19 May 1952, London, Ministry of Defence (Air Historical Branch), Slessor Papers, XLIIIH.

50. Ibid.

51. CAS to VCAS, 13 August 1952, London, Ministry of Defence (Air Historical Branch), Slessor Papers, XLIIIH.

52. Radical Review - USAF Contribution to ADUK, undated, London, Public Record Office (P.R.O.), AIR20/7561.

53. History of the 406th Fighter Bomber Wing, July-September 1952, Maxwell AFB, USAF Historical Research Center.

54. ACAS(Ops) to ACAS(P)/AUS(A), 10 August 1953, London, Public Record Office (P.R.O.), AIR20/7561.

55. Secretary of State for Air to Prime Minister, 3 Jan. 1957, London, Public Record Office (P.R.O.), PREM11/2188.

56. JP(59)17(Final), 9 Feb. 1959, London, Public Record Office (P.R.O.), DEFE4/116.

57. Sir Oliver Franks to Foreign Office, 14 Jan. 1952, London, Public Record Office (P.R.O.), PREM11/620.

58. Thetford, *Aircraft of the RAF since 1918*, pp. 114-15, 414-415, 448-449.

59. Note by Minister of Supply, 18 June 1952, London, Public Record Office (P.R.O.), PREM11/620.

60. Botti, *The Long Wait*, p. 117.

61. For details of NSC 162 see *FRUS 1952-54*, II, pp. 488-534, 545-6 and 562-97.

62. Brief for CAS on Meeting with Admiral Radford, Chairman US JCS, 3 Nov. 1953, London, Public Record Office (P.R.O.), AIR8/1852.

63. 'Meeting with the British, 1700, December 13, Hotel Talleyrand', 13 Dec. 1953, London, Public Record Office (P.R.O.), DEFE13/222.

64. ACAS(P) to VCAS, 30 March 1953 and A/ACAS(P) to CAS, 11 April 1953, London, Public Record Office (P.R.O.), AIR8/1853.

65. Richard Powell to Lord Alexander, 17 Dec. 1953, London, Public Record Office (P.R.O.), DEFE13/222.

66. Lord Alexander to Charles Wilson, 17 Dec. 1953, London, Public Record Office (P.R.O.), DEFE13/222.

67. Charles Wilson to Lord Alexander, 17 Feb 1954; Alexander to Wilson, 23 Feb. 1954, London, Public Record Office (P.R.O.), DEFE13/222.

68. Sir Roger Makins to Foreign Office, 2 July 1954, London, Public Record Office (P.R.O.), DEFE13/222.

69. Wilson to Alexander, 12 March 1954, London, Public Record Office (P.R.O.), DEFE13/222.

70. General Sir Nevil Brownjohn to General Sir John Whitely, 24 June 1954, London, Public Record Office (P.R.O.), DEFE11/101.

71. Colonel Potter to Mr. Wheeler, 16 Sept. 1955, London, Public Record Office (P.R.O.), DEFE13/222.

72. NSC 162, 30 October 1953, *FRUS, 1952-54*, II, p. 593.

73. General Sir Nevil Brownjohn to General Sir John Whitely, 24 June 1954, London, Public Record Office (P.R.O.), DEFE11/101.

74. Sir Richard Powell to Minister of Defence, 4 Dec. 1954, London, Public Record Office (P.R.O.), DEFE7/942.

75. 'Record of Meeting at British Embassy, Paris', 17 Dec. 1954, London, Public Record Office (P.R.O.), DEFE7/942.

76. 'Brief for Mr. Lincoln Gordon over Plan 'K' Aid Discussion', undated, London, Public Record Office (P.R.O.), DEFE7/942.

77. Colonel Potter to Wheeler, 16 Sept. 1955, London, Public Record Office (P.R.O.), DEFE13/222.

78. Sir Richard Powell to Minister of Defence, 1 April 1955, London, Public Record Office (P.R.O.), DEFE7/942.

79. VCAS to Maj-Gen. James W. Spry (Chief, Military Aid Advisory Group, UK), undated, London, Public Record Office (P.R.O.), DEFE7/942.

80. Sir Harold Parker to Minister of Defence, 23 Sept. 1955, London, Public Record Office (P.R.O.), AIR8/1912.

81. MISC/M(56)40 Meeting between Sir Richard Powell and Mr. Winthrop Brown, 23 Feb. 1956, London, Public Record Office (P.R.O.), DEFE13/222.

82. Memorandum of Conversation between the Prime Minister and President, 22 March 1957, London, Public Record Office (P.R.O.), DEFE7/984 and Kikuyana, 'Britain and Short-Range Nuclear Weapons', pp. 539-560.

83. Young (ed.), *The Foreign Policy of Churchill's Peacetime Administration*, pp. 39-43.

84. ACAS(P) to CAS, 17 Sept. 1957, London, Public Record Office (P.R.O.), AIR8/2161.

85. Sir Richard Powell to Minister of Defence, 4 Dec. 1954, London, Public Record Office (P.R.O.), DEFE7/942.

86. 'Inter-Allied Organisation' Maj-Gen. Sir Ian Jacob, 12 Dec. 1952, London, Public Record Office (P.R.O.), DEFE7/744.

87. Secretary of State for Air to Minister of Defence, 23 March 1955, London, Public Record Office (P.R.O.), DEFE11/101.

88. 'The Size of the Bomber Force' forwarded by Secretary of State for Air to Minister of Defence, 23 March 1955, London, Public Record Office (P.R.O.), DEFE11/101.

89. Ibid.

90. Ibid.

91. Ibid.

92. Ibid.

93. Ibid.

94. D.D.Pol(AS)1 to ACAS(P), 21 Sept. 1955, London, Public Record Office (P.R.O.), AIR20/9850.

95. 'The Size of the Bomber Force' forwarded by Secretary of State for Air to Minister of Defence, 23 March 1955, London, Public Record Office (P.R.O.), DEFE11/101.

96. Ibid.

97. Cross, 'The Origins and Development of the British Strategic Nuclear Deterrent Forces, 1945-1960', pp. 40-43.

98. 'The Size of the Bomber Force' forwarded by Secretary of State for Air to Minister of Defence, 23 March 1955, London, Public Record Office (P.R.O.), DEFE11/101.

99. Secretary of State for Air to Minister of Defence, 23 March 1955, London, Public Record Office (P.R.O.), DEFE11/101.

100. Ibid.

101. 'The Size of the Bomber Force' forwarded by Secretary of State for Air to Minister of Defence, 23 March 1955, London, Public Record Office (P.R.O.), DEFE11/101.

102. 'The Size of the Bomber Force' forwarded by Secretary of State for Air to Minister of Defence (marginal notes), 23 March 1955, London, Public Record Office (P.R.O.), DEFE11/101.

103. Clark and Wheeler, *British Origins of Nuclear Strategy*, pp. 216-7.

104. Ibid., p.217.

105. 'The Size of the Bomber Force' forwarded by Secretary of State for Air to Minister of Defence, 23 March 1955, London, Public Record Office (P.R.O.), DEFE11/101.

106. Secretary of State for Air to Minister of Defence, 8 Sept. 1955, London, Public Record Office (P.R.O.), AIR8/2044.

107. Ball, 'Bomber Bases and British Strategy in the Middle East, 1945-1949', passim.

108. Deighton (ed.), *Britain and the First Cold War*, p. 149.

109. 'Draft Paper on Defence Policy and Global Strategy' Slessor to Secretary, COS, 20 March 1950, London, Ministry of Defence (Air Historical Branch), Slessor Papers, XIVA.

110. Ibid.

111. Ovendale, *The English-Speaking Alliance*, p. 126.

112. Slessor to CinC MEAF, undated, London, Ministry of Defence (Air Historical Branch), Slessor Papers, XXXB.

113. Slessor to Sir Pierson Dixon, London, Public Record Office (P.R.O.), AIR8/1806.

114. 'Some First Reactions to the Foreign Office Draft Annex to COS2029/16/10/52' PS to CAS to D.of Plans, 17 Oct. 1952, London, Ministry of Defence (Air Historical Branch), Slessor Papers, XIVD.

115. Slessor to CIGS, 10 Oct. 1952, London, Ministry of Defence (Air Historical Branch), Slessor Papers, XIVD.

116. Young (ed.), *The Foreign Policy of Churchill's Peacetime Administration*, p. 137.

117. Interview with T.C.G. James. James was Lord De L'Isle's private secretary during his tour of the Middle East in 1952.

118. Young (ed.), *The Foreign Policy of Churchill's Peacetime Administration*, p. 139.

119. Ibid., p. 150.

120. 'Use of the RAF in Time of Peace' Note by Secretary of State for Air, July 1953, London, Public Record Office (P.R.O.), AIR20/7561.

121. 'Radical Review - RAF Medium Bomber Policy' Report by VCAS, 5 Feb. 1953, London, Public Record Office (P.R.O.), AIR20/7560.

122. ACAS(Ops) to AUS(A), 14 Aug. 1953, London, Public Record Office (P.R.O.), AIR20/7561.

123. Brief by Ops(Tac)3, 19 Nov. 1953, London, Public Record Office (P.R.O.), AIR20/7554.

124. ACAS(P) to CAS, 5 Oct. 1954, London, Public Record Office (P.R.O.), AIR8/1880.

125. ACAS(P) to CAS, 19 Oct. 1954, London, Public Record Office (P.R.O.), AIR8/1880.

126. COS(55)77th, 27 Sept. 1955, London, Public Record Office (P.R.O.), AIR20/7554.

127. JP(56)29(Final), 24 Feb. 1956, London, Public Record Office (P.R.O.), DEFE4/84.

128. JP(56)61(Final), 15 March 1956, London, Public Record Office (P.R.O.), DEFE4/85.

129. 'The Size of the Bomber Force' forwarded by Secretary of State for Air to Minister of Defence, 23 March 1955, London, Public Record Office (P.R.O.), DEFE11/101.

130. Young (ed.), *The Foreign Policy of Churchill's Peacetime Administration*, pp. 159-61.

131. JP(59)107(Final) 'Review of Baghdad Pact Military Planning', 19 August 1959, London, Public Record Office (P.R.O.), DEFE4/120.

132. 'The Size of the Bomber Force' forwarded by Secretary of State for Air to Minister of Defence, 23 March 1955, London, Public Record Office (P.R.O.), DEFE11/101.

133. ACAS(P) to CAS, 12 June 1956, London, Public Record Office (P.R.O.), AIR8/2116.

134. C-in-C MEAF to VCAS, 3 Dec. 1956, London, Public Record Office (P.R.O.), AIR20/10096.

135. ACAS(P) to VCAS, 5 Dec. 1956, London, Public Record Office (P.R.O.), AIR20/10096.

136. Land/Air Warfare Committee Policy Statement No.1 (Third Revise) Air/Ground Operations in the Tactical Area, 11 Feb. 1955, London, Public Record Office (P.R.O.), AIR2/9748.

137. DRP/P(55)16, 4 April 1955, London, Public Record Office (P.R.O.), DEFE7/763.

138. COS(55)51 Confidential Annex, 29 June 1955, London, Public Record Office (P.R.O.), DEFE7/763.

139. 'The Strategic Situation in the World Today Through UK Eyes' Address by CAS to C-in-Cs at Exercise 'Onward', 14 June 1955, London, Public Record Office (P.R.O.), AIR8/2048.

140. COS(55)51 Confidential Annex, 29 June 1955, London, Public Record Office (P.R.O.), DEFE7/763.

141. Baylis et. al. (eds.), *Contemporary Strategy*, pp. 258-9.

142. COS(55)51 Confidential Annex, 29 June 1955, London, Public Record Office (P.R.O.), DEFE7/763.

143. JP(55) Note 20(Final), 11 Oct. 1955, London, Public Record Office (P.R.O.), DEFE4/80.

144. First Lord of the Admiralty to Minister of Defence, 9 July 1958, London, Public Record Office (P.R.O.), DEFE7/679.

145. Ibid.

146. Clark and Wheeler, *British Origins of Nuclear Strategy*, p. 222.

147. 'The Size of the Bomber Force' forwarded by Secretary of State for Air to Minister of Defence, 23 March 1955, London, Public Record Office (P.R.O.), DEFE11/101.

148. Land/Air Warfare Committee Policy Statement No.1 (Third Revise) Air Ground Operations in the Tactical Area, 11 Feb. 1955, London, Public Record Office (P.R.O.), AIR2/9748.

149. 'Defence Policy in Economic Crisis' Memorandum by Sir John Slessor, 20 Oct. 1952, London, Ministry of Defence (Air Historical Branch), Slessor Papers, XIVD.

150. AUS(A) to Secretary of State for Air, 16 March 1953, London, Public Record Office (P.R.O.), AIR8/1853.

151. Note by A/ACAS(P) on (1) Ground Forces Required to Meet Paratroop Attack on UK (2) RAF Plans for 2nd TAF - Radical Review Questions, 27 July 1953, London, Public Record Office (P.R.O.), AIR20/7561.

152. Air Chief Marshal Sir Hugh Saunders to CAS, 30 April 1953, London, Public Record Office (P.R.O.), AIR8/1853.

153. Ibid.

154. D(53)14 Memorandum by Minister of Defence, 2 March 1953, London, Public Record Office (P.R.O.), CAB131/12.

155. N. C. D Brownjohn to Prime Minister, 25 March, London, Public Record Office (P.R.O.), PREM11/369.

156. Ibid.

157. Sir Norman Brook to Prime Minister, 25 March 1953, London, Public Record Office (P.R.O.), PREM11/369.

158. D(53)5th, 26 March 1953, London, Public Record Office (P.R.O.), PREM11/369.

159. CC(53)28th, 21 April 1953, London, Public Record Office (P.R.O.), PREM11/369.

160. FO Telegram No.127 Chancellor of Exchequer to Prime Minister, 24 April 1953, London, Public Record Office (P.R.O.), PREM11/369.

161. CC(53)29th, 28 April 1953, London, Public Record Office (P.R.O.), PREM11/369.

162. T. J. Beagley to General Brownjohn, 17 July 1953, London, Public Record Office (P.R.O.), DEFE7/743.

163. Future NATO Policy - Ministry of Defence Meeting, 20 July 1953, London, Public Record Office (P.R.O.), DEFE7/743.

164. Field Marshal Lord Montgomery to Prime Minister, 26 June 1953, London, Public Record Office (P.R.O.), PREM11/370.

165. C(53)234 'A Revised Policy Directive for NATO' Memorandum by Lord President of the Council, 17 August 1953, London, Public Record Office (P.R.O.), PREM11/369.

166. Sir Norman Brook to Prime Minister, 24 August 1953, London, Public Record Office (P.R.O.), PREM11/369.

167. CC(53)50th, 25th August 1953, London, Public Record Office (P.R.O.), PREM11/369.

168. DFM.95/53, 13 Nov. 1953, London, Public Record Office (P.R.O.), PREM11/369.

169. Sir Norman Brook to Prime Minister, 1 Dec. 1953, London, Public Record Office (P.R.O.), PREM11/369.

170. BC(F)53 4th Meeting, 6 Dec. 1953, London, Public Record Office (P.R.O.), PREM11/369.

171. BC(P)(53)3rd, 6 Dec. 1953, London, Public Record Office (P.R.O.), PREM11/369.

172. COS(53)144th Confidential Annex, 22 Dec. 1953, London, Public Record Office (P.R.O.), PREM11/369.

173. WU.1072/180G 'Record of the Restricted Meeting of Ministers of North Atlantic Council on December 16, 1953', London, Public Record Office (P.R.O.), PREM11/369.

174. Clark and Wheeler, *British Origins of Nuclear Strategy*, pp. 178-182.

175. General N.C.D. Brownjohn to Parliamentary Secretary, Ministry of Defence, 4 Sept. 1953, London, Public Record Office (P.R.O.), DEFE11/101.

176. Young (ed.), *The Foreign Policy of Churchill's Peacetime Administration*, pp. 95-98 and Young and M. Dockrill (eds.), *British Foreign Policy, 1945-1956*, pp. 160-162.

177. ACAS(P) to VCAS, 6 October 1954, London, Public Record Office (P.R.O.), AIR8/1881.

178. VCAS to Sir Walter Dawson (SHAPE), undated, London, Public Record Office (P.R.O.), AIR8/1881.

179. 'The Implications of the Foreign Secretary's Recent Undertaking Regarding the Retention of UK Forces on the Continent in Relation to Future Plans for 2nd TAF' Air Ministry, 18 Oct. 1953, London, Public Record Office (P.R.O.), AIR8/1881.

180. CAS to ACAS(P), 9 Nov. 1954, London, Public Record Office (P.R.O.), AIR8/1881.

181. Note by CAS, 21 Feb. 1955, London, Public Record Office (P.R.O.), AIR8/1881.

182. JP(54)99(Final), 2 Dec. 1954, London, Public Record Office (P.R.O.), DEFE4/74.

183. Ibid.

184. COS(54)133rd Confidential Annex, 22 Dec. 1954, London, Public Record Office (P.R.O.), DEFE4/74.

185. JP(55)147(Final), 13 Dec. 1955, London, Public Record Office (P.R.O.), DEFE4/81.

186. Ibid.

187. COS(55)104th, 15 Dec. 1955, London, Public Record Office (P.R.O.), DEFE4/81.

188. ACAS(P) to CAS, 12 Sept. 1955, London, Public Record Office (P.R.O.), AIR20/9399.

189. Ibid.

190. DC(55)8th, 26 August 1955, London, Public Record Office (P.R.O.), CAB131/16.

191. ACAS(P) to CAS, undated, London, Public Record Office (P.R.O.), AIR8/2044.

192. MISC/P(55)47, undated, London, Public Record Office (P.R.O.), AIR8/1912.

193. ACAS(P) to CAS, undated, London, Public Record Office (P.R.O.), AIR8/2044.

194. D.of Plans and S.6 to Secretary of State for Air and CAS, 1 Oct. 1955, London, Public Record Office (P.R.O.), AIR8/2044.

195. ACAS(P) to CAS, 30 Sept. 1955, London, Public Record Office (P.R.O.), AIR8/2044.

196. COS(55)80th, 6 Oct. 1955, London, Public Record Office (P.R.O.), DEFE4/79.

197. JP(55) Note 19(Final), 4 Oct. 1955, London, Public Record Office (P.R.O.), DEFE4/79.

198. JP(55)151(Final), 1 Dec. 1955, London, Public Record Office (P.R.O.), DEFE4/81.

199. D(55)5 'Information Made Public on the Effects of Thermo-nuclear Weapons' Note By Minister of Defence, 13 Jan. 1955, London, Public Record Office (P.R.O.), CAB131/15.

200. DRP/P(55)16, 4 April 1955, London, Public Record Office (P.R.O.), DEFE7/963.

201. SM(55)4th, 4 May 1955, London, Public Record Office (P.R.O.), DEFE7/963.

202. General Sir Nevil Brownjohn to Field Marshal Sir John Harding, 9 June 1955, London, Public Record Office (P.R.O.), DEFE7/963.

203. Minister of Defence to First Lord of the Admiralty, 9 July 1955, London, Public Record Office (P.R.O.), DEFE7/963.

204. Note to CAS, 8 Nov. 1955, London, Public Record Office (P.R.O.), AIR8/1912.

205. LDP/M(55)1, 10 May 1955, London, Public Record Office (P.R.O.), DEFE7/963.

206. COS(57)278, 18 Dec. 1957, London, Public Record Office (P.R.O.), DEFE5/80.

207. DC(55)2nd, 2 May, London, Public Record Office (P.R.O.), DEFE7/1111.

208. 'The RAF 1955/6 to 1962/3', 13 June 1955, London, Public Record Office (P.R.O.), AIR19/660.

209. Sir Frederick Brundrett to Minister of Defence, 18 Nov. 1954, London, Public Record Office (P.R.O.), DEFE13/66.

210. Sir Frederick Brundrett to Sir Richard Powell, 12 April 1955, London, Public Record Office (P.R.O.), DEFE7/1111.

211. MISC/M(55)69, 12 July 1955, London, Public Record Office (P.R.O.), DEFE7/963.

212. Minister of Defence to Prime Minister, 28 Dec. 1956, London, Public Record Office (P.R.O.), DEFE7/1111.

213. MISC/M(55)69, 12 July 1955, London, Public Record Office (P.R.O.), DEFE7/963.

214. Minister of Defence to First Lord of the Admiralty, 9 July 1955, London, Public Record Office (P.R.O.), DEFE7/963.

215. Secretary of State for Air to Minister of Defence, 14 July 1955, London, Public Record Office (P.R.O.), DEFE7/963.

216. COS(55)57th Confidential Annex, 15 July 1955, London, Public Record Office (P.R.O.), DEFE7/963.

217. Secretary of State for Air to Minister of Defence, 14 July 1955, London, Public Record Office (P.R.O.), DEFE7/963.

218. MISC/M(55)76, 2 Aug. 1955, London, Public Record Office (P.R.O.), DEFE7/963.

219. Interview with Lord De L'Isle.

220. COS(55)51st Confidential Annex, 29 June 1955, London, Public Record Office (P.R.O.), DEFE7/963.

221. JP(55) Note 19(Final), 4 Oct. 1955, London, Public Record Office (P.R.O.), DEFE4/79.

222. ACAS(P) 'Review of the Defence Programme - In light of Minister of Defence's Memorandum', 19 Sept. 1955, AIR8/1912.

223. ACAS(P) to CAS, 30 Sept. 1955, London, Public Record Office (P.R.O.), AIR8/2044.

224. ACAS(P) to CAS, 6 Oct. 1955, London, Public Record Office (P.R.O.), AIR8/2044.

225. Minister of Supply to Minister of Defence, 30 Aug. 1955, London, Public Record Office (P.R.O.), AIR19/660.

226. Clark and Wheeler, *British Origins of Nuclear Strategy*, p. 226.

227. AUS(A) to CAS, 19 Oct. 1955, London, Public Record Office (P.R.O.), AIR8/1912.

228. CAS to Secretary of State for Air, 13 Sept. 1955, London, Public Record Office (P.R.O.), AIR8/2044.

229. Secretary of State for Air to Minister of Defence, 8 Sept. 1955, London, Public Record Office (P.R.O.), AIR8/2044.

230. Secretary of State for Air to Minister of Defence, 8 Sept. 1955, London, Public Record Office (P.R.O.), AIR8/2044.

231. Ball and Richelson (eds.), *Strategic Nuclear Targeting*, p. 46.

232. CAS to Secretary of State for Air, 13 Sept. 1955, London, Public Record Office (P.R.O.), AIR8/2044.

233. Cross, 'The Origins and Development of the British Strategic Nuclear Deterrent Forces, 1945-1960', pp. 43-4.

234. Ball and Richelson (eds.), *Strategic Nuclear Targeting*, pp. 45-7.

235. CAS to Secretary of State for Air, 13 Sept. 1955, London, Public Record Office (P.R.O.), AIR8/2044.

236. Secretary of State for Air to Minister of Defence, 8 Sept. 1955, London, Public Record Office (P.R.O.), AIR8/2044.

237. CAS to Secretary of State for Air, 13 Sept. 1955, London, Public Record Office (P.R.O.), AIR8/2044.

238. Secretary of State for Air to Minister of Defence, 8 Sept. 1955, London, Public Record Office (P.R.O.), AIR8/2044.

239. MISC/P(55)47, October 1955, London, Public Record Office (P.R.O.), AIR8/1912.

240. 'V' Bomber Force: 176 U.E. Force, London, Public Record Office (P.R.O.), AIR8/1912.

241. 'V' Bomber Force: 200 U.E. Force, London, Public Record Office (P.R.O.), AIR8/1912.

242. AUS(A) to Secretary of State for Air, 19 Oct. 1955, London, Public Record Office (P.R.O.), AIR8/2044.

243. Secretary of State for Air to Minister of Defence, 5 Oct. 1955, London, Public Record Office (P.R.O.), DEFE7/1111.

244. DC(55)13th, 4 Nov. 1955, London, Public Record Office (P.R.O.), CAB131/16.

5

The Reassessment of Strategy: 1956-1960

The V-bomber Force and the
Policy Review Committee

In the mid-1950s two broad but interlocked approaches had been developed towards the V-force and British nuclear weapons. The first approach was based on the belief that a British nuclear force made the United Kingdom a great power; the second on the contention that it would give the British government influence over American policy. The first rationale included three main propositions. First, that the possession of nuclear weapons gave Britain influence in its three major alliances, NATO, the Baghdad Pact and SEATO. Second, that a nuclear force was a symbol of power; nuclear weapons were the measure of military strength and only the USA, the Soviet Union and Britain had developed and could deliver them. Third, given the emergence of a doctrine of extra-European limited nuclear war, a nuclear force acted as a deterrent to aggression from countries other than the Soviet Union and had war-fighting potential as a substitute for large conventional forces.

The place of the V-force in Anglo-American relations was also divided into three parts. It was claimed that the British force was a militarily significant contribution to an overall Western deterrent and therefore the Americans would wish to enter into joint nuclear planning with Britain in order to ensure that that deterrent was effective. It was hoped that this co-operation would lead to a more general influence over American policy. Second, the British nuclear force was seen as an independent threat to the Soviet Union. Since the Americans did not have all nuclear decision-making under their own control they would be obliged to consider the British position on a whole range of issues and would be constrained from making rash nuclear decisions. Third, by vitiating any hope of limiting a nuclear war to the European continent, the British nuclear force would help to preserve the American nuclear guarantee to Western Europe once the USA became vulnerable to nuclear attack.

The dominant consensus on these issues was, however, fragile since it had emerged from a round of defence debates marked by an inability to reach agreement on the pressing practical questions of weapons procurement and force levels. Harold Macmillan, who became Chancellor of the Exchequer in December 1955, Sir Walter Monckton, Selwyn Lloyd's successor as Minister of Defence, and the Cabinet Secretary, Sir Norman Brook, were all frustrated by the failure of the Long Term Defence Review process to produce firm decisions about future strategy and weapons procurement. They combined to insist that Eden set in motion a new defence review which would limit service influence and allow ministers and senior civil servants to take the necessary decisions. From March to June 1956 a group of officials under Brook worked on a report on Britain's position in world affairs. The report endorsed the RAF's view that the hydrogen bomb had revolutionised strategy. It argued that Russia and China were very unlikely to resort to aggression and that conventional forces were, therefore, of diminished importance. The report also argued that since the war Britain had overextended itself in many fields leading to recurring economic crises. Unless substantial economies were made soon the country's ability to play a role in world affairs would be greatly diminished. This report was submitted to a ministerial Policy Review Committee (PRC) which undertook an intensive review of defence policy in June and July only to be interrupted by the Suez crisis. The Policy Review Committee resumed work briefly in December 1956 before the change of government in the next month.[1] Although it is difficult to be categorical about which parts of the case for a British nuclear bomber force developed in 1954-5 were the most influential with the PRC, since its records are not available, it would seem that the balance of strategic argument about the British nuclear force did change in 1956 and that this change was linked more with the PRC's intensive review of policy than the Suez crisis itself.

The Chiefs of Staff were unaware of the exact nature of the first part of the policy review and only received the Brook group's paper, 'The Future of the United Kingdom in World Affairs', on 6 June to coincide with the first meeting of the PRC[2] but they had been told to expect a further defence review starting around Easter.[3] Thus, as far as the British nuclear force was concerned, three issues were already being considered: the nature of thermonuclear war which would form the background to any decisions about the exact size of the force, the decision on the size of the

V-force itself, and the procurement decisions for the weapons which would succeed the V-bomber force.

The Chiefs of Staff could agree that Britain needed both atomic and thermonuclear weapons[4] but were divided over their exact role. In January 1956 they advised the government that it was against British interests not to continue the development of the hydrogen bomb. In doing so they endorsed the role of British nuclear weapons both as a integral part of great power status and of Anglo-American relations.

> Any such action [not developing the H-bomb] would remove the foundation stone of United Kingdom strategic policy which was based on our remaining an independent power possessing, and being able to deliver, the primary deterrent. ... If we did not develop megaton weapons we would sacrifice immediately and in perpetuity our position as a first-class power. We would have to rely on the whim of the United States for the effectiveness of the whole basis of our strategy. Furthermore our views would no longer have any weight with Russia and our status would be lowered in the eyes of the United States.[5]

The chiefs further agreed that Britain's leading position in NATO rested on the possession of megaton weapons, that it was impossible to justify force reductions in Europe without them and that any British decision to abandon their programme would destabilise the alliance.

These arguments seem to have been generally accepted by ministers[6] but the First Sea Lord, Lord Mountbatten, and the Chief of the Imperial General Staff, Sir Gerald Templer, refused to accept that their views on nuclear weapons amounted to an endorsement of a V-bomber force anywhere near the size of 200 agreed at the end of 1955. They based their case on the proposition that once Russia attained nuclear parity with the United States, and the Joint Intelligence Committee estimated that the Soviet Union would have the ability to carry out effective two-way bombing operations against America from 1959,[7] the strategic environment would change. First, they argued, once both sides had the ability to use thermonuclear weapons each would be deterred from doing so, raising the possibility that major limited wars would be fought under the H-bomb threshold. According to Mountbatten:

> It [the hydrogen bomb] will only deter thermo-nuclear war. Once again we shall have to face the possibility of war being fought with conventional weapons (possibly with tactical atomic weapons), because thermo-nuclear action by two power blocs, each with the maximum destruction in its possession, would mean world suicide. Anyone holding such a view must surely agree that it would be an act of lunacy to plan, during the temporary period when the West is predominant in nuclear power, to disband our conventional forces.[8]

Their second argument was that once the United States became vulnerable its nuclear guarantee to Europe would be suspect and the West would need the complementary deterrent of large-scale conventional forces in Europe.[9] Implicit in their case was a rejection both of the belief that Britain could deter the Soviet Union independently or that the British nuclear force would give the United Kingdom any significant influence over the United States government. Given the support all the chiefs had given to the British hydrogen and atomic bomb programme it would seem that Mountbatten and Templer were arguing for a minimal bomber force capable of demonstrating British capability to develop and deliver such weapons rather than one which had any particular military significance to either the United States or the Soviet Union.

The Air Ministry case for the force rested on the definition of an 'effective deterrent'. Whereas the Army and the Navy claimed this meant Western nuclear preponderance the RAF defined it as the ability of both sides to destroy one another.[10] The Air Ministry case rested upon the proposition that a nuclear balance would continue to create the conditions for mutually effective deterrence since no government would embark on any sort of war which risked its own destruction. It dismissed the fear of Western self-deterrence on two grounds. First, that NATO would be unwilling to allow Europe to be overrun without resorting to its most powerful weapon. Second, that a true nuclear balance would not, in practice, emerge since it would still be easier for America to attack Russia than vice-versa in the foreseeable future. The British nuclear force would prevent the thermonuclear decision from resting wholly in American hands thus dissuading either the United States or the Soviet Union from forming the assumption that a war could be limited to Europe. To back up these views they also argued that nuclear escalation could not be controlled: NATO land forces had to be equipped with atomic weapons to give them any hope of posing a serious military threat to a Soviet offensive but it was unrealistic to believe that once such weapons were used this would not inevitably lead to the use of hydrogen bombs.[11]

Neither side would compromise so separate appreciations had to be forwarded to ministers.[12] The PRC accepted the views of the RAF.[13] This was an important decision since it reaffirmed the primacy of the bomber force in British defence policy. The exact size of the force, however, remained undecided. Following the suspension of the PRC's work in late July Monckton issued a directive to the Service ministries in early August outlining substantial cuts to the planned 1958/9 defence estimates. The RAF's budget was to be cut by 15% to £505 million. Although the main blow fell on Fighter Command the proposed front-line of the V-bomber force was reduced from 200 to 184. The RAF protested about the political impact of this reduction in the negotiations about a new NATO strategy[14] but it is probable that the Air Staff were not unduly concerned by the reduction from 200 to 184. To continue to fight for a bigger front-line would have had a severe effect on other parts of the RAF.[15] Acquiescence was also a matter of practical politics: no-one else would support a bigger force. The Ministry of Defence had already proposed that the front-line should be 176 in 1955, Sir Walter Monckton was not a strong supporter of an independent British force,[16] and it seems that Macmillan suggested to the PRC that 100 or 120 bombers would be enough.[17]

The debate in the Chiefs of Staff committee shows that by mid-1956 the decision on the size of the V-force appeared to rest on a calculation of how many bombers would be needed to influence the United States. It was recognised that the force could not be justified in purely military terms since the 200 strong front-line had been arrived at by simply removing Valiants from earlier plans. The RAF argued that emphasis should be placed on building up the force as quickly as possible in order to gain influence with the Americans, achieve joint targeting and obtain a supply of bombs before the British could supply their own. The availability of British weapons seems to have been a marginal consideration in deciding the size of the force since Sir Dermot Boyle noted that 'the delivery of 100 bombs did not mean 100 megaton weapons', but included nuclear weapons of all sizes. The size of the force was not 'calculated on the availability of 100 megaton bombs ... until we had a sufficient force to persuade the United States to co-ordinate their planning with us, we could not say with certainty what targets and, consequently what weapons, we would need.'[18] According to the Chief of the Air Staff, therefore, the size of the V-bomber force did not rest on British hydrogen bomb production or on the need to attack a particular number of identifiable targets but on the need to co-ordinate planning with the Americans; only once this had been achieved would the exact role of the bomber force be decided.

The force's critics cast doubts on the influence which would flow from its possession. Sir Gerald Templer argued that although Britain should be a member of the 'H-club' the V-force provided no more deterrent than SAC alone, that there were no targets of vital importance to the United Kingdom which were not also of sufficient importance to the United States to appear in SAC plans, and that British influence would be as great if not greater if she maintained substantial conventional forces. According to Templer 'they [the Americans] might well say that our best solution would be to retain effective conventional forces and make some small contribution to the deterrent'.[19]

The shift in the argument towards the importance of the V-bombers in influencing the Americans clearly predated Suez. Although its most forthright exposition came from Macmillan in the aftermath of the crisis he had been one of the main figures in the PRC who had argued for a significant reduction in the V-bomber force. In November 1956 he once more pressed his senior ministerial colleagues to both rethink strategy and reduce defence expenditure. Macmillan wanted to cut the bomber force on the grounds that the true deterrent was American nuclear potential. He believed that this deterrent would be relatively secure until the United States developed an ICBM and so ceased to need British bases. The role of the bomber in his eyes was to convince the Americans that Britain was a worthwhile ally. His aim was to maximise Britain's access to the American missile programme. Macmillan did not argue that Britain did not need an independent nuclear force or that the potential problems of nuclear parity between the United States and the Soviet Union were not worrying but that the time-frame of the debate was awry. British concern should be focused on the late 1960s rather than the late 1950s. As in 1955 Macmillan was unwilling to accept the Air Ministry's argument that the USA was an unreliable ally which could be coerced by Britain's possession of an independent nuclear force. Nevertheless, since his main criticism of British defence policy was directed against conventional rather than nuclear forces in practice he was minded to give more support to the Air Staff than the opposition to the V-force led by Templer and Mountbatten.[20]

Macmillan's views were important not only because he succeeded Eden as Prime Minister in January 1957 but because he was the prime mover behind the 1956 review. He was therefore responsible for a shift towards an emphasis on the role of the British nuclear force in Anglo-American relations rather than its independent value. This shift had significant consequences when the successor force to the V-bombers came to be debated.

Other senior ministers did not necessarily share Macmillan's view on the role of the bomber force, even if they agreed with his opinion that nothing was sacrosanct in the face of the post-Suez financial crisis. For example, Lord Salisbury believed:

A reduction of the V-bomber force to about 100 would not enable the United Kingdom to make a significant contribution to the deterrent. The figure of 184 aircraft proposed by the Minister of Defence was the minimum which would be consistent with the general policy. ... Moreover, any smaller number would increase the difficulties of persuading the RAF to accept the other reductions proposed. On the other hand, there would be no certainty at this stage that the national economy could afford the cost of maintaining a bomber force of this size.[21]

Although Salisbury was not a central figure in the defence debates of 1957, he resigned in March over Cyprus, similar views were not uninfluential in the Conservative Party. This suggests that, although such considerations were not cited directly, Macmillan was under political constraints which prevented the adoption of the 100 strong 'membership of the H-club' force advocated by Templer and Mountbatten.

1956 saw a winnowing of V-bomber rationales by Macmillan and the PRC. The most important casualty was the military justification for the force. The PRC refused to accept that Britain needed a bomber force whose primary aim would be to reduce damage to the United Kingdom by attacking Soviet air bases and nuclear facilities which would not be targeted by SAC. This role was questioned because of the impossibility of preventing a Soviet first-strike delivering enough hydrogen bombs to utterly devastate the United Kingdom, because Britain did not have the capability to attack the 150 targets identified as posing a threat and because it was not necessarily true that these targets did not appear in SAC targeting plans. Any continuation of a counterforce role only made sense as part of an Anglo-American targeting plan. The second military argument rejected by the PRC was that that SAC alone would be incapable of posing a credible deterrent, either because it was unable to penetrate Soviet defences or to cause enough destruction. The RAF's contention that the V-force could 'tip the balance' between success and failure was no longer regarded as credible.

The second category of rejected arguments centred around the risk of nuclear decoupling. Macmillan claimed that the American thermonuclear guarantee could be relied upon until the late 1960s. Thus the V-force was not important in making Britain a second centre of nuclear decision, although its successor force could potentially be called upon to fulfil that role. Conversely the case that from the early 1960s it would be necessary to prepare for a conventional or limited nuclear war in Europe was also rejected.

The symbolic role of the V-force and its weapons, the membership of the 'H-club', retained its importance. So too did another potentially independent role, bombers as a deterrent and war fighting force overseas. Templer even argued that the size of the force should be tied to the latter role.[22] The RAF, not unnaturally, refused to accept his suggestion but the policy of the Macmillan administration on overseas deployment shows that it was of considerable importance. The primary role Macmillan ascribed to the bomber force, however, was to convince the Americans that Britain remained an important ally. Implicit in his argument was the view that the Americans would not be able to ignore the British nuclear force whereas they could afford to discount conventional forces. Support was given to this view in December 1956 when the Americans finally agreed to open talks on joint nuclear targeting. Macmillan believed that these contacts could be deepened to include technology transfers thus guaranteeing British influence over decades rather than years.

The Chancellor's views did not go unchallenged; the Air Staff objected that the V-force was the only means of having a foreign policy which did not slavishly follow that of the United States.[23] Both Macmillan and the Air Staff saw the United States nuclear guarantee as potentially unreliable; they disagreed over whether American reliance on British bases was a sufficient interim guarantee. Both wanted an independent nuclear force but neither believed Britain could stand alone against Russia. An independent deterrent had always been seen as a means rather than an end of policy: the force was never meant to deter Russia without American help but to ensure that the American nuclear guarantee remained in place. It was essential to ensure that whatever political developments took place in the United States the Soviet Government could never be certain that the nuclear guarantee had effectively been withdrawn. If a force was to exist it was easy for Macmillan, as Prime Minister, to agree to independent targeting plans as an extra guarantee of American good faith. Although plans of this nature had additional implications for the size and composition of the force there were already political constraints on its reduction.

The Suez crisis did not provoke a new demand in the defence establishment for an independent nuclear force capable of deterring Russia. Although the Air Staff disagreed with Macmillan's rejection of a V-force capable of posing an independent threat to Russia they did so on the basis of arguments consistently advanced in previous years.

Macmillan, Sandys and the V-bomber Force

The exact size of the V-bomber force did not play an explicit part in the debate over the 1957 Defence White Paper. The central issue in the early part of the year was the decision to abolish national service. There was no carefully discussed linkage between reduction in manpower and the number of nuclear armed bombers needed as a replacement.[24] In a wider sense, however, the White Paper did adopt the ideas about nuclear substitution proposed by the RAF since the early 1950s. It was also predicated on the decisions taken in 1956 that the nuclear rather than conventional forces would have first priority in the defence budget.

In February 1957 Macmillan ruled that 'we should ... have within our control sufficient weapons to provide a deterrent influence independent of the United States'.[25] Sandys accepted Air Staff arguments that the force should consist of 184 front-line aircraft including 120 Mark 2 Victors and Vulcans armed with powered guided bombs rather than the 176 aircraft with only 40 Mark 2 bombers then on order.[26] Although any immediate decision was blocked by the Chancellor of the Exchequer, Peter

Thorneycroft, the importance of the Mark 2 V-bombers was accepted by all parties. Sandys and Thorneycroft agreed that although the final force could be anywhere between 120 and 184 strong there would be at least 80 Mark 2 aircraft.[27] The final decision on the size of the force was taken in August 1957.

Although Macmillan accepted that 'the total capital and running costs of 184 V-bombers together with the necessary nuclear weapons would not represent more than 7-10% of total defence costs' and that a 'force of this order was an effective means of maintaining British prestige throughout the world and represented an extremely economic use of manpower'[28] his previous positions on the force suggested that he would be amenable to some compromise. Sandys put a strong case for the 184 aircraft force. He acknowledged that any figure was not calculated on precise military grounds but said he was convinced of the operational arguments for the force. He also expressed concern that given the tone of his recent White Paper it would be politically unwise to announce a reduction in the British nuclear force. He was met by the alternative view of the Chancellor that since each Mark 2 V-bomber cost about £750,000 and the total costs of the force were continually rising it should be limited to 144 bombers with 96 Mark 2 aircraft. The Defence Committee agreed on the compromise of a force of 144 aircraft with 104 Mark 2 bombers. This decision was influenced by one major and one minor consideration. The major consideration was the belief that since the V-bombers would never be needed to attack the Soviet Union on their own some financial saving was acceptable.[29] The minor consideration was the recognition that the Mark 2 bombers would be much more effective and that Mark 1 aircraft could be deployed in overseas theatres once the more advanced aircraft became available.[30] The final decision on the front-line of the the V-force, taken after years of tortuous debate, amounted to an exercise in cost cutting balanced by the desire for an operationally effective force.

In both 1955 and 1956 Macmillan had rejected the argument that the primary role of the V-force was to prevent nuclear decoupling. The Prime Minister did not, however, deny that decoupling was a long-term danger. Within the Air Ministry it continued to be seen as a major justification for an independent nuclear force. This was reflected in the counter-city independent targeting plan developed for the V-force.

The RAF had always kept a number of target systems under review but since the early 1950s the officially stated role of the British bomber force had been a counterforce mission aimed at reducing the damage done to Britain in a nuclear attack. Within the defence establishment it was recognised that this role was no longer credible. The original concept had been based on either the prevention of the Soviet launch of a second wave of nuclear attacks or the destruction of Soviet nuclear capability in the event of a major conventional war in Europe. Analysis of the destructive potential of hydrogen weapons since 1955 had shown the damage caused by a Soviet first-strike with thermonuclear weapons would be so great as to make the prevention of another attack of marginal importance. The growth in the number of Soviet air bases from which attacks could be launched on the United Kingdom meant that the British nuclear force would never be sufficiently strong to attack them all. The start of formal planning with the Americans meant that targeting could be rethought.

Anglo-American Nuclear Targeting and the Cities Criterion

The 1954 Wilson/Alexander agreement had committed the RAF bomber force to the support of NATO ground forces. It had also provided for the creation of links with SHAPE to facilitate such use. The Americans showed few immediate signs of following up the agreement. In August 1955, however, Sir William Dickson, the Chief of the Air Staff, was invited to meet with General Nathan Twining, the USAF's Chief of Staff. This invitation followed talks between Selwyn Lloyd, then Minister of Defence, and General Norstad, during a visit to SHAPE, about the role Bomber Command could play alongside SAC in support of the land battle. Norstad had suggested that Bomber Command should take on twenty targets for SHAPE and Lloyd felt that this plan lay behind Twining's invitation.[31] As the Chiefs of Staff suggested the gap in American interest between February 1954 and March 1955 could be explained by the fact that the first Valiant squadron did not form until January 1955 and did not become operational until later in the year.[32]

The negotiations and a brief for CAS were approved by Eden on 16 August 1955. The approved British negotiating position sought greater association on defence strategy worldwide. The British argued that since Bomber Command and SAC were planning to attack the same target complex a full exchange of information leading to co-ordinated target planning would prevent either wasteful overlapping or omissions. At the same time the British government was at pains to stress the independence of its force and the political and military unacceptability of an American supreme commander, in peacetime, who could pressure the United Kingdom to modify its plans in a direction and to an extent which it could not afford.[33]

Macmillan as Foreign Secretary was cautiously optimistic about the negotiations. He told Eden: 'It seems unlikely that the Americans will be prepared to reveal to us at this stage the full plans for their SAC; but our V-bomber force and our H-bomb are coming along and I think the suggested approach might produce some good results.'[34]

Macmillan's analysis was largely correct; it took over a year for the Americans to agree to detailed targeting discussions. During that year Sir Dermot Boyle lobbied the USAF, a Valiant bomber visited the 1956 SAC bombing competition and the first air drop of a British atomic weapon took place.[35] In late 1956 a USAF team visited Britain to discuss the capabilities of the V-force. The USAF team came to the conclusion that target co-ordination and detailed joint planning were necessary. The Chiefs of Staff gave permission for this planning to go ahead in early 1957. On the British side the basis of these negotiations was to be an understanding that Britain would not be tied to any specific number of bombers or H-bombs and that 'operational plans would not in any way imply any relinquishment of our national control of the RAF bomber force'. One of Duncan Sandys' first acts as Minister of Defence was to approve further RAF-USAF talks on this issue[36] and they were further discussed and approved by Macmillan and Eisenhower at the Bermuda Conference in March 1957.[37] At this stage there were disagreements between the USAF and the RAF especially over American plans for a war longer than a few days.[38] By May 1958, however, two meetings had taken place between Strategic Air Command and Bomber Command and 'the co-ordination between the two nuclear strike forces was ... entirely satisfactory, and no real difference of view had become apparent.' Dermot Boyle informed the Chiefs of Staff that 'although we had not yet a full knowledge of the entire United States strike plan, we knew their intentions regarding any targets which could possibly provide a threat to the United Kingdom - i.e. - all targets within 2500 nautical miles of the United Kingdom.'[39]

Sir Richard Powell has recalled that 'in the joint plan we retained the targets of primary interest to us. There was not a great readjustment'.[40] This suggests that, initially, the British put forward their counterforce targets, about 150 Soviet air bases, as part of the joint effort. Presumably the first aim of the British negotiating team was to ensure that SAC would supplement Bomber Command's planned effort with sufficient forces to ensure that all sources of Soviet nuclear threat to the United Kingdom would be destroyed. During the debate on the 1959 Defence White Paper, however, Sandys quoted General Powers, SAC's commanding general, as saying that 'having regard to Britain's closer proximity we rely on her V-bombers to provide an important part of the first wave of an allied retaliatory force'.[41] This statement could be taken as implying that the V-force, in conjunction with American bombers based in Britain, would prepare the way for the main SAC offensive. In order to fulfil this role the United Kingdom based force would need to attack the Soviet air defence system. Taken in conjunction with Boyle's May 1958 report on Anglo-American negotiations Sandys' statement would suggest that American assurances, given in 1958-9, that SAC would attack all the targets of interest to Britain enabled the RAF to agree to a targeting plan which abandoned British counterforce targeting and committed the V-force to a defence suppression mission. Although not of direct use in limiting damage to Britain Sandys seems to have contemplated such a role as early as 1957 since it made more sense in terms of a joint plan.[42]

This joint plan was the preferred way forward for the British nuclear force.[43] The primary aim of British policy was to deter the Soviet Union from invading Western Europe with either nuclear or conventional forces. The deterrent was conceived as a threat to inflict unacceptable damage on the Soviet Union itself with atomic and thermonuclear weapons. That policy had rested for more than a decade solely on American capability. The secondary aim of British policy was to limit damage to the United Kingdom in the event of war. Both aims would be served by a formally agreed Anglo-American plan for their respective nuclear forces. Yet looking back to 1957, when he was Deputy Secretary at the Ministry of Defence, Sir Richard Way has commented: 'No one could be sure that the Americans would have reacted with the use of their deterrent to a purely conventional advance across Europe. I think there is no doubt at all that at this time it [the V-bomber force] was regarded in one sense as entirely independent of the Americans.'[44] As the result of such thinking considerable thought was given to an independent nuclear force as a means of deterring Russia both directly and indirectly, by guaranteeing the availability of the American deterrent. It was the RAF's contention that such a force would have to be militarily credible. It would have to be able to survive a Russian attack, penetrate Russian air defences and inflict massive devastation by using megaton weapons on Russian cities.

The role of the V-bombers as a guarantee of American reliability was laid clearly before ministers in 1957. In May Lord Mountbatten reported on talks with the Chief of Naval Operations and SACLANT which suggested that as a result of the feared future threat of Soviet submarines armed with ballistic missiles, there 'was ... a very real danger that this possibly direct threat to the United States itself would result in their taking less interest in the defence of Europe and their NATO commitments.'[45] The Chiefs of Staff endorsed a statement to the effect that:

> this was the first indication of the US reaction to a possible Soviet capability of direct nuclear action against the United States. He [Sir Richard Powell] foresaw considerable political difficulty in the future of maintaining United States interest and forces in Europe. He suggested that there might well be value in examining now probable United States and Soviet strategy when both were in possession of inter-continental ballistic

missiles. Would a future war be trans-polar with Europe only on the touch line? Should such a development tend to draw away United States interest in Europe, it might be a factor in determining the size of the United Kingdom V-bomber force and this point should be brought to the attention of ministers.[46]

Although such statements could be interpreted as a call to prepare for the eventuality of Britain standing alone in support of Europe the actual thrust of British policy was aimed at influencing the United States in order to prevent any risk of decoupling from Europe rather than to make provision for Britain to stand alone if the Americans did retreat into isolationism. A two-track targeting policy was developed with this end in mind. By the autumn of 1957 the chiefs had produced a policy document which dealt both with 'the highly improbable course of unilateral retaliation by the United Kingdom' for which cities were 'the most effective target system for our limited resources' and an offensive in conjunction with the Americans. Mountbatten wanted to make clear that 'the Chiefs of Staff would be over-stating the case to give ministers the impression that, in the event of the United Kingdom being forced to take independent retaliatory action against the USSR, we could quickly break the Russian will to continue the war.' Although Boyle defended the power of the V-bombers and argued that they could inflict very severe damage on the Soviet Union he agreed that it was unwise to give ministers the impression that a unilateral British strike would necessarily be decisive. His primary concern was to obtain authority to continue planning with the USAF on the basis of a Chiefs of Staff policy which laid stress on Anglo-American co-operation but also explicitly discussed British capacity for unilateral action.[47]

Boyle's insistence on the importance of the British nuclear force in influencing the Americans and, in the final instance, of forcing them to act was made clear by a refusal to agree to any statement which suggested 'the onus of deciding whether to start a general nuclear war was on the Russians.' He believed 'it [the initiative] would also rest with the Western powers, since, if it appeared that the Russians were winning a limited contest we should have the same decision to make.'[48] He was also sceptical of American reliability based only on 'paper promises' and, therefore, opposed any plans to place too much emphasis on acquiring American nuclear weapons on the grounds that if the Americans possessed the 'key to the cupboard' it would not be safe to assume they would make such weapons available to the British even if the United Kingdom was under direct attack.[49]

The RAF case was that, to be credible, the British bomber force had to pose the threat of destroying a considerable number of Soviet cities. The suggested number in 1958 was thirty[50] although this number was subsequently reduced to ten[51] in the early 1960s. Despite the existence of a Joint Global War Committee which had grown out of Admiralty war games on the duration and course of global war[52] these figures do not seem to have been based on any complex calculations. The RAF saw the Committee, which reported in March 1959 that war termination would require 304 hydrogen bombs dropped on 300 Soviet cities,[53] as a tool for suggesting that the V-force was militarily negligible.[54] It does seem likely, however, that the 30 cities criterion had some effect in determining the size of the V-bomber force. In 1957 Sandys acknowledged that it was the Mark 2 V-bombers which would be capable of attacking Russia in the 1960s[55] and that he agreed with the Air Staff's operational calculations.[56] Between February and July 1957 the requirement for British hydrogen bombs to be manufactured by 1961 was increased from 40[57] to 100.[58] Given previous calculations 104 V-bombers would have seemed a reasonable number to attack 30 targets.

The final force level figure of 104 Mark 2 V-bombers was accepted on the grounds that Britain was not attempting to build a unilateral deterrent.[59] At the end of 1956 Macmillan had stated unequivocally that he believed that the only justification for the British nuclear force was as a lever to exert influence over the Americans. He had maintained that American bases in the United Kingdom were a sufficient guarantee of American nuclear power in the short-term and had offered no support to unilateral deterrence. It is thus clear that the first policy aim of the Macmillan government was co-ordination with the Americans. Nevertheless, it can be inferred from the attention given to the the cities criterion that paper guarantees were not deemed sufficient. Indeed this position was stated very clearly during the 'nuclear sufficiency' debate during 1958. Sandys concluded that although it was hard to produce a firm model of international relations for the time when America and the USSR had enough weapons to destroy each other 'he could envisage circumstances in which the *threat* that we would use our nuclear deterrent independently of the United States would be the only method of preserving the peace.'[60] At the same time Macmillan directed that the principal determinants of the size of the independent nuclear force should be: first, the need to threaten to use independent nuclear power to secure United States co-operation and, second, to persuade the Russians that Britain could retaliate independently if the United States was aloof or preoccupied outside Europe.[61]

The British government was aware that its policy was both complex and controversial and, in consequence, attempts to explain the policy in public were avoided.[62] Published sources, such as Defence White Papers, are, therefore, unreliable guides to British policy. The Foreign Office was fearful that if stress was placed on the independent, coercive nature of the force, indicating a lack of confidence in the United States, European morale would be undermined. If the force was justified with specific reference to United States policy American goodwill could be affected. It was agreed policy that public statements would not reflect the actual debate in the defence establishment but have 'emphasis laid on the British contribution to the Western deterrent.'[63]

Despite this sensitivity to the American government the British chose to disregard the view of its representatives that 'one may well doubt whether the British needed the H-bomb and whether their decision to possess it was wise or provident either from their own view or that of the West generally'. Uncomplimentary American opinions of the V-force were also filtered out. In 1957, for example, the United States Chiefs of Mission advised the Ambassador in London, John Whitney, that 'while recognising the ability of Bomber Command to perform its mission as an atomic striking force within the limits of its meagre numbers ... the effectiveness of the RAF in 1962 will be only such as to a contributing force to assist as an ally of the United States in any combat activity and could not on its own present any great threat through offense or any great deterrent through defense.'[64] Although decisions about the V-bombers were underpinned by the closeness of co-operation on nuclear weapons between the RAF and the USAF between 1955 to 1958, which was much greater than has previously been thought, the force was, nevertheless, based on British calculations about Anglo-American relations rather than on any agreed bilateral basis.

RAF-USAF Nuclear Relations

In January 1955 Lord De L'Isle reported to Churchill that Anglo-American nuclear relations were bearing little fruit. Following talks between Eisenhower and Duncan Sandys, then the Minister of Supply, in 1954 the USAF had been authorised to give the RAF technical information which would allow it to modify aircraft to carry American nuclear weapons. The USAF had, however, remained reluctant to do so because of differing interpretations of the 1954 Atomic Energy Act. De L'Isle concluded that although 'the United States, are ... doing something to implement the understanding with the President ... [and] there is thus a prospect that, in war, we may be able to obtain some nuclear bombs from the United States stockpile in this country ... I do not think we can count on the Americans changing their present attitude so as to allow us to acquire physical possession of any of their bombs in peace.'[65]

Later in the same year the United States and Britain signed parallel civil and military agreements for co-operation on atomic energy based on the Atomic Energy Act of August 1954. These agreements raised hopes for closer Anglo-American atomic relations. Using evidence based on statements made to Congress John Simpson has argued that these hopes were dashed.

> The signing of the military agreement led to a meeting between British and American representatives at Quantico, near Washington, in mid-1955, at which it was agreed that the United Kingdom should be given details of the size, weights and attachment systems of American nuclear bombs, thus ensuring that the V-bombers could be adapted to carry them if circumstances permitted. Such information had been made the legal property of the AEC by both the 1946 and 1954 Acts and, in December 1955, the Department of Defense requested that it be transferred to the UKAEA in order to implement the agreement. The Commissioners refused on the grounds that the 1954 Act gave them no legal authority to do so, thus initiating a prolonged dispute over which organisation was authorised to determine military interchange with other states ... the President chose not to intervene in this conflict, or exercise his legal authority over military issues, thus creating a decision making vacuum ... Thus the limited scope for dialogue offered by the 1954 Act rapidly diminished once the AEC chose to place restrictive interpretations on its language.[66]

In fact the United States military largely ignored these restrictions. The supply of information on atomic and thermonuclear weapons to the RAF by the USAF remained, however, a matter of the highest secrecy. Even now virtually all information on this aspect of Anglo-American co-operation is closed. My reconstruction is based on Treasury records of funding requests for the project.

The first mention of Project 'E' occurs in December 1955 as a 'project for special security operations at Farnborough'.[67] At the end of December 1955 the Ministry of Supply asked the Treasury to authorise funding for a thirty-two man project.[68] In March 1956 the Ministry of Supply informed the Treasury that the first task of Project 'E', to be completed by the end of the year, was to modify and clear Canberras to use the American Low Altitude Bombing System (LABS) for the delivery of American atomic weapons. The Royal Aircraft Establishment had already been able to start trials with twenty dummy bombs obtained from the USAF by the Air Ministry.[69] Thus the British were in full possession of the data about the dimensions, weights and attachment systems of American atomic weapons which the United States Atomic Energy Commission had sought to deny them.

In the same month there is also mention of another project at Farnborough involving 'work of a similar nature going on ... on the carriage and release on future generations of this store. (Project 'X')[70] It is even harder to obtain information on Project 'X' than on Project 'E'. Virtually nothing is available in writing and ex-officials still refuse to talk about it. It would seem, however, that from early 1956 onwards there were Anglo-American plans to equip the RAF with American thermonuclear weapons.

In May/June 1956 the RAF proposed to modify a total of 150 Canberras under Project 'E' in order to provide establishments of 50 in Bomber Command and 48 in 2nd TAF. The Air Ministry argued that these modified bombers would be an added contribution to the deterrent and would be used to help justify reduced conventional forces to SACEUR. The Treasury found it 'difficult to deny importance of these proposals as a contribution to greater co-operation between the American and British Air Forces and as a means of reducing our existing undertakings to SACEUR.' It did, however, have doubts about the need for tactical nuclear bombers if international tension relaxed or strategy changed.[71] These and other worries led the Treasury to seek a meeting with the RAF. The Treasury team were satisfied on the practical point that different bomb racks were needed in the same Canberra types for American and British built weapons and that the necessary changeover between the two could be quickly accomplished. Their main concern, however, was the exact nature of Anglo-American understandings on the availability of nuclear weapons. According to one official present at the meeting 'the RAF swear that there is a clear understanding about the availability of American weapons in case of need and say this is known to and approved by the appropriate Congressional Committee.'[72]

Yet the nature of the arrangements the RAF claimed it had secured reamined unclear. The RAF team could have been referring to the Quantico meeting but that meeting does not seem to have been reported to the Congressional Joint Committee on Atomic Energy until 1958.[73] In any case the Treasury was sceptical of RAF assurances. Treasury officials worried that the United States could be in a position to dictate where the Canberras would be deployed in Europe and about the cost of the conversion. In order to address the cost problem they, initially, demanded that the RAF seek American aid for the conversions.[74] This demand was, however, dropped in July 1956 suggesting that the British government's main concern was not cost but the possibility that word of the arrangement would be disclosed in the United States through its financial details.[75]

In August 1956 the Ministry of Supply informed the Treasury that the Air Ministry wanted to modify the V-bombers to carry American nuclear weapons.[76] The Treasury refused to countenance this new development on two grounds. First, the only agreement on weapon availability Treasury investigations had discovered was an informal one made between Sir William Dickson, when CAS, and General Twining, presumably during Dickson's visit to the United States in September 1955. Second, Treasury officials believed that the case for modifying the

V-bombers had nothing to do with SACEUR but was simply a ploy to increase the United Kingdom's independent nuclear force beyond the strength available from British manufactured weapons.[77] In order to try and persuade them otherwise the Air Ministry set out in detail its understanding of Anglo-American agreements on nuclear weapons.

> There is ... no formal detailed agreement between ourselves and the Americans about the supply and availability of weapons. The basis of the present scheme rests on discussions with President Eisenhower. Some discussions, of which we have no record in the Air Ministry, took place in the Bermuda Conference of 1953.[78] Subsequently there were some further discussions between the then Minister of Supply and the President in the course of which the latter gave certain gerenal [sic] assurances ... a note about these discussions was included in a paper DP(54)8 ... the Cabinet Office called for the return of this paper shortly after issue. ... Further I understand there has been a much more recent exchange between the Prime Minister and the President about possible publicity on these arrangements, with which the President could not agree at this time.[79]

The Treasury civil servants were horrified to find that a large part of British policy on military nuclear weapons had been constructed around a fragile set of arrangements based on general verbal promises given by Eisenhower. Nevertheless, given this general enabling power, the two air forces had set to work making practical arrangements for the transfer of nuclear weapons in time of crisis. There had been an agreement between the two senior officers in each air force and the USAF had provided practical help such as supplying dummy bombs and details of LABS. The Air Ministry made the point that there was a cleavage between parts of the USAF which recognised the value of the V-bombers and 'other elements' in the United States which refused to link aid of any kind to the MBF.[80]

No further decisions were taken until June 1957. The Canberras were equipped to carry American nuclear weapons but the V-bombers remained unconverted. Following the Bermuda Conference, however, the Deputy Chief of the Air Staff visited the United States for staff talks on joint targeting. As a result of the talks the Air Ministry contended that 'as part of the process of co-ordinating Anglo-American strategic bombing plans, it was essential to work out the details of providing US atomic weapons for the V-force and to implement these details as far as can be done within the existing laws of the two countries. In particular we now not only have the Americans assurance in principle that the weapons will be made available, but in order planning and action can go ahead, we shall have to send the Americans information at six monthly intervals on the capability of our bomber aircraft to use their weapons.'[81]

The Air Staff's success in negotiating an Anglo-American joint targeting agreement compelled the Treasury to remove its block on V-bomber modification. The RAF then proposed a bomb carrying system for the V-bombers which would not only be suitable for both American weapons and British manufactured atomic and thermonuclear bombs but also needed only minor modifications to switch from a British to an American bomb under operational conditions. 120 Victors and Vulcans were converted, 60 of each, along with 56 Valiants. The conversion of the Valiants was considered vital since it provided an immediate, rather than a planned, capability to use American weapons and thus fulfilled the Anglo-American joint targeting agreement.[82]

In 1957 and 1958 Anglo-American nuclear relations improved greatly. The initial impetus for this improvement came from a desire on both sides to repair the damage done by the Suez crisis. More importantly, however, American attitudes to co-operation were transformed by the launch of Sputnik in October 1957.[83] At the meeting of the NSC on 10 October 1957 the acting Secretary of State, Christian Herter, described 'foreign policy reactions [to Sputnik] as "pretty somber".' He called for the United States 'to do a great deal to counteract them and, particularly, to confirm the existence of our military and scientific strength.' Eisenhower's response to this appeal was to stress that 'the fact remained that the US couldn't possibly set up a whole vast scientific program of basic research in areas about which we didn't know anything, and then attempt to outdo the Russians in each aspect of such a program. We must above all seek a military posture the Russians respect.'[84] Debate about the nature of the American response to Sputnik continued until the approval of NSC5801/1 in July 1958[85] but even before the debate had fully evolved it was clear that co-operation with Britain on nuclear weapons was logical either as part of the diplomatic response advocated by Herter or as a means of limiting the expansion of the defence technological-industrial base as Eisenhower insisted. In pursuit of this second goal the United States had a heightened interest in gaining access to certain elements of nuclear weapons technology pioneered by the independent British programme.[86]

The Eisenhower administration was effectively able to repeal the McMahon Act by amending the 1954 Atomic Energy Act and by signing bilateral agreements with Britain in July 1958 and May 1959 which allowed the transfer of nuclear technology. The American archives have failed to yield a full picture of what these agreements entailed. The American historian who has studied them most closely concluded that Congress effectively excluded the exchange of information on thermonuclear weapons from the 1958 agreement and that it was unclear whether such weapons were included in the terms of the 1959 agreement. He speculated that the British and United States governments must have made an agreement about the exchange of data on hydrogen weapons sometime after 1959.[87] Further work on the American archives led Jan Melissen to conclude that by the end of 1958 the Americans had given Britain virtually complete details on how to make certain American thermonuclear weapons in the United Kingdom.[88] In fact the British archives suggest that American government had also started to supply Britain with nuclear weapons in 1958; possibly even before the July 1958 agreement was signed. Evidence is, unsurprisingly, sparse but Treasury records show that in November 1958 the Air Ministry informed other departments that the United States had agreed to supply H-bombs rather than A-bombs to the V-force. 72 V-bombers were re-equipped to carry American thermonuclear weapons.[89]

It could be argued that the Americans had merely promised that, in the event of war, weapons would be transferred to the RAF but there is also evidence to suggest some form of physical transfer. In January 1958 the Minister of Defence asked the Air Ministry whether there had ever been any public statement about plans for the RAF to possess American nuclear weapons.[90] At the same time there was some disquiet amongst senior RAF officers who raised the objection, with specific reference to the extension of Project 'E' to the V-bombers,[91] that too much of the British nuclear force was passing under the control of the United States. A few days later Sandys instructed the Chief of the Air Staff to inform him when the first American nuclear bombs would be delivered to the RAF. Sandys was briefed verbally on this issue by Sir Geoffrey Tuttle in an unrecorded meeting.[92] There is no record of discussions about American thermonuclear weapons in the minutes of Sandys' meetings with the Secretary of Defense, Neil McElroy, in September 1958 but comments made during talks on other issues suggest that not only were nuclear weapons available to the RAF but that they were airborne in V-bombers under American supervision. During a meeting between the Secretary of Defense and the Minister of Defence the Deputy Chief of the Air Staff, Sir Geoffrey Tuttle, raised the issue of the RAF's interest in the USAF's air-to-air nuclear missile 'Genie'. The Deputy Secretary of Defense told him that 'Genie' could be made available on the same terms as nuclear weapons for the V-bombers. During the ensuing discussion Tuttle stated that 'there would be a need to get this weapon airborne *more* frequently in a single-seater aircraft'[93] His remarks imply that American weapons were already airborne in British aircraft since he was arguing for an increased degree of control not suggesting a completely different arrangement.

Upgrading the V-bomber Force

In addition to negotiating joint targeting and nuclear sharing arrangements with the United States senior RAF officers were also intimately involved in discussions, held between March 1956 and November 1958, about the deployment of American Thor IRBMs in Britain. The Air Staff had initially favoured this deployment but came to oppose it on the grounds that the USA was offering a bad deal.[94] Macmillan ignored military advice since he saw the missiles as, above all, a political symbol of a revivified post-Suez Anglo-American partnership.[95] During the Thor debates the Air Ministry, whilst championing an independent nuclear force, demonstrated that it was well aware of the practical advantages offered by close co-operation with the USA. Such ambivalence meant it was far from clear what kind of nuclear force should replace the Mark 2 V-bombers in the mid-1960s. In 1959 a high-level working group was set up under Sir Richard Powell to consider the future of the independent deterrent and all the weapon systems available after 1963, including the American Skybolt and Polaris missiles. In 1960 the government decided to cancel the British Blue Streak ballistic missile and Blue Steel Mark 2 air-to-ground missile and to adopt Skybolt. Within this process the RAF's main contribution was the decision to back Skybolt rather than the home produced Blue Steel Mark 2.

Harold Macmillan visited Washington in October 1957, immediately after the launch of Sputnik. He found his American hosts, faced with the spiralling costs of their own missile programmes, more inclined than hitherto to consider joint research and development projects with the British. As a result of Macmillan's visit a US-UK-Canada Technical Committee was set up and first met in December 1957. It agreed that the next generation of American and British air-to-ground missile programmes should be reviewed in order to achieve some degree of integration. A USAF-RAF Task Group started work in April 1958 on a comparison between the American Hound Dog and Advanced Air-to-Surface Missile (ASM) and the British Blue Steel and OR1159 (Blue Steel Mark 2). The two air forces discovered that they had very different requirements. The USAF regarded the ASM as a secondary weapon. It was to be carried 4000 miles by a B-52 bomber before release and its main role was to attack 'hard' point targets. The RAF wanted an ASM as its primary weapon. It was planning for a bomber/missile operational radius of 2500 miles. The missiles launched from the bombers were to be targeted on cities. The technical specifications for the planned weapon systems did not, therefore, seem compatible although both sides were keen to keep open channels for the interchange of technical information.[96]

In October 1958 the USAF changed its operational requirement for the Advanced ASM. This new operational requirement renewed Air Staff interest in the American missile. Its technical representative in the United States noted that although the ASM was still regarded as a secondary system by the USAF it was assuming increased importance. The USAF still believed that pinpoint attacks on enemy offensive capability would be more important than city attacks but the technical difficulty of achieving very fine accuracy led them to a requirement that 'might be a basis of interdependence'.[97] The Air Staff quickly developed a two-pronged approach to the air launched nuclear missile. It backed both the continued development of OR1159 and co-operation with the Americans. In December 1958 the RAF and the USAF formally agreed that the Advanced ASM would be considered as the main strategic weapon for the V-bombers.[98] At the same time the Air Ministry sought funding for the continued development of Blue Steel Mark 2. Sandys approved this cautious approach. He told Macmillan 'I am concerned with the decision on Blue Steel Mk.2. The weapon is already late; to incur further delays ... risks doing damage to the 'V' bomber force out of all proportion to the money saved. ... I am sure the right course is to press on with the development of Blue Steel Mk.2 and in no way reduce effort until and unless an effective American weapon can be seen to be available with certainty.'[99] Macmillan, however, wanted to cancel Blue Steel Mark 2 and acquire an American missile. The prime minister would only authorise the short-term funding for Blue Steel Mark 2 proposed by the Ministry of Supply.[100]

Although the Air Staff hoped that a choice between the two weapons would not be necessary until the end of 1959[101] this was not a tenable position in the long-term. Britain risked expenditure on the development of two competing missile systems. A more pressing problem, however, was the USAF's presumption that the British government had an active interest in its missile. British civilian officials based in Washington assumed that, given the air force's close relationship with the American press, this interest would soon become public.[102]

Whilst the Air Staff was delighted with USAF enthusiasm for a joint development project it warned against a commitment to the American weapon or nothing. The Air Staff argued that it was too early to make a decision on Blue Steel Mark 2. Its concern focussed on the warhead of the American missile. The American warhead was a type which the British were unable to construct. The Air Staff feared that, if the Americans made full design details available, the independence of the nuclear force would be compromised. It also identified a further problem: the American warhead was expensive in fissile materials which the British nuclear programme could ill-afford to produce.[103]

A major turning point in the British approach was reached in January 1959. Sir Frederick Brundrett, the Ministry of Defence's Chief Scientist, travelled to the United States to discuss the American missile further. During his visit Brundrett became convinced that Britain should adopt the American weapon immediately. He advised the Ministry of Defence that 'I do not personally believe we should go on with Blue Steel Mk.2 because the American weapon will be a better one, whichever of the various technical approaches they finally adopt. The only danger of cancelling our production that I can see is that our weapon may have a lower yield ... in these circumstances my recommendation would be cancel Blue Steel Mk.2 now and arrange small manpower contribution to the United States project office at earliest time.'[104]

The Air Staff was horrified by Brundrett's opinion. It wished the dual-track policy, agreed by Sandys only the previous month, to continue. The Air Staff warned of 'the risks we run in putting all our faith in the American weapon when we know so little about it'[105] and concluded that it would be 'absolutely wrong' to accept Brundrett's advice. Yet although the Air Staff once again stressed the independence of the deterrent and the warhead problem it was willing to concede that if these problems could be solved the RAF should adopt the American weapon.[106]

By late January 1959 the the balance of opinion, despite serious Air Staff reservations, had swung in favour of accepting the American missile. A key meeting of the Defence Research Policy Committee produced general support for Skybolt from all parties, although each had a slightly different viewpoint. Brundrett stressed that the Americans were keener on this joint project than any other and felt that once the technical difficulties were resolved there would not be any further problems. Sir Geoffrey Tuttle was more cautious but agreed that the project had to be supported and made to work. Sir Claude Pelly, the Controller, Aircraft at the Ministry of Supply, agreed and pointed out that 'one reason for American keeness was their desire to ensure the weapon was retained in the US budget. If we took on a joint project with them and there was any subsequent pressure in the USA to cancel it, its US sponsors could reply that to do so would mean letting down an ally.' It was agreed that everything should be done to ensure that a joint project went ahead.[107]

By April 1959 more details about the American missile project had emerged. The USAF expected to select a prime contractor for its missile, now designated WS138A, by the middle of the year. The Ministry of Supply reported that the arrangements for assessing the technical proposals jointly with the USAF were operating smoothly and British views were being taken into account.

The nature of the warhead and arrangements for Anglo-American financing of the missile remained major problems. The two issues were closely linked since the warhead decision would have major implications for the cost of the weapon to the United Kingdom. The USAF had chosen a warhead which was considerably lighter, had a lower yield and made less efficient use of fissile material than the equivalent British Red Snow warhead. The common adoption of Red Snow would seriously degrade the missile's performance and was unacceptable to the USAF. To make the American warhead in Britain would disrupt the British nuclear weapons programme and lead to the production of less warheads since four Red Snows could be made for every one American warhead. It was expected that if the warhead was procured directly from the United States there would be strings attached and the whole future of the British nuclear force could be jeopardised.[108]

The warhead issue caused doubts about the viability of the whole project. Three options were canvassed. The United States could be asked to supply the entire weapon; any conditions it attached would be accepted. Britain could continue to develop the OR1159. Britain could ensure that that the WS138A was compatible with the V-bombers but not procure it. Reversing his earlier enthusiasm Sir Frederick Brundrett argued that the last option, twinned with the development of a modified Blue Steel Mark 1, should be adopted. Once again his position was unacceptable to the Air Staff. It wanted a successor system to prolong the RAF's independent nuclear role into the 1960s and 1970s.[109]

Despite this rebuff Brundrett continued to press his changed view that 'this exercise is pretty nearly over'. He stressed information emanating from the American defence establishment which suggested that the WS138A, far from being secure in the budget, was merely a USAF project under assessment. He complained that it was impossible to make the Americans understand British shortages of fissile material and dismissed their warhead development as unsatisfactory.[110]

Although Tuttle and Pelly visited the United States in June 1959 to continue negotiations Brundrett, in his role as Chairman of the Defence Research Policy Committee, interpreted statements by the Chiefs of Staff and the Minister of Defence to be a decision that if the WS138A could not carry the Red Snow warhead the United Kingdom would not become involved in a joint project. Britain would simply continue to ensure that the missile was compatible with the V-bombers in order to allow eventual procurement under Project 'E'.[111]

The Air Ministry viewed Brundrett as a dangerous meddler. It feared that his ideas could become official policy, either by default or because they would eventually attract political patronage. The ministry was appalled by the prospect of a British nuclear force under strict American control even if it was supplemented by, inadequate, British weapons. The Air Ministry argued that the long-range guided bomb was not 'another' independent deterrent but the only one possible in the medium-term.

The V-bombers would be ineffective without an air launched missile after 1963 and Blue Streak would not be operational in any numbers until the late 1960s. According to the Air Ministry if Britain was to have an independent deterrent it needed either OR1159 or an American weapon without 'strings'. The availability of such an American weapon was regarded as improbable. 'If we fail to establish this', noted the Assistant Under-Secretary attached to the Air Staff, 'not only do we stand to lose the independence of the V-bomber deterrent; we shall have prejudiced the case for maintaining a force as large as 144 bombers, which was accepted ... almost entirely on the argument that the force must possess an independent deterrent capability. We shall also have prejudiced the case for an independent British successor, whether missile or manned, to the V-bomber. ... Our case for OR 1159 obviously enjoys no sympathy on the part of the First Sea Lord or CIGS who doubtless favour Sir Frederick Brundrett's approach as the potential basis of dismantling the deterrent in favour of familiar War Office and Admiralty interests.'[112]

At the behest of the Air Staff George Ward attempted to persuade Duncan Sandys that Britain risked ending up with no independent, effective nuclear weapons. Ward argued that not only was the British government not in a position to choose its own strategic weapon until the end of 1959 but that the American government had made no final decision of its own on WS138A. Although he reaffirmed his preference for the RAF's dual-track policy, which would continue development of OR1159, at least until the end of 1959, he also promised to carry out a more favourable reassessment of WS138A. Thus, in effect, Ward and his advisers proposed a major change of policy. The Air Ministry would support the procurement of WS138A rather than OR1159 if the Americans decided to proceed with their missile and were willing to supply both missile bodies and warheads to the RAF on terms which guaranteed the independence of the British nuclear force. In support of this new statement of policy the Air Staff produced a technical report which was to prove even more crucial to the eventual decision to procure Skybolt. RAF technical experts reappraised the service's need for fissile material and decided it needed far less than previously thought. The downward revision of RAF fissile material requirements meant that production of the American warhead in the United Kingdom would not pose insuperable problems.[113] Duncan Sandys approved of the Air Ministry's new approach and accepted it as the way forward for the next stage of decisions about the British strategic force.[114]

The Air Staff's paramount aim, whatever its ambivalence about the role of an American weapon, was to guarantee the existence of an airborne independent nuclear force. It is unclear, therefore, whether the Air Staff's lowering of its fissile material requirement was genuine or whether it was a political ploy. The changed requirement certainly seems to have tipped the balance in favour of procuring Skybolt.

By the end of 1959 it had been decided that if there was to be an airborne nuclear force it would comprise Mark 2 V-bombers equipped with Skybolt missiles. All of the non-RAF members of the Defence Policy Research Committee agreed, especially after it was revealed that, because of technical changes, it would not be operational until 1967, that Blue Steel Mark.2 would be the least effective means of preserving the British deterrent in the late 1960s and 1970s. Sir Dermot Boyle was ambivalent. He argued that the weapon should continue to be funded in order to ensure that the V-bombers were not rendered prematurely redundant. Boyle portrayed Blue Steel Mk.2 as an insurance policy rather than an unavoidable necessity and stated that the RAF would prefer WS138A if the Americans adopted it and it proved compatible with the V-bombers. The Chiefs of Staff decided that if the United States was willing to provide Britain with the WS138A without political conditions the offer should be accepted. At the time they took this decision all of the chiefs were convinced that there would be little difficulty in equipping Skybolt with a British warhead. These arguments were forwarded to the British Nuclear Deterrent Study Group for a final decision but from November 1959 Blue Steel Mk.2 was effectively cancelled and Skybolt became, partly by default, the RAF's candidate for the airborne deterrent.[115]

This decision was of central importance because at the time it was taken the other British nuclear delivery system under consideration, the ground-to-ground ballistic missile Blue Streak, fell out of favour. Blue Streak's demise in the winter of 1959/60, although seemingly rapid, had its roots in developments which can be traced back to 1956.

The need to find a successor system to the V-bombers had been one of the biggest problems faced by the defence establishment from 1956 onwards. In March 1956 a report of the Defence Research Policy Committee presented to the Chiefs of Staff had made clear that the scientific and engineering resources of the country were insufficient to meet the demands put on them by the defence programme and that the proportion of scientific manpower devoted to defence research was already too high. The report had recommended that not only should research and development be concentrated on projects of strategic worth but more specifically upon those which it was possible to bring into production at realistic agreed dates.[116]

In response to this report the PRC attempted to impose the deepest cuts on weapons research and development. Sir Walter Monckton's August 1956 directive on defence expenditure called for a research and development budget of £175 million a year from 1958/9, a 33% cut on the proposed budget and more than double the cut the government intended to impose on the Air Estimates. The Air Ministry was painfully aware that any such cuts would affect the RAF much more than the other services since not only did the Admiralty control its own development programme but most of the high cost projects related to aircraft or missiles. A committee chaired by Brundrett was set up to suggest projects that could be cancelled. Its proposals included the abandonment of either the Mark 2 Victor or Vulcan and the RAF's proposed supersonic bomber, OR330. The Air Staff opposed the cancellation of OR330 on the grounds that it provided a safeguard against the failure of either Blue Streak or Blue Steel Mark 2 and that without it the reconnaissance capability needed for the nuclear force would disappear. As a fall-back position it argued that if OR330 was cancelled a Mark 3 V-bomber would have to be developed. Blue Streak was expected to come into service in 1965 and form a large part of the nuclear force by 1970. It was hoped that Blue Steel Mark 2 with a 1000 mile range would keep the V-bombers effective until that date. The Air Staff's view was that the proposed cancellations were unacceptable but that if the £175 million budget was imposed it could develop a Mark 3 V-bomber, Blue Streak, Blue Steel Mark 2 and the necessary thermonuclear and atomic warheads.[117]

Within the Air Council, however, there was criticism of Blue Streak. The Controller, Aircraft at the Ministry of Supply described its development as a massive scientific effort with no useful application in any other field. The Secretary of State and the Chief of the Air Staff criticised it as having no use apart from deterring the Soviet Union from launching an all-out attack on Europe. Boyle also expressed his preference for a stand-off guided bomb in its stead. All, however, agreed that it was not politically possible to propose Blue Streak's cancellation.[118]

During the first six months of 1956 there was a lively internal debate about the future size, composition and role of the RAF. In the part of this debate concerned with strategic forces Blue Streak received strong support from within the Air Staff. In studies carried out on the RAF from 1960-65 and from 1965-70 some officers outlined the concept of a V-bomber force, primarily concerned with deployment overseas to deter limited war, which would be superseded by 100 OR330 bombers which in turn would be replaced by 100 ballistic missiles. At this stage senior officers intervened to insist that there would always be a need for a mixed bomber/missile force.[119] The Secretary of State for Air, Nigel Birch, endorsed the view that there would always be a role for the manned bomber.[120] Nevertheless, Sir Ronald Ivelaw-Chapman, the Vice-Chief of the Air Staff, and Sir Geoffrey Tuttle, the Deputy Chief of the Air Staff, both recommended that the development of a British ballistic missile should be given the highest priority.[121]

The effort put into planning the future of the RAF is notable because the dashing of hopes for a mixed force played a significant part in the development of subsequent thinking. Despite Sir Dermot Boyle's scepticism there was considerable interest shown in ballistic missiles. The decisions taken by Sandys in early 1957, not only to cancel OR330, which had seemed likely after the 1956 review in any case, but to announce that Britain was in possession of its last generation of manned aircraft and to push ahead with the deployment of Thor and the development of Blue Streak, effectively dampened this interest. The Air Staff was diverted towards preserving the best manned force possible. This effort lay behind its lukewarm support for Blue Streak and its emphasis on a 'flying platform' as the basis for the next British nuclear force. Much of the energy the Air Staff could have expended on lobbying for Blue Streak was used, instead, on the fight to secure the development of the TSR2.

The TSR2 design started life as a Canberra replacement and as such survived Sandys' initial cancellation programme. The operational requirement was completely rewritten and issued in March 1957. The aircraft was given no less than five roles. First, to deliver tactical nuclear weapons at low altitude, long-range, in all weathers, day or night. Second, to undertake day and night photographic reconnaissance. Third, to undertake all-weather electronic reconnaissance. Fourth, to deliver nuclear weapons from medium altitude. Fifth, to carry out visual attacks with conventional weapons.[122] According to the Air Staff's own operational requirements staff 'the problem of trying to define priorities lies in the fact that we are attempting to produce one aircraft to do a number of tasks in a practically unlimited range of political situations. It is analogous to football pools; the chance of getting a fully correct priority line is small.'[123] The reconnaissance role was included in order to ensure Army support for the project. The Air Staff was much more concerned with the bomber role. The Air Ministry managed to keep the aircraft in the defence budget primarily because of its limited war role.[124] Yet always lurking in the background was the belief 'that such an aircraft, with range increased by flight refuelling, would pose a low level threat to Russia and thus contribute to the primary deterrent'.[125] The absolute insistence on the ability to penetrate the most advanced fighter and missile defences 'on all major targets in Russia, Europe and on special points of interest in zones of Soviet influence in the Middle East'[126] justified the rejection of all alternatives, whether V-bombers in the limited war role, the development of the NA.39 (Buccaneer) favoured by Sandys, an American or French alternative, or indeed a simplified version of the TSR2 itself.[127] Worries that, given the history of British aircraft development, the aeroplane would take at least ten years to develop, might be obsolete when it did arrive and would take up too much of the research and development budget were brushed aside on the grounds that no interim aircraft was considered suitable. The TSR2 would simply have to be ready by 1964.[128]

Meanwhile the official Air Ministry approach to Blue Streak was summed up by the Secretary of State, George Ward, in early 1958. 'In pressing the Ministry of Defence to give every priority to Blue Streak we must nevertheless be careful to avoid giving an opening to them to cancel other projects which were also regarded as vital. Despite this risk the future of Blue Streak must be watched with the greatest care and no effort spared to make the weapon a success.'[129] Sir Dermot Boyle, however, remained much more hostile to Blue Streak. He 'was not convinced that the ballistic missile was the future cornerstone of our deterrent policy'[130] and believed that 'to maintain the validity of the deterrent the long range guided bomb ought to be developed.'[131] In December 1958 the Air Ministry formally proposed that the next generation of the independent nuclear force should be based around a 'flying platform' rather than a ballistic missile.[132] Sandys remained a strong supporter of Blue Streak but even he would have preferred a different system if the Americans had been willing to help build one without putting any restrictions on British use. In February 1957 Macmillan had described the best way forward for the British nuclear force as 'a modest programme of research so we could still make a contribution to the United States development programme.' He had, nevertheless, acknowledged that there was no guarantee that a programme could be agreed which would marry American missiles and British warheads. In early 1957 there was general concern in the Defence Committee that if Britain gave up a full ballistic missile programme 'the responsibility for the deterrent would pass entirely to the United States.'[133] From the start of the Macmillan-Sandys era policy was clear. Britain should have a nuclear force completely under its own control but Blue Streak was a second-best option in lieu of any satisfactory alternative arrangement with the Americans.

Policy was therefore reconsidered in 1958 when the United States repealed the McMahon Act. Sandys proposed that Blue Streak should be cancelled on the grounds that it would cost £200 million to develop yet was technically inferior to American missiles. He believed that the Americans would offer full information on lightweight megaton warheads. If this was the case there were a number of options for ensuring the continuance of the British nuclear force: the development of a more advanced missile with American help, acquisition of Thor to be fitted with a British warhead based on a lightweight American design, the development of Blue Steel Mark 2 or even a partnership with Western Europe.[134] These hopes were dashed by Sandys' visit to the United States in September 1958. During Sandys' talks with Neil McElroy it became clear that the Americans were uninterested in developing a missile suitable for British purposes. McElroy also emphasised that the United States would prefer to develop a NATO missile under the control of SACEUR.[135] Sandys was forced to reverse his recommendation to the Cabinet and argue that Blue Streak should be continued with whatever technical assistance the Americans were willing to offer.[136]

At this stage Blue Streak, already labelled a second-best solution, came under increasingly heavy attack from the Treasury. The Chancellor, Derick Heathcoat Amory, argued that if the defence budget was to be kept at £1500 million at least one major military capability would have to be abandoned.[137] His main target was Blue Streak, which the Treasury believed could cost anything from £400 million to £600 million. Costs were set to spiral even further due to the requirement to house the missile in underground silos in order to reduce its vulnerability. Heathcoat Amory called for Blue Streak to be cancelled 'even if this meant that at some time in the 1960s we should cease to have an independent nuclear deterrent.'[138] As an alternative to complete abandonment of the British nuclear force he suggested that Britain should acquire the submarine launched Polaris system and stretch the life of the V-bombers and Thor in the interim.[139]

Although Macmillan was unwilling to agree to Heathcoat Amory's most radical prescription of abandoning the nuclear force in the 1960s[140] all senior ministers seemed to agree that Blue Streak should be abandoned if any replacement which met the criterion of complete operational independence could be found. In some ways Polaris seemed the most attractive alternative. Sandys, however, did not believe that its development was advanced enough to warrant placing the whole future of the British deterrent on its success.[141] In addition, there were doubts if the missile would have sufficient range to meet British requirements.[142] At Sandys' insistence the working group on the future of the British nuclear force set up under Sir Richard Powell in January 1959 was to consider all alternatives, including the RAF's 'flying platform', rather than carry out a simple comparison between Blue Streak and Polaris.[143]

In December 1959 the Powell Working Group recommended that the best way forward for the British nuclear force was the acquisition of an American system; either WS138A or the submarine-launched Polaris. At the same time it argued for the continued development of Blue Streak 'until we are quite certain that the United States will agree to our procuring WS138A or Polaris on the conditions ... referred to.' In February 1960 the further development of Blue Streak was challenged by the Chiefs of Staff. According to the chiefs 'we have received much more reassuring information about WS138A than was available to the Study Group, and we consider our initial approach should be designed to secure this weapon.' The Chiefs of Staff objected to Blue Streak on the grounds that it was only useful as a first-strike weapon. Harold Watkinson, Sandys' successor as Minister of Defence, accepted their views. Later in the month he presented the Defence Committee with what became the definitive statement on British nuclear policy.

We shall wish to continue to maintain under our undivided control the ability to deliver a significant number of megaton weapons ... it is not, however, indispensable to our objective that the means of delivery should be of our own design or manufacture, provided we can buy what we want without political conditions ... it is settled policy that we should produce our own nuclear warheads.[144]

The most surprising supporter of Skybolt was the Royal Navy but the advice proffered by the Chiefs of Staff makes clear its motives. 'An assessment will be required of the relative merits of the launching of WS138A from a new type of aircraft and launching Polaris from a nuclear submarine, to determine the form of our deterrent from 1970 onwards.'[145] The Admiralty wanted the Royal Navy to provide the ultimate successor system to the V-bombers. It saw Skybolt as an interim system. This cautious approach has usually been explained by doubts within the Navy whether any independent nuclear force was useful. These doubts were exacerbated by the fear that Polaris would divert resources from the conventional role in the east Atlantic and 'East of Suez' which was being pressed on the government, with considerable success, at the end of the 1950s.[146] Recent research has, however, shown that Lord Mountbatten, who had recently moved from the post of First Sea Lord to be Chief of the Defence Staff, had an additional reason for avoiding a direct challenge to Skybolt in late 1959 or early 1960. The United States Chief of Naval Operations, Admiral Arleigh Burke, who was a key player in the procurement of Polaris did not want a joint Anglo-American programme. He believed that such a programme would slow down Polaris development and weaken the project's bureaucratic position in the United States. Burke was only willing to support the Royal Navy's aspirations once the United States Navy was guaranteed an operational capability. Admiral Burke's position strongly suggested a timetable for British acquisition of Polaris weighted towards the late 1960s.[147]

Various successor systems were under consideration for the British nuclear force by the end of the decade. There was, however, a secular trend towards an air-launched system since the Mark 2 V-bombers and Blue Steel Mark 1 were already in the pipeline. The Air Ministry was determined to resist Polaris and was only a reluctant supporter of Blue Streak. Blue Steel Mark 2 had been killed off by Skybolt rather than Blue Streak.[148] The American offer to supply Skybolt did not arrive unexpectedly in March 1960 although up to that point there had been some doubt about the seemingly favourable terms which were eventually agreed. Skybolt was an important part of British thinking from October 1958 and the subject of a preliminary agreement with the Americans from December of the same year.

In hindsight it is interesting to note that doubts about the missile's security in the United States budget were aired several times at an early stage. Skybolt's precarious position was actually seen as an advantage since it increased the importance of British participation in the project.

In terms of British strategy the most important development was the emergence of the concept of an independent British deterrent provided by an American weapon. There was a great deal of ambivalence about this concept but its adoption was hastened by the competitive bureaucratic process which made programmes like Blue Steel Mark 2 and Blue Streak, already vulnerable because of cost and technical difficulties, seem less attractive. Doubts about American unreliability were overcome by a desire for American technology and financial assistance. The shift in British strategy towards greater reliance on the United States in the late 1950s should also be seen as a function of American rather than British policy. The British had desired closer co-operation before 1956 whilst the Americans had been unwilling to countenance it. Arguably, therefore, the twin shocks of Suez and Sputnik did more to alter American attitudes. Greater American willingness to enter into nuclear co-operation actually caused doubt and inconsistency in British policy-making. Yet as the analysis of RAF behaviour over joint targeting, Thor and Skybolt shows this inconsistency was not a result of battles between identifiable pro- or anti-Americans or between champions of independence and interdependence.

The deployment of Thor shows the RAF shifting from cautious support to vocal opposition in response to changing American offers and an emerging gap between the attitudes of senior officers and politicians. The procurement of Skybolt shows individuals changing their views in response to the increasing practical possibility of acquiring an American weapon 'without strings'. The Air Ministry initially advocated the dual-track policy of proceeding with Blue Steel Mark 2 whilst considering a possible American alternative but then shifted to firm support of Skybolt. This change did not come about because of any change in personnel or in views about the nature of Anglo-American relations but because of practical considerations. An American system was on offer, the other services refused to support a British weapon and there were doubts about the technical feasibility of Blue Steel Mark 2. There was no move to make the Britain more independent of the United States following Suez. Rather the RAF played a part in maintaining the pre-Suez political consensus that an irreducible minimum aim of British policy was to possess a nuclear force wholly under British control.

The Independent Nuclear Force and
Peripheral Nuclear Strategy

Although the debate about the V-bomber force and its successor was conducted mainly in terms of Anglo-American relations the force's role in maintaining Britain's great power status remained important. Since 1955 the role of nuclear weapons overseas had been a central part of the defence establishment's thinking. The decision on the size of the V-bomber force was taken on the basis that the bombers would have, from about 1960 onwards, the important secondary role of providing an extra-European nuclear capability. This concept retained its importance since it appeared to bridge the gap between the prestige of possessing a nuclear force and a practical means of supporting British power. The ability to deploy bombers and nuclear weapons worldwide seemed to give Britain influence with allies. It also obviated the necessity of the large overseas troop concentrations which would be increasingly difficult to achieve as national service was phased out in the early 1960s. Along with other developments at the end of the 1950s, such as enhanced mobility through a much enlarged Transport Command, the V-bomber force still lent comfort to those who believed that Britain could and should maintain its power worldwide.

In practice, however, it proved difficult to produce realistic scenarios in which nuclear weapons had an important role. The general proposition that nuclear weapons enhanced British power overseas was thus more influential than any detailed consideration of their actual usefulness. As a result the strategic consensus on this issue was influential in the late 1950s but it was also fragile.

An argument for the retention of balanced and independent British forces overseas emerged from the debate about the nature of limited war which had divided Sandys and the Chiefs of Staff in 1957 and 1958.[149] The role of tactical nuclear weapons in such scenarios did not play a part in the debate on the 1957 White Paper and was not considered until the summer of 1957.[150] When the question of tactical nuclear weapons overseas was considered it threw up a different balance of bureaucratic forces than the main debate over the independent nuclear deterrent. All three services wanted such weapons and it was the Army who led the campaign to ensure that they would be developed. The Chief of the Imperial General Staff, Sir Gerald Templer, argued that although the Joint Intelligence Committee estimated that only the United States, Britain and the Soviet Union would possess nuclear weapons before 1965 a number of countries would develop such weapons in the medium term. Britain therefore needed nuclear weapons specifically for limited war outside Europe, whatever decisions were taken about their use on the continent.[151] All three services agreed that once nuclear parity was a reality the Soviet Union would become more aggressive and the United States more cautious. The risk of limited wars would increase and British forces would need to be equipped with tactical nuclear weapons.[152]

Sandys had directed that only a modest contribution should be made to the Baghdad Pact, or CENTO as it became in August 1959, and SEATO. The Chiefs of Staff had ruled that the two treaty organisations should in no way be considered analogous to NATO.[153] Yet as Phillip Darby once commented on the role of SEATO and CENTO in Defence White Papers, 'each year these alliances were brought out to justify the continued worldwide distribution in very much the same way as NATO was used to argue the case for Europe.'[154] The extra-European alliances were important for the RAF since they formed the basis for the case that nuclear armed bombers could replace conventional forces. Indeed of the five-fold overseas role the RAF defined for itself at the 1957 Commonwealth Prime Ministers Conference three roles, the main V-bomber deterrent, light bombers for the Baghdad Pact and a rapid deployment force of V-bombers for the Middle and Far East, were nuclear, the other two being strategic transport and a garrison air force in Malaya.[155]

In South-East Asia Plan 'Hermes' for the defence of Malaya had been 'pigeon-holed' in 1956.[156] During the course of 1957 senior commanders in the region argued that it should be scrapped completely. The regional commanders cited two reasons why the plan should be abandoned. First, it was militarily unrealistic since there were not enough land forces to mount an effective defence of the peninsula. Second, the United States would have nothing to do with the defence of Malaya. The Americans argued that there was no threat to Malaya except from a large-scale Chinese attack and that such an attack would not take place unless the West lost the general war; an outcome to be prevented by nuclear attacks on the Chinese mainland. The alternative war plan proposed by the senior RAF officer in the region involved the re-equipment of FEAF with modern jet light and fighter-bombers and provision for V-bomber reinforcements to conduct counter-air operations against Indochinese or Thai airfields and to use nuclear weapons on the Kra Isthmus in order to prevent any invasion.[157] His views were accepted by the Air Staff which also believed that the 'operation of medium bombers in the theatre in limited war ... is the cornerstone of our Far East strategy.'[158] The Chiefs of Staff advised Macmillan in preparation for his tour to the area that 'the SEATO strategic concept is based on the use of nuclear weapons and it is the view of the Chiefs of Staff that in limited war the FEAF should be reinforced by three squadrons of medium bombers with a nuclear capability'.[159]

In the summer of 1957 Sandys seems to have promised the Australians that a force of nuclear capable V-bombers would be stationed in the Far East.[160] The Australian government placed enough importance on nuclear deterrence in the region to consider the purchase of nuclear weapons to be put under joint Anglo-Australian control.[161] In February 1958 Sandys proposed in the Defence Committee that a V-bomber runway and nuclear storage facilities should be constructed at Tengah airbase in Singapore. The committee agreed that if Britain was to retain its position in South-East Asia the capacity to send nuclear armed bombers to the region was essential.[162]

The acquisition of nuclear capability in the Far East was undertaken with the intention of improving co-operation with the Americans within the region.[163] Nevertheless, the British government also wanted to maintain a position independent of the United States. Although, in the end, it was impossible to form a Commonwealth bloc in Asia since the Australians were always too concerned about the lukewarm American attitude to ANZAM Sandys certainly hoped in 1957 to strengthen ANZAM and increase British influence in SEATO by presenting a united Commonwealth front.[164]

Despite fears about the threat from Indonesia[165] China continued to be assessed as the main threat. It was assumed that both nuclear deterrence and limited nuclear war-fighting had a role in dealing with this threat. According to the BDCC(FE):

> It has been assessed that in 5 or 10 years China could, by her own efforts, achieve a nuclear capability. Should help be coming from the Soviet Union, then this period would be reduced. In the event of a limited war in the Far East, existing plans allow for the deployment of up to three squadrons of medium bombers to bases in Malaya and Singapore. Under present conditions, the lapse of several days before this force would be ready for operations, would be acceptable. However once China achieves a nuclear capability, we consider it would be necessary for our own nuclear power to be able to be be brought to bear without delay and, in order to provide a convincing deterrent to war, would have to be in position in peacetime. This could be achieved by stationing at least one medium bomber squadron in the theatre or, if this is not possible, less efficiently by ensuring that tactical aircraft have a nuclear capability and a range to reach their targets from RAF bases. In any event nuclear capability of support aircraft is necessary to implement the declared SEATO policy of using nuclear weapons in any war with China or the Democratic Republic of Vietnam.[166]

Exchanges between the Air Ministry and the Ministry of Defence concerning the proposed provision of a permanent nuclear force in the Far East show the uncertain direction of British policy. The Air Ministry intended to develop further nuclear capability in the region including the construction of a V-bomber base on Labuan in Borneo.[167] This proposal was vetoed by the Ministry of Defence. One official commented: 'as far as the RAF requirements are concerned, I think this brings us once more to the slippery slope leading to the bottomless pit'. Ministry of Defence officials argued that the plans for permanent stationing could not be based on a Chinese nuclear capability since if such a capability existed the bombers would be vulnerable to a surprise attack. In order to minimise the threat of such an attack the bombers would need costly dispersal airfields and air defence facilities. The civilian officials also pointed out that, if the main emphasis of British defence policy in South-East Asia was on limited war, the nuclear force was not actually very important - its only purpose would be to deter the use of nuclear weapons by other countries.[168]

In the Middle East strategy was based partially on the peripheral nuclear strategy first adumbrated in the 1940s. As the military brief for Macmillan's visit to Moscow in 1959 noted:

> The present deployment of Western nuclear forces is probably known to the Russians. They will appreciate that the larger the number of bases from which an attack on Russia can be carried out, the more flexible will be the Western plan of attack and the more difficult it will be to neutralise. They must therefore be expected to take into account every base capable of operating aircraft with a nuclear offensive capability. They will, of course, attach special importance to those bases which normally support the main Allied strategic air forces. ... The retention of peripheral air bases will remain an essential part of Western deterrent strategy until the reliable delivery of the nuclear deterrent by ballistic missiles of at least intermediate range, either from land or sea, can be assured.[169]

The RAF planned to disperse some V-bombers to the Middle East in periods of tension. This tactic was intended to decrease their vulnerability and complicate the task of the Russian air defence system.[170] The RAF also planned to deploy the V-bombers, armed with conventional weapons, in the Middle East in a limited war role.[171]

Nuclear weapons were seen as having further importance for the Middle Eastern theatre. The main vehicle for British power in the Mediterranean and Northern Tier was the Baghdad Pact. The pact's supposed military aims were to deter Soviet aggression in the Middle East and to secure the right flank of NATO in the event of conflict. The British contribution to the Pact was four squadrons of nuclear-armed Canberras based in Cyprus. More accurately these aircraft were included in the Pact's Interim Capabilities Plan. As the United Kingdom Military Deputy to the Pact pointed out in December 1957 'the plan was inaccurate in some respects and in particular where it assumed that the

RAF in Cyprus already had a nuclear capability. This was not yet the case and would not be for, perhaps, two years'. He was refused permission to either offer conventional forces in lieu or to tell Britain's allies of the true position lest they lose confidence.[172] Nuclear facilities were not, in fact, provided until late 1961.[173] There was thus a distinct mismatch between British aims and capabilities.

Nuclear planning had no clear link with the Pact's political aims. Part of its purpose was to encourage American involvement in the region. In June 1957 the United States became a full member of the Baghdad Pact's Military Committee and agreed to fill the post of deputy director of the Central Military Planning Staff. The Pact's nuclear planning remained, however, largely irrelevant to American involvement. The Americans had bilateral agreements with each of the regional Pact members and supplied them with military aid. The British were well aware that these members, especially Iran, used the Pact as a diplomatic channel for exerting pressure for more aid and that, in reality, it was little more than a cover organisation for this process.[174]

As far as the British military were concerned one of the initial aims of the Pact had been to secure its position in Iraq and in 1957 Iraq remained the lynchpin of the alliance.[175] In July 1958 the pro-British Nuri Said and King Feisal were overthrown and murdered in a coup. A military reappraisal of the Pact was carried out in the summer of 1958 but no change of policy ensued. It was recognised that the Pact was a facade. The strategy of relying on the strategic air offensive and tactical nuclear weapons, although approved by the Military Committee, commanded no real support from the regional members who were interested in conventional weaponry. Nevertheless, it was concluded that the existence of the Pact produced political advantage at limited cost and the nuclear strategy was re-endorsed.[176] Britain continued to plan on the basis of the Canberra force and very limited financial aid, which amounted to £500,000 for the construction of a radar early warning system in Iran and £30,000 for training Pact personnel in the United Kingdom. These sums were dwarfed by the American programme which in 1960 included the transfer of four minesweepers, four patrol boats and 56 F-86 aircraft to Iran alone.[177] The British believed, however, that their approach to planning was justified.

> Planning within the Baghdad Pact has so far been limited to global war. The United Kingdom has devoted much effort to persuading regional members to concentrate on the major Soviet threat. She has done this in an attempt to discourage possible dangerous thoughts about Syria, Iraq, Afghanistan and India and to avoid getting embroiled in local situations. It has been felt that preparedness to deal with the global war threat ensures more than adequate strength to control local situations. Moreover, the

United Kingdom has been more easily able to conceal her own shortcomings in the context of global war.[178]

The Pact's nuclear planning did, however, have an important impact on British policy in the region since, despite the Chiefs of Staff's bitter claim that lack of consultation over this issue was one of Sandys' 'Intolerable Acts',[179] there was no compelling strategic justification for attempting to retain Cyprus as a colony as long as secure base facilities under full British control could be guaranteed. In 1959 British requirements in an independent Cyprus were set at an Army brigade group for use anywhere in the Middle East, seven permanent RAF squadrons, including the four bomber squadrons committed to CENTO and facilities for the V-bombers.[180]

The role of nuclear weapons outside Europe remained controversial. Indeed the question of limited nuclear war was reconsidered in 1959. A report drawn up for the Defence Committee argued that the only possibility of using nuclear weapons in such a war would be as a last resort against Chinese aggression. Yet Sir Frances Festing, the CIGS, 'believed that in six or seven years time the use of nuclear weapons in limited war might be more readily acceptable'.[181] Harold Watkinson was sceptical of such views. He ruled that there was no possibility of limited nuclear war in the Middle East or Africa although he admitted that the presence of nuclear equipped forces might have some deterrent effect. Watkinson also ruled that although the use of nuclear weapons might be considered in response to all out aggression by the Chinese such a policy ran the risk of triggering a global thermonuclear war.[182]

The failure of the post-Suez period to bring about any radical changes in national strategy and military deployment can be explained largely in terms of imperial nostalgia, fear of Soviet infiltration and service self-interest.[183] The RAF did, however, contribute to this inertia. The Air Ministry offered the nuclear legitimisation of existing policy. Britain was already committed to its role as a nuclear weapons state for reasons explored earlier. Resources would have been concentrated on nuclear rather than conventional forces even if a major withdrawal from the Far East had been agreed upon. The physical availability of nuclear weapons was combined with the twin beliefs that they would deter limited aggression and could be used in a geographically limited war. This combination effectively short-circuited challenges, based on the premiss that Britain no longer had the military resources to sustain a global role, to existing policy. Britain did not have the strength to defend the Middle East against Soviet aggression; but there would be no limited Soviet attack in the area because the Soviets would be fearful of provoking a global war. Britain could not defend Malaya against a Chinese conventional invasion but China would not attempt such an invasion

because of the American nuclear threat to the mainland and the RAF's ability to destroy invading forces with nuclear weapons. Regional powers would be impressed or deterred by Britain's ability to deploy nuclear weapons.

The arguments of the late 1950s about extended deterrence and peripheral nuclear strategy became less convincing once the debate about the utility of nuclear weapons for war-fighting was more fully explored in the context of NATO strategy.[184] In addition nuclear weapons proved to be of little relevance to the actual military challenges Britain had to face in the 1960s. V-bombers were deployed to Singapore during the Indonesian confrontation. Nuclear armed Canberras were stationed in Cyprus until 1969 and then replaced by Vulcans which were finally withdrawn in 1975.[185] They proved to be of little value when Britain needed to react to the invasion of the island by Turkey, its NATO ally, in 1974.[186] Nuclear weapons continued to play a part in overseas strategy but the ideas which underpinned East of Suez in the late 1950s no longer seemed particularly compelling when the Labour government decided to abandon it in the late 1960s.

The Bomber Force and NATO Strategy:
Tripwire and Limited Liability

The nuclear armed bomber and British land forces in Europe were uneasy bedfellows throughout the 1950s. As Sir William Dickson, the Chairman of the Chiefs of Staff, wrote in 1957, 'although I subscribe to the Deterrent/Shield concept in my heart of hearts, I think it wrong in the longer term that the UK should be forced to maintain an army on the Continent.'[187] The nuclear armed bomber seemed to offer the prospect of limiting Britain's continental commitment whilst enabling her to remain a world power. Although planning for both land and nuclear air forces co-existed it was not the result of a coherent strategy. There was a political necessity of retaining a visible military commitment to Europe. Under the cloak of this committment different bureaucratic constituencies propounded competing strategies.

One clear decision taken by the Policy Review Committee in 1956 was that NATO should adopt a new strategy. This policy was rigorously followed through with determined support from officials in the Ministry of Defence and Foreign Office. The services were united in their distaste for the PRC. Yet this distaste did not prevent them from refining arguments over NATO strategy in order to undermine each other. Not only did the RAF advocate a new strategy but the Air Staff found a name for it. 'There is a fundamental difference between our thinking and that of the Army about the purpose of land forces in Europe', wrote the Air Staff's senior planning officer, 'we see them mainly as a sort of "trip wire" and, as such, part of the deterrent. They see them more as capable of playing a significant part in holding up a Russian attack. To our way of thinking, therefore, the main considerations are political and psychological rather than military.'[188]

The Air Staff suggested a method of proceeding.

> NATO was originally set up as a global war agency. It is doubtful if it can be legitimately regarded as such today; indeed the complacency with which the virtual disappearance of the French contribution has been accepted is indicative that it cannot be so regarded. Too abrupt a rundown of the forces we have declared to NATO would be disastrous to our cold war aims. In any case, however, orderly administration would demand a gradual rundown and it should be possible during the rundown period to replace the cold war value of the present NATO military dispositions by a revised strategic concept and by political and economic ties as already clearly foreshadowed by Mr. Dulles.[189]

The Air Staff recommendations were adopted by the PRC. The review committee's report on the issue called for a new NATO strategic concept 'that can be interpreted in terms of lower but militarily definable force levels, and a planned and coherent Allied effort ... it might perhaps be based mainly on the idea of a "plate glass window" or "trip-wire"'.[190]

The proposal that NATO strategy should be completely revised went far beyond British inter-service disputes. The United States government, other NATO countries and SACEUR had to be convinced. Nevertheless, the preparation of the new strategic directive shows that the internal imperatives of British policy were important. Britain drove forward the strategic review despite strong objections from elsewhere in NATO.

In June 1956 Sir Roger Makins, the British Ambassador in Washington, proposed to the United States government that NATO should adopt a new military directive. Foster Dulles responded that the British proposal was too spectacular and would cause a serious public crisis in NATO. Dulles suggested that a series of military studies carried out by NATO itself was a better way to proceed. Makins refused to countenance such studies on the grounds that they would not produce the required, predetermined, result.[191] By mid-July Dulles had realised the seriousness and urgency of the British position and he promised that he and Eisenhower would hold talks with the British government before American force plans were finalised in August.[192]

Eden then wrote to Eisenhower with a clear statement of British policy. He pledged his support for any project to increase the political cohesion of the Alliance but pointed out that the essential attribute of NATO was its military strength and posture. He argued that the strategic situation had been revolutionised by the development of thermonuclear weapons. In the British government's view since NATO and the Soviet

Union possessed nuclear weapons both realised that their use would lead to mutual annihilation. The public of Western nations were well aware that the threat of war had receded but that if it came it would be of a totally new kind. In this climate there was little public support for large-scale conventional forces. Eden acknowledged that it was senseless for the United States and United Kingdom to pursue a 'peripheral strategy': land forces stationed in Western Europe would be needed indefinitely. Yet the size of these ground forces could be kept relatively small. 'A "shield" of conventional forces is still required; but it is no longer our principal military protection', wrote the Prime Minister, 'its primary function seems now to be to deal with any local infiltration, to prevent external intimidation and enable aggression to be identified as such. It may be that it should also be capable of imposing some delay on the progress of a Soviet land invasion until the full impact is felt of the thermonuclear retaliation which would be launched at the Soviet Union.'[193]

Eden suggested that NATO's aim should be to change the nature and size of forces, especially those in Germany, since 'it is on the thermonuclear bomb and atomic weapons that we now rely, not only to deter aggression, but to deal with aggression should it be launched.'[194]

The American response to Eden's proposals was decided at a meeting between Dulles, Secretary of Defense Wilson, the Chairman of the JCS, Admiral Radford, and SACEUR, General Gruenther. The United States opposed a new directive and warned against the withdrawal of American and British divisions from Europe. American leaders were, however, willing to trim between 25,000 and 50,000 troops from existing NATO formations.[195]

General Gruenther lobbied the British government to proceed cautiously. In June he wrote to Sir Walter Monckton arguing that it would be premature to conclude that NATO forces could be cut before SHAPE finished their own studies for the 1958 to 1965 period. He urged the British to enter into further consultations with SHAPE and their allies before announcing reductions as part of British defence policy in case the force cuts triggered a military rundown of NATO.[196]

The Air Staff was concerned about Gruenther's activities since it believed that the War Office was co-ordinating its own proposals with SACEUR in an attempt to retain conventional forces in Europe.[197] On the other hand, parts of the American defence establishment offered support for Air Staff views. During a visit to Britain the Secretary of the Air Force, Donald Quarles, confirmed that the United States itself had plans to reduce the United States Army to 800,000 men and to re-equip it with nuclear weapons. He agreed with the RAF on two strategic issues. First, that the deterrent effect of thermonuclear weapons would remain the same even after the Russians achieved near parity with the United States.

Second, that military planners should assume the use of atomic weapons in all future wars. Nevertheless, even Quarles, who favoured the substitution of nuclear wepons for ground troops, insisted that Britain should continue to play a major military role in the alliance. He warned the British government that if it put the case for reform badly, stressing force reductions rather than improvements in weapons technology, American public opinion might come to favour withdrawal of the United States from NATO.[198]

At the same time as Quarles and Gruenther were putting diplomatic pressure on the British government Lord Montgomery also urged a change in NATO strategy rather than a mere reduction in forces. Montgomery regarded global war as extremely unlikely but felt that NATO had to clearly and publicly state that aggression would be resisted by all means including thermonuclear weapons. He foresaw the replacement of tactical air forces by land forces armed with nuclear weapons but argued that the alliance would continue to need conventional forces in order to combat minor infiltrations at the peripheries of the NATO area such as Turkish Thrace or North Norway.[199]

Over the summer of 1956 the British government was bombarded with a range of advice concerning the feasibility of an attempt to change NATO strategy, the exact content of that strategy and the implications for the armed forces. The Chiefs of Staff, who recognised that if they did not produce coherent advice their role in strategic policy-making would be usurped, made their own submission on NATO strategy to the Minister of Defence in July. The Chiefs of Staff document reflected Army and Royal Navy rather than RAF views. It started from the premiss that the risk of global war had decreased and was decreasing due to the thermonuclear deterrent posed by SAC. This American nuclear guarantee rested on its involvement in NATO. Thus although the strengthened deterrent lessened the military importance of conventional forces they remained important in preventing the political unravelling of the alliance. According to the Chiefs of Staff there had to be a stable balance between East and Federal German forces, between American, British, French and West German forces and the forces of the major powers and those of the smaller countries. The MC.48 concept was outmoded because it called for forces which could defeat a surprise attack and prevent the rapid overrun of Europe. The obsolescence of current doctrine did not, however, obviate the need for conventional forces. Russia was in the process of building up a thermonuclear stockpile and the forces to deliver it. Once this aim had been achieved the United States would be reluctant to commit thermonuclear suicide. In the medium-term, therefore, conventional forces, equipped with nuclear weapons, would be needed to deal with limited aggression, such as an attack on Berlin by the East Germans. Land forces would have to be large enough to ensure that any aggression they could not deal with was a full-scale attack on Western Europe. Air forces should be determined by the same logic as land, not because of their contribution to the primary deterrent, and would be retained as a nuclear support force until the land forces had the missile capability to replace them.[200]

The actual directive to be proposed for NATO, written by senior officials in the Ministry of Defence, took some account of this case but reflected more closely views put forward by the RAF.[201] Indeed the Air Staff felt that '[the directive]... reflects the views you [CAS] have consistently put forward in the recent discussions on future strategy. It is therefore acceptable to us though ... it will be attacked by your colleagues.'[202] The draft directive stated the premiss that since the death of Stalin and the detonation of the Russian H-bomb the Russian government had re-examined its strategy and tactics. The Soviet leadership appreciated the catastrophic nature of thermonuclear war and realised that even if nuclear parity was achieved NATO could still destroy the USSR. Soviet policy was to avoid global war and such war was, therefore, unlikely. Long-term Soviet goals, such as the disruption of NATO and the subversion of the the West outside the NATO area were unchanged. The Soviets could be left in no doubt that if they committed any act of aggression against NATO it would immediately trigger a full scale thermonuclear attack on the USSR. Within a policy of massive retaliation NATO military forces in Europe had four roles: to maintain confidence in NATO as a military alliance, to deal with local infiltration and subversion, to identify Soviet and satellite aggression and to secure facilities for the strategic bomber offensive. The directive was clear on two key issues: thermonuclear parity did not in any way weaken massive retaliation; and stronger tactical nuclear forces in Europe were not necessary since such forces were to be little more than a warning screen.[203]

Impressed by the forcefulness of the British approach and worried that the pressure within NATO might damage the alliance Dulles recognised that a new strategic directive was inevitable. The purpose of NATO ground forces, in the eyes of the Secretary of State, was the protection of western Europe against all aggression, including that of Soviet satellites. An effective shield of conventional ground forces was needed to avoid inflexibility. 'Accordingly, we find unacceptable any proposal which implies the adoption of a NATO strategy of total reliance on nuclear retaliation.'[204] Admiral Radford believed that Dulles was overstating the implications of British policy, that NATO would be reduced to complete reliance on nuclear weapons, and claimed that Britain were merely following an American lead and adopting the 'New Look'. Dulles believed, however, that whereas the United States might rely on the 'New Look' European countries subject to conventional and insurrectionary attacks could not. Although Dulles' doubts were transmitted to the British a week later they submitted an unchanged draft of a new directive to the North Atlantic Council.[205]

If Britain's position was made diplomatically delicate by the State Department's lukewarm response it was further complicated by General Gruenther's vigorous espousal of the 'sword and shield' concept. Gruenther presented the view that within a few hours of the initial nuclear offensive Soviet land forces would invade NATO territory. The atomic counter-offensive would fail to stop or sufficiently disorganise them and NATO countries would have to undertake conventional military operations for about thirty days to stabilise the front. As an antidote to the British draft directive SHAPE produced its own study of the armed forces needed by NATO in order to wage such a campaign.[206]

SACEUR's report predicted that from 1960 onwards both sides would have adequate stockpiles of nuclear weapons. Once 'nuclear sufficiency' was reached Russia would only be discouraged from considering nuclear war if NATO was prepared to fight a general war. The Cold War role of NATO forces was to provide an environment of nuclear security and to demonstrate that anything other than a full attack would be contained. The main threat would then be a massive surprise nuclear offensive followed by a land, sea and air campaign to seize and isolate Europe. A Soviet attack of this nature would lead to a two-phase war, violent organised fighting, with an intense nuclear exchange in the first few days, lasting up to a month, followed by a period of reorganisation and limited military activity. SACEUR defined a threefold mission for himself: to assist in deterring aggression by showing the readiness, capability and will to use nuclear weapons; to maintain confidence in NATO; and to defend NATO Europe. For these tasks he wanted air defences, including early warning, high readiness nuclear strike forces, conventional land, sea and air forces to ensure that the only aggression possible was an all-out Soviet offensive and ready reserves of mobile forces to be deployed as required. Gruenther called for material changes in NATO's force structure. On land these changes included the deployment forward in depth, increased integration of nuclear forces and the elimination of all forces with a long lag in mobilisation. In the air he called for an increased nuclear strike force, a reduction in conventional strike forces, a reduction in heavy anti-aircraft guns and their replacement with surface-to-air missiles, a reduction in day fighters and an increase in all-weather fighters, and a large increase in reconnaissance aircraft.[207]

SACEUR's campaign completely cut across British policy. Although it envisaged changes to MC.48, with more emphasis on immediately available forces and a mobile reserve, it allowed for no reduction in expenditure or net reduction in British force levels, put NATO forces in the category of a primary deterrent along with strategic air forces and retained a modified concept of two-phase war.[208]

In order to have the new directive adopted at the Ministerial meeting of the North Atlantic Council held in Paris during mid-December 1956 Britain needed the support of the American government. This support could only be acquired through a diplomatic response to American concerns. On 11 December 1956 Macmillan, Lloyd, Head and Sir William Dickson met with Dulles, Wilson, Secretary of the Treasury Humphrey and Admiral Radford. At this meeting the British argued their case to an American audience. Under the WEU Treaty, Macmillan's team argued, the United Kingdom was bound to provide four divisions and a tactical air force to NATO but the the size of these forces was not fixed. MC.48 already implied that these forces should be equipped with atomic weapons. If the European countries felt the treaty had been breached there would be serious political consequences. Political disruption of NATO could, however, be avoided if SACEUR would certify that the forces proposed under the new strategic directive were of 'equivalent fighting capacity'. Since British capability to deploy tactical nuclear weapons was less advanced than American there would then be a politically stabilising changeover period. Under the new directive it would be possible to work out a compromise between 'trip-wire' and a World War Two type organisation. The Americans still felt that the directive went too far in stressing nuclear forces. They argued that NATO forces should not be so dependent on atomic weapons. Even if reliance was to be placed on nuclear weapons in the event of major attack NATO would continue to need conventional forces in order to provide flexibility in a crisis. The bulk of the manpower for these forces had to come from Britain and the United States since the French army was concentrated in North Africa.

Dulles did finally agree to use his political influence in support of Britain on the grounds that 'we were planning to reduce the number of men in our divisions for our own purposes and saw no reason why the UK should not do the same, and perhaps do it faster.' He promised to bring General Gruenther's successor, Lauris Norstad, into line. 'The UK should work with SACEUR, perhaps with US help, to get him to accept that reduced UK forces would provide equivalent fighting ability. Perhaps some pressure on SACEUR might have to be exerted. SACEUR must of course be alive to the realistic facts involved.' Nevertheless, Dulles issued a stern warning against pushing the changes too far. 'The US felt that no unsound strategic concept should be forced on NATO to meet financial problems. They could not support the view that ... NATO should go entirely on a 'trip-wire' basis, nor could the US accept the idea that there was no need for substantial manpower because any attack would set off massive retaliation. ... While in about 90% of the possible situations nuclear retaliation would cover the situation there were ... particularly with respect to Berlin, certain types of risks requiring the presence of German troops. Secretary said the trip wire theory would, he feared, perhaps mean there would be no German troops at all'.[209]

General Norstad, who had become SACEUR in November 1956, was informed by Anthony Head that Britain intended to run down BAOR to 50,000 men and to halve 2nd TAF. Norstad expressed concern that the 'measles of reduction' would spread to other NATO countries. He also continued to press the case for a NATO force of 30 divisions in 1960-2 to act as a 'human fence' in order to prevent local adventures leading to nuclear war.[210] Although he refused to accept any strategic justification for the British reductions he acknowledged that they would not constitute a major catastrophe.[211]

Britain had amassed enough diplomatic support to have its proposals accepted by the North Atlantic Council. The Standing Group was instructed to produce a new political directive, MC.14/2, and a new strategic directive, MC.48/2, based around them. There was general satisfaction in the defence establishment that British arguments had been so well received, at least in public. The Minister of Defence had argued that, in the light of manpower difficulties and the costs of new weapons, a reduction in NATO contributions balanced by improved effectiveness and continued large-scale support for NATO forces in Europe was necessary. The Chancellor of the Exchequer had presented a case based on the proposition that Britain had a balance of payments problem and was already spending a much greater proportion of its national income on defence than any other European country and must, therefore, be allowed some decrease.[212]

The successful campaign to get a NATO political directive based on massive retaliation was one of the most important underpinnings of the 1957 Defence White Paper. Indeed the force cuts in Europe announced by Sandys resulted directly from policies pursued by the Eden administration. In response to the 'Head Directive' of December 1956 the RAF proposed a 2nd TAF, assuming the Germans took over its air defence role in 1961, of 50 Canberra nuclear strike aircraft, a reconnaissance contingent for this force based in Germany and two tactical reconnaissance squadrons for the Army, 104 aircraft in all.[213]

Little emphasis should be put on the well-known Dullesian texts in assessing the British version of massive retaliation. Policy was relatively unrefined and revolved around the practical problems of force levels. The emphasis was on thermonuclear deterrence both of a Soviet invasion of Western Europe and nuclear attack against Europe and the United Kingdom. There was no hint of 'brinkmanship'. The British aim was to reinforce the certainty of the massive nuclear response not its uncertainty. Neither was any form of 'active' deterrence involved in British calculations: the aim was purely to deter a large-scale Soviet invasion of Western Europe. The RAF version of massive retaliation had elements of mutually assured destruction contained within it since it assumed that the strategy would be equally as valid under conditions of nuclear parity. The Soviets would be deterred by the risk of annihilation; what was needed from the West was a posture which left the Russians in no doubt of its willingness to use nuclear weapons.

There was little thought given to any doctrine of limited nuclear war, despite the intention to contribute a nuclear armed Canberra force to SACEUR. The idea of an RAF Canberra force had more to do with long-term force plans than any consideration of limited nuclear war. Such a force had, in fact, been mooted, armed with conventional weapons, as long ago as the late 1940s. The concept had been further developed in the early 1950s when it was thought that that an atomic offensive against the Soviet Union would not immediately stop the Red Army. In 1956 the RAF opposed proposals to equip 2nd TAF fighter-bombers with nuclear weapons, a stance which suggested that the Air Staff did not believe that tactical nuclear weapons were merely high-powered 'conventional' munitions.[214] The idea that SACEUR's nuclear forces were as much part of the primary deterrent as SAC or Bomber Command was specifically rejected. In the debate over 'nuclear sufficiency' the RAF argued that any nuclear war in Europe would almost immediately escalate into a full-scale thermonuclear conflict.

The adoption and vigorous espousal of this strategy by Britain owed less, however, to RAF arguments in 1956 than the cumulative effect of the case it had made between 1952 and 1955 in every defence policy-making forum for a greater reliance on nuclear weapons in Europe. It also became clear that the position adopted by the British government had a number of flaws. These flaws were shown up over the next two years. The new NATO strategic directive was put into place under the lash of economic necessity[215] and its opponents were left unconciliated. These opponents were able to regroup and challenge declaratory policy during the debate over the force level requirement, MC.70, drawn up to put the new strategy into effect. MC.14/2 itself made the case for warning and anti-infiltration forces,[216] as had the British draft upon which it was based. It could be argued that these forces should be of the magnitude of Norstad's thirty divisions. The arguments put forward by SACEUR and the army and naval staffs in Britain were obviously self-interested but their criticisms, especially of the lack of flexibility a strict intepretation of MC.14/2 would entail, carried considerable force.

Between 1957 and 1959 there were two main aspects of British strategic policy towards NATO. First, a governmental attempt to frame force structure proposals to follow its success in achieving a new declaratory strategy. Second, the use by the Army and Navy of the debate within NATO, and particularly the ideas put forward by SACEUR, to influence British defence policy.

The aim of British policy was to balance maximum force reductions with the maintenance of the alliance's cohesion. Ministry of Defence officials advised Sandys when he took office in January 1957 that the United Kingdom was overcommitted to NATO. War in Europe was very unlikely and preparations for it were taking up too large a proportion of resources. 'In theory, we should not spend any money on this objective at all', wrote Richard Powell and Richard Chilver, 'global war would be so catastrophic that we cannot divert resources from preventing it to preparations for surviving after a fashion if it should come'. 'But', they continued, 'we cannot wholly eliminate this part of our contribution, because of the effect on our allies (including the loss of influence in allied counsels) and because of the effect at home.'[217]

Sandys' civil servants believed that a reduction in 'shield' forces to about half of those envisaged by the Paris Agreements would be politically acceptable. These political constraints on British policy were accepted by Macmillan. He told the Cabinet Defence Committee in July 1957: 'The effectiveness of the deterrent depended to large extent on maintaining the vital link with the United States and other allies in NATO. It was therefore essential that we should be able to demonstrate to the Soviet Union that we were determined both to keep the sea routes across the Atlantic open and to continue to provide effective support for the North Atlantic Alliance. If we reduced that support, the United States might withdraw from Europe and NATO might disintegrate.'[218]

Nevertheless, Macmillan, Sandys and Ministry of Defence and Air Ministry officials believed that large reductions in NATO forces were both politically possible and strategically desirable. The RAF repeated its proposed reduction of 2nd TAF to 104 aircraft. By 1961 this force was to be mainly made up of four squadrons of nuclear armed Canberras under the control of SACEUR.[219] The Ministry of Defence also planned to reduce BAOR to 43,000 men by 1962.[220]

Although Britain was strongly criticised in Europe for the reduction of BAOR from 77,000 to 64,000 men announced in the 1957 White Paper[221] the British government believed it had considerable political latitude. The West German government, which was not a member of the North Atlantic Council, had been effectively excluded from the decision to adopt a new NATO strategy but it had already initiated a restructuring of the Bundeswehr in October 1956 which placed more reliance on nuclear weapons and less on manpower.[222] From Paris Gladwyn Jebb reported that the French Minister of Defence, Bourges Maunoury, 'far from opposing our proposals about force reductions, was really in favour of them, as being in accordance both with our economic possibilities and strategic realities.' The French refused to help in public because they did not want British logic applied to their own forces. Jebb believed, however, that if Britain made some concessions on 'phasing' reductions 'any formal and continuing objection from the French will not be sustained to breaking point'.[223]

There was also a certain amount of support for the British position within the American government. At the time of the Bermuda Conference Eisenhower expressed the view that that Britain was following the policy of the 1953 New Look by trying to support its alliances whilst maintaining a viable economy. He commented: 'I certainly admire the courage and nerve with which Britain has undertaken it'.[224] During Macmillan's visit to the United States in October he and Dulles seemed to agree that nuclear weapons would have an ever increasing role in both defence and offence and that 'as the cost of nuclear developments increase, there is less and less capacity, and perhaps utility, in carrying out the "shield" concept.' Yet both sides acknowledged that disbelief amongst the non-nuclear powers that Britain and America would risk their own destruction was an important political problem which needed careful management.[225] In fact Macmillan made concessions. He acceded to SACEUR's suggestion that the planned 5000 troop strategic reserve would be left in Europe rather than be permanently based in the United Kingdom.[226]

The Americans still had some serious concerns about British policy.[227] They saw a danger of Britain squeezing every possible force reduction out of NATO thus making American plans to withdraw fifteen USAF squadrons and two battle groups from one of their five divisions in Europe in 1958, as the first stage in the draw-down of United States forces worldwide to 2.5 million men, damaging politically.[228] In addition they felt that the British emphasis on nuclear weapons brought into question the whole concept of 'sword and shield' and increased the possibility that France would develop nuclear weapons.[229] Since the British government had expressed its own desire to exclude France from the 'nuclear club'[230] Norstad attempted to play on British sensitivities. He pointed out that the United States had already provided France with F-84F atomic capable fighter-bombers and was training the French air force in the use of atomic weapons in an attempt to deflect calls for a French atomic bomb.[231] Underlying Norstad's remarks was a belief that American attempts to control French nuclear ambitions would be undermined if Britain continued to flaunt its own nuclear power and its bilateral relationship with the USA. As a result of these considerations the United States government was generally sympathetic to the Britain's position but tried to steer a careful course away from supporting radical steps by the British.[232]

Within these broad political constraints, and there was little hesitation in moving ahead without consulting European allies and dismissing German sensitivity about the over emphasis on nuclear weapons,[233] the primary motivation of the British government was to reduce the proportion of the defence budget allocated to Europe. As Sir Richard Powell put it 'the United Kingdom contribution would be based on what we could afford without endangering economic stability'.[234] In January 1958 a further reduction in BAOR to 55,000 was announced and in May Britain and Germany signed a support costs agreement envisaging only 45,000 troops by 1961.[235] The reduction in the RAF, which was regarded as less politically sensitive, went ahead rapidly although plans to withdraw all fighters were delayed by the slower than expected build up of the Luftwaffe.[236]

Despite the overall direction of government policy an important strategic debate developed over the nature of limited war. The United Kingdom had framed the new political directive with the firm intention that nuclear retaliation would be the main deterrent with some complementary shield forces. This concept was watered down, and therefore open to different interpretations, because of the need to have a superficially agreed NATO policy. The British had agreed to changes in order to preserve unanimity with the caveat that 'our agreement to specific words would not materially affect the level of our NATO forces'.[237] The policy proposed by the British was that such forces should be able to deal with local infiltrations. If these infiltrations were broadened or prolonged all types of nuclear weapons would be used. No concept of limited war was involved. The American Embassy in London reported to Dulles that 'United Kingdom doubts nuclear weapons can be used tactically on European Continent and Sandys and his senior officials think that principal benefit so-called 'tactical' nuclear weapons is to add strength to nuclear deterrent by convincing Russians NATO will not meet aggression with conventional weapons and that any Communist aggression in the NATO area raises grim possibility of all-out nuclear war both on Communist spearheads and on Communist vitals.'[238]

Yet both SACEUR and SACLANT argued that NATO should plan for limited war. In his force capabilities submission SACLANT stated that 'the danger of preparing for all-out nuclear war may lie in the failure or refusal of the Allies to counter limited aggression without resort to nuclear weapons.' In an oral presentation to the North Atlantic Council SACEUR argued that thermonuclear parity imposed on NATO the need to deal with situations short of general war with measures short of massive retaliation.[239] Norstad developed his position that the force levels proposed in MC.70 were already less than those proposed under MC.48 in 1954 because the difference had been made up by tactical nuclear weapons. He pointed out that the whole purpose of NATO was to defend its territory. Thirty divisions was the minimum needed for a holding action to force the Soviet Union to commit a definite act of aggression. He dismissed suggestions of a 'tripwire' or 'plate glass' strategy as dangerous. An aggressor could make territorial gains with little force and NATO would then be faced with the piecemeal loss of territory or massive retaliation. He argued that the 'shield' had to be strong enough to deny the Soviet Union of the option of launching limited attacks on western Europe. MC.70 was thus the 'ultimate cost' which could only be reduced by fatally damaging the alliance.[240]

The British government attacked Norstad's arguments on the grounds that any war involving a Warsaw Pact country would not be limited. Since neither side wanted to provoke a global war satellite aggression would only occur as the precursor to an all-out Soviet offensive. The British denounced his ideas as an espousal of the rejected doctrine of 'graduated deterrence' and claimed that if the explicit aims of MC.70 - 'defending the land, sea and air frontiers of NATO Europe' and 'to hold the invaders until the nuclear battle had been won' - were accepted the defence programme would be much too ambitious. Britain's formal position was that it was militarily impossible to defend NATO Europe.[241]

Despite the statements of their own government the Royal Navy and the Army agreed with SACEUR's position on force levels. Early in 1957 Sir Gerald Templer argued that strategy should be based either on the assumption that the deterrent would not fail, and that NATO forces were a major part of such a deterrent, or that by miscalculation or the failure of deterrence a war would start and gradually develop into a thermonuclear conflict, in which case the 'shield' forces had to be of sufficient size to hold the enemy whilst the strategic offensive took effect. Lord Mountbatten dismissed talk of days and phases of global war as dangerous for the whole concept of deterrence. He pointed out that the Russians might not act as the West predicted. They might believe Soviet forces could maintain and win a long war in which case the Allies should plan to continue the struggle until the Soviet Union was defeated.[242] Following the tense December 1957 NATO heads of government meeting[243] at which British defence policy was severely criticised by other European countries[244] Templer and Mountbatten tried again. The First Sea Lord claimed that nuclear parity would be achieved in the near future and CIGS argued that this would entail a wholly new evaluation of limited war.[245] Although some army officers in Germany did not believe in the early use of nuclear weapons and 'gave at least equal emphasis in training for conventional operations'[246] neither the British Army[247] nor SHAPE[248] were thinking it terms of war with conventional weapons. Both expected the forces maintained in Western Europe to be heavily armed with nuclear weapons.

It was left to the RAF to make the case fully supporting British strategy. The Air Staff's representatives argued that 'it was most dangerous to assume that it would be possible to fight a limited war in Europe with atomic weapons without starting a general conflict'[249] and that 'the success of Sputnik did not necessarily mean that Russia was ahead of the Americans in ICBMs. This particularly applied to the problems of accuracy and re-entry into the atmosphere. The availability of fissile material was the controlling factor and as far as could be foreseen the West would always have more than Russia.'[250] In the event of a war British forces would fight for as long as possible but no emphasis should be put on this role since it would lead to requirements for greater forces or reserves.[251]

British policy towards NATO from 1956 was governed by the belief that too much was being spent on defence and too great a proportion of defence resources was being directed to Europe. Although British military planners were not particularly attuned to European sensibilities there was, nevertheless, an acute awareness that force reductions had political limits. The role of strategy in force structure decisions was limited but important. The development of strategic thinking by the RAF in the mid-1950s helped create the climate of belief about the nature of nuclear war, the logical culmination of which was the new NATO directive of December 1956. Thereafter it was important to have a strategy which, although subject to intense criticism both from within the defence establishment and from outside commentators, was, arguably, the most credible nuclear option at a time when American and British nuclear forces lacked a guaranteed second-strike capability.

The most significant influence on the changes in strategy can be best seen in the way Britain's most senior military officer portrayed her role in NATO circles. 'As regards British policy: we are a global power. NATO, until recently, had blinkers on ... but we and the US, have to think globally; we have to think of the Far East and the Middle East as well as NATO.' Dickson argued that the Baghdad Pact, despite Iraq's loss, and SEATO were vital for European security as were British bases in Gibraltar, Malta, Cyprus, Aden, Kenya, Hong Kong and Singapore both as a means of instilling psychological resistance to Russian aggression and because they protected the oil countries of the Middle East.[252] Although there were changes of emphasis, the Baghdad Pact was downgraded for instance, the message remained much the same to the end of the decade.[253] British policy towards NATO was not only governed by a desire to decrease defence expenditure. The recasting of NATO nuclear strategy was intended to help maintain a fully global role for Britain. At the end of the 1950s it seemed that, with American acquiescence, the shift from European to overseas commitments could be achieved. With the increase in tension in Europe over Berlin and the arrival of the Kennedy administration, which had drawn very different conclusions from the strategic debate in the United States than its predecessor, this aim proved unrealisable. Yet the developments of the early 1960s should not cloud the actual policy aims of the late 1950s.

Notes

1. James, 'The Impact of the Sandys Defence Policy on the Royal Air Force', pp. 11-13.

2. Ibid.

3. Minister of Defence to Chairman, COS, 31 Jan. 1956, London, Public Record Office (P.R.O.), AIR8/2045.

4. Atomic tests were planned for Monte Bello in spring 1956 and for Maralinga in the autumn. Fears about an international ban on atmospheric testing gave the programme an even greater urgency. In June 1956 a team arrived at Christmas Island to prepare for what was supposedly Britain's first H-bomb test. It now seems that the British government was involved in a sleight of hand. The thermonuclear device tested in May 1957 was an interim development. A British fusion bomb was actually tested only in 1958. Norman Dombey and Eric Grove, 'Britain's thermonuclear bluff' and Norris, *British, French and Chinese Nuclear Weapons*, pp. 34-42.

5. COS(56)4th Confidential Annex, 10 Jan. 1956, London, Public Record Office (P.R.O.), DEFE32/5.

6. In 1954 Nigel Birch, then a junior minister at the Ministry of Defence, had been the only minister to suggest that a British hydrogen bomb programme would complicate efforts to achieve nuclear disarmament by encouraging further proliferation. Pierre, *Nuclear Politics*, p. 91.

7. COS(56)13th, 31 Jan. 1956, London, Public Record Office (P.R.O.), DEFE4/83.

8. First Sea Lord to CAS, 11 July 1956, London, Public Record Office (P.R.O.), AIR8/2064.

9. COS(56)271, 13 July 1956, London, Public Record Office (P.R.O.), DEFE32/5.

10. Ibid.

11. ACAS(P) to CAS, 11 July 1956, London, Public Record Office (P.R.O.), AIR8/2064.

12. First Sea Lord to CAS, 11 July 1956, London, Public Record Office (P.R.O.), AIR8/2064.

13. James, 'The Impact of the Sandys Defence Policy on the Royal Air Force', p. 14.

14. 'The Policy Review: The RAF Programme 1957/8 and 1958/9' Note by Air Ministry, August 1956, London, Public Record Office (P.R.O.), AIR8/2046.

15. Cooper, 'The Origins and Development of the British Strategic Nuclear Deterrent Forces, 1945-1960', p. 30.

16. Sir Richard Powell, 'King's Seminar', p. 29.

17. James, 'The Impact of the Sandys Defence Policy on the Royal Air Force', p. 14.

18. COS(56)70th, 17 July 1956, London, Public Record Office (P.R.O.), DEFE32/5.

19. Ibid.

20. Chancellor of the Exchequer to Minister of Defence, 24 November 1956, London, Public Record Office (P.R.O.), AIR8/2046.

21. GEN564/1st, 19 Dec. 1956, London, Public Record Office (P.R.O.), CAB130/122.

22. COS(56)70th, 17 July 1956, London, Public Record Office (P.R.O.), DEFE32/5.

23. ACAS(P) to CAS, 29 Nov. 1956, London, Public Record Office (P.R.O.), AIR8/2046.

24. Navias, *British Nuclear Planning*, pp. 134-141.

25. D(57)2nd Confidential Annex, 27 Feb. 1957, London, Public Record Office (P.R.O.), CAB131/18.

26. GEN570/2nd, 30 May 1957, London, Public Record Office (P.R.O.), CAB130/122.

27. Ibid.

28. D(57)6th, 31 July 1957, London, Public Record Office (P.R.O.), CAB131/18

29. D(57)7th, 2 August 1957, London, Public Record Office (P.R.O.), CAB131/18.

30. D(57)7th, 2 Aug. 1957, London, Public Record Office (P.R.O.), CAB131/18

31. Minister of Defence to Prime Minister, 12 Aug. 1955, London, Public Record Office (P.R.O.), PREM11/846.

32. Thetford, *Aircraft of the RAF since 1918*, p. 571.

33. Minister of Defence to Prime Minister, 12 Aug. 1955, London, Public Record Office (P.R.O.), PREM11/846.

34. Foreign Secretary to Prime Minister, 22 Aug. 1955, London, Public Record Office (P.R.O.), PREM11/846.

35. 'The Origins and Development of the British Nuclear Deterrent Forces, 1945-1960', pp. 53, 40, 13.

36. Cecil James, 'Kings Seminar', p. 21.

37. GEN570/2nd, 30 May 1957, London, Public Record Office (P.R.O.), CAB130/122.

38. COS(57)3rd Confidential Annex, 8 Jan. 1957, London, Public Record Office (P.R.O.), DEFE4/94.

39. COS(58)46th Confidential Annex, 30 May 1958, London, Public Record Office (P.R.O.), DEFE4/107.

40. Sir Richard Powell, 'King's Seminar', p. 22.

41. Pierre, *Nuclear Politics*, p. 174.

42. Cecil James, 'King's Seminar', p. 21.

43. Ibid.

44. Sir Richard Way, 'King's Seminar', p. 20.

45. COS(57)35th, 10 May 1957, London, Public Record Office (P.R.O.), DEFE4/97.

46. COS(57)35th, 10 May 1957, London, Public Record Office (P.R.O.), DEFE4/97.

47. COS(57)78th Confidential Annex, 15 Oct. 1957, London, Public Record Office (P.R.O.), DEFE4/100.

48. COS(57)86th, 12 Nov. 1957, London, Public Record Office (P.R.O.), DEFE4/101.

49. COS(58)77th, 3 Sept. 1958, London, Public Record Office (P.R.O.), DEFE4/111.

50. Ibid.

51. Sir Richard Way, 'King's Seminar', p. 20.

52. COS(56)1st, 3 Jan. 1956, London, Public Record Office (P.R.O.), DEFE4/82.

53. COS(JGW)(59)4(Final), 25 March 1959, London, Public Record Office (P.R.O.), DEFE5/90.

54. 'Report on the Nature, Course and Duration of Global War' (= COS(57)237) ACAS(P) to CAS, 12 Dec. 1957, London, Public Record Office (P.R.O.), AIR20/10092.

55. GEN570/2nd, 30 May 1957, London, Public Record Office (P.R.O.), CAB130/122.

56. D(57)7th, 2 Aug. 1957, London, Public Record Office (P.R.O.), CAB131/18.

57. D(57)2nd, 27 Feb. 1957, London, Public Record Office (P.R.O.), CAB131/18.

58. D(57)14 'Fissile Material for Nuclear Weapons' Note by Secretary, 27 July 1957, London, Public Record Office (P.R.O.), CAB131/18.

59. D(57)7th, 2 Aug. 1957, London, Public Record Office (P.R.O.), CAB131/18.

60. D(58)24th, 5 Nov. 1958, London, Public Record Office (P.R.O.), CAB131/19.

61. Ronald Melville (DUS, Air Ministry) to Sir Richard Powell, 15 Sept. 1958, London, Public Record Office (P.R.O.), AIR8/2220.

62. Sir Richard Powell to L. J. Sabatini, 16 Jan. 1959, London, Public Record Office (P.R.O.), DEFE7/991.

63. Sir Derek Hoyer-Millar to Sir Richard Powell, 12 Jan. 1959, London, Public Record Office (P.R.O.), DEFE7/991.

64. Recent UK Defence Developments - A Review for Ambassador Whitney (Chiefs of Mission Meeting, Paris, May 1957), Washington, National Archives.

65. Secretary of State for Air to Prime Minister, 10 Jan. 1955, London, Public Record Office (P.R.O.), DEFE11/101.

66. Simpson, *The Independent Nuclear State*, pp. 115-116.

67. Note for the Record, Project 'E', R. T. Armstrong, 5 Dec. 1955, London, Public Record Office (P.R.O.), T225/645.

68. Myers (Ministry of Supply) to Armstrong, 29 Dec. 1955, London, Public Record Office (P.R.O.), T225/645.

69. Leitch (Ministry of Supply) to Macpherson, 14 March 1956, London, Public Record Office (P.R.O.), T225/645.

70. Lynch to Armstrong, 28 March 1956, London, Public Record Office (P.R.O.), T225/645.

71. Macpherson to Serpell, 1 June 1956, London, Public Record Office (P.R.O.), T225/645.

72. Serpell to Macpherson, 'Project 'E' Discussion with RAF', 5 June 1956, London, Public Record Office (P.R.O.), T225/645.

73. Simpson, *The Independent Nuclear State*, p. 290.

74. Macpherson to Serpell, 1 June 1956, London, Public Record Office (P.R.O.), T225/645.

75. Serpell to Melville (Air Ministry), 3 July 1956, London, Public Record Office (P.R.O.), T225/645.

76. Leitch (Ministry of Supply) to Macpherson, 22 Aug. 1956, London, Public Record Office (P.R.O.), T225/645.

77. Macpherson to Serpell, 4 Oct. 1956, London, Public Record Office (P.R.O.), T225/645.

78. At Bermuda Churchill asked for weapons data so that British bombers could be equipped with American nuclear weapons. Admiral Strauss rejected this request on the grounds that compliance would be illegal under the McMahon Act. Botti, *The Long Wait*, p. 127.

79. Haynes (Air Ministry) to Macpherson, 24 Oct. 1956, London, Public Record Office (P.R.O.), T225/645.

80. Ibid.

81. Penney (Air Ministry) to Bligh, 19 June 1957, London, Public Record Office (P.R.O.), T225/645.

82. Penney (Air Ministry) to Bligh, 19 June 1957, London, Public Record Office (P.R.O.), T225/645.

83. Compare Sir Harold Caccia to Foreign Office, 14 Sept. 1957 with Sir Harold Caccia to Foreign Office, 6 Oct. 1957, London, Public Record Office (P.R.O.), PREM11/2554.

84. *FRUS ,1955-1957*, XXIV, pp. 163-65.

85. For this process see 'Deterrence and Survival in the Nuclear Age' Report by the Science Advisory Panel of the Security Resources Board, 7 November 1957 (the Gaither Report), Minutes of the 363rd Meeting of the NSC, 24 April 1958 and the Minutes of the 364th Meeting of the NSC, 1 May 1958 as well as NSC5801/1, May 1958 itself.

86. Dombey and Grove, 'Britain's thermonuclear bluff'.

87. Botti, *The Long Wait*, p. 248.

88. Melissen, *The Struggle For Nuclear Partnership*, pp. 51-52.

89. Herbecq to Bligh, 11 Nov. 1958, London, Public Record Office (P.R.O.), T225/645.

90. PS to Secretary of State for Air to Head of S.6, 23 Jan. 1958, London, Public Record Office (P.R.O.), AIR19/942.

91. ACSC(58)2nd, 20 Jan. 1958, London, Public Record Office (P.R.O.), AIR19/942.

92. Secretary, COS Committee to CAS, 27 Feb. 1958 and CAS Note, undated, London, Public Record Office (P.R.O.), AIR8/2164.

93. 'Record of Meetings held at the Pentagon and State Department, Washington, DC, September 22 to September 25 1958', 14 Oct. 1958, London, Public Record Office (P.R.O.), DEFE13/180.

94. ACSC(58)2nd, 20 Jan. 1958, London, Public Record Office (P.R.O.), AIR19/942; AC 3(58), 30 Jan. 1958, London, Public Record Office (P.R.O.), AIR6/111; 'American IRBMs', CAS to COS, 28 Jan. 1958, London, Public Record Office (P.R.O.), AIR19/942; 'Note of talk between Admiral Sir Michael Denny and First Lord' First Lord of the Admiralty to Prime Minister, London, Public Record Office (P.R.O.), PREM11/2868.

95. Horne, *Macmillan, 1957-1986*, p. 26.

96. 'Report of the Joint USAF-RAF Task Group on Air-to-Ground Weapons', Interdependence Sub-Committee 'D' (Delivery Systems), April 1958, London, Public Record Office (P.R.O.), AIR2/14711.

97. DDOR9 (BAFS) to ACAS(OR), 19 Nov. 1958, London, Public Record Office (P.R.O.), AIR2/14711.

98. 'Strategic ASM Interdependence Short Summary', DCAS to Sir Frederick Brundrett, 22 Dec. 1958, London, Public Record Office (P.R.O.), AIR2/14711

99. Minister of Defence to Prime Minister, 30 Dec. 1958, London, Public Record Office (P.R.O.), AIR2/14711.

100. Secretary of State for Air to Minister of Defence, 24 June 1959, London, Public Record Office (P.R.O.), AIR2/15261.

101. ACAS(OR) to PS to Secretary of State for Air, 11 Dec. 1958, London, Public Record Office (P.R.O.), AIR2/14711.

102. Follett (BJSM, Ministry of Supply Staff) to Sir Frederick Brundrett, 31 Dec. 1958, London, Public Record Office (P.R.O.), AIR2/14711.

103. DCAS to Brundrett, 1 Jan. 1959, London, Public Record Office (P.R.O.), AIR2/14711.

104. Brundrett to Powell, 8 Jan. 1959, London, Public Record Office (P.R.O.), AIR2/14711.

105. ACAS(OR) to PS to Secretary of State for Air, 8 Jan. 1959, London, Public Record Office (P.R.O.), AIR2/14711.

106. DCAS to Powell, 9 Jan. 1959, London, Public Record Office (P.R.O.), AIR2/14711.

107. DRP/M(59)1, 27 Jan. 1959, London, Public Record Office (P.R.O.), AIR2/15261.

108. DRP/P(59)38 'Interdependence - Strategic Air-to-Surface Weapons' Note by Controller of Aircraft Production, 14 April 1959, London, Public Record Office (P.R.O.), AIR2/15261.

109. DRP/M(59)6, 21 April 1959, London, Public Record Office (P.R.O.), AIR2/15261.

110. Brundrett to DCAS, 1 May 1959, London, Public Record Office (P.R.O.), AIR2/15261.

111. DRP/M(59)7, 2 June 1959, London, Public Record Office (P.R.O.), AIR2/15261.

112. AUS(A) to DCAS, 3 June 1959, London, Public Record Office (P.R.O.), AIR2/15261.

113. Secretary of State for Air to Minister of Defence, 24 June 1959, London, Public Record Office (P.R.O.), AIR2/15261.

114. Minister of Defence to Secretary of State for Air, 14 July 1959, London, Public Record Office (P.R.O.), AIR2/15261.

115. COS(59)72nd Confidential Annex, 24 Nov. 1959, London, Public Record Office (P.R.O.), DEFE4/122.

116. COS(56)33rd, 20 March 1956, London, Public Record Office (P.R.O.), DEFE4/85.

117. AC(56)85 'Reductions in the Ministry of Supply's Defence Research and Development Programme to £175 million in 1958/9' Note By DCAS, London, Public Record Office (P.R.O.), AIR19/855.

118. Air Council Conclusions 21(56) Annex A, London, Public Record Office (P.R.O.), AIR19/855.

119. VCAS Meeting, 20 April 1956, London, Public Record Office (P.R.O.), AIR8/1912.

120. AC 13(56)(Special), 15 June 1956, London, Public Record Office (P.R.O.), AIR8/2068.

121. ACSC (56)16 'Future Size and Shape of the RAF' Note by VCAS, London, Public Record Office (P.R.O.), AIR8/2068 and AC(56)85 'Reductions in the Ministry of Supply's Defence Research and Development Programme to £175 million in 1958/9' Note By DCAS, London, Public Record Office (P.R.O.), AIR19/855.

122. Air Staff General Operational Requirement No. GOR 339 Tactical Strike/Reconnaissance Aircraft, March 1957, London, Public Record Office (P.R.O.), AIR20/10732.

123. D.OR(A) to ACAS(OR), 26 Sept. 1957, London, Public Record Office (P.R.O.), AIR20/10732.

124. AC 18(57) Secret Annex 'B', 25 July 1957, London, Public Record Office (P.R.O.), AIR20/10732.

125. AC(57)60 'Tactical Strike/Reconnaissance Aircraft' Note by DCAS, 22 July 1957, London, Public Record Office (P.R.O.), AIR20/10732.

126. DOR(A) to Chief Staff Officer to CDS, 27 Oct. 1958, London, Public Record Office (P.R.O.), AIR2/14843.

127. AUS(A) to F.W. Mottershead (MoD), 30 Sept. 1958; DCAS to ACAS(OR), 29 Aug. 1958; ACAS(OR) to DCAS, 10 Sept. 1958; Minister of Defence to First Lord of the Admiralty, 10 Oct. 1958; DCAS to Secretary of State for Air, 17 Oct. 1958; Minister of Defence to Secretary of State for Air, 13 Nov. 1958, London, Public Record Office (P.R.O.), AIR2/14843.

128. DOR(A) to VCAS, 5 Aug. 1959, London, Public Record Office (P.R.O.), AIR2/14843 and 'An Assessment of Risk assuming a system to GOR 339 is not available until 1967/8' Draft Air Council Paper, undated, London, Public Record Office (P.R.O.), AIR2/10732.

129. AC 4(58) Top Secret Annex, 13 Feb. 1958, London, Public Record Office (P.R.O.), AIR6/111.

130. COS(57)30th Confidential Annex (2), 12 April 1957, London, Public Record Office (P.R.O.), DEFE4/96.

131. COS(57)73rd Confidential Annex, 24 Sept. 1957, London, Public Record Office (P.R.O.), DEFE4/100.

132. Sir Richard Powell to L. J. Sabatini, 6 Jan. 1959, London, Public Record Office (P.R.O.), DEFE7/991.

133. D(57)2nd, 27 Feb. 1957, London, Public Record Office (P.R.O.), CAB131/18.

134. D(58)47, 8 Sept. 1958, London, Public Record Office (P.R.O.), CAB131/20

135. 'Record of Meetings held at the Pentagon and State Department, Washington, DC September 22-25 1958', 14 Oct. 1958, London, Public Record Office (P.R.O.), DEFE13/180.

136. D(58)57, 3 Nov. 1958, London, Public Record Office (P.R.O.), CAB131/20

137. D(58)14th, 23 July 1958, London, Public Record Office (P.R.O.), CAB131/19.

138. D(58)24th, 5 Nov. 1958, London, Public Record Office (P.R.O.), CAB131/19.

139. D(58)69, 17 Nov. 1958, London, Public Record Office (P.R.O.), CAB131/20.

140. D(58)31st, 22 Dec. 1958, London, Public Record Office (P.R.O.), CAB131/19.

141. D(58)57, 3 Nov. 1958, London, Public Record Office (P.R.O.), CAB131/20.

142. CWP/P(58)11 'The Possibilities of Alternatives to Blue Streak', 7 May 1958, London, Public Record Office (P.R.O.), DEFE13/193.

143. COS(59)4th Confidential Annex, 13 Jan 1959, London, Public Record Office (P.R.O.), DEFE4/115.

144. Elliot, 'The Cancellation of the 'Blue Streak' Missile System and its Relevance to British Nuclear Thinking and Strategy, 1954-1960' pp. 126-127.

145. Ibid., p. 125.

146. Grove, *Vanguard to Trident*, p. 236.

147. Elliot, 'The Cancellation of the 'Blue Streak' Missile System and its Relevance to British Nuclear Thinking and Strategy, 1954-1960', pp. 93-99.

148. Horne, *Macmillan, 1957-1986*, p. 275 mistakenly makes this claim.

149. Sir Richard Powell to Minister of Defence, 16 Jan. 1957, London, Public Record Office (P.R.O.), DEFE13/237; COS(57)13th Confidential Annex, 18 Feb. 1957, London, Public Record Office (P.R.O.), DEFE32/5; 'Report of a Working Party on the Future Organisation of the Defence Services' Air Ministry, May 1957, London, Public Record Office (P.R.O.), AIR8/2156; COS(58)155 'Definitions Applied to War', 13 June 1958, London, Public Record Office (P.R.O.), DEFE5/84; Recent UK Defence Developments - A Review for Ambassador Whitney (Chiefs of Mission Meeting, Paris, May 1957), Washington, National Archives; Sir Richard Powell to Minister of Defence, 11 July 1957, London, Public Record Office (P.R.O.), DEFE13/237; Duncan Sandys to Prime Minister, 9 July 1958, London, Public Record Office (P.R.O.), PREM11/2639; COS(59)23rd, 2 April 1959, London, Public Record Office (P.R.O.), DEFE4/117; D(58)14th, 23 July 1958, London, Public Record Office (P.R.O.), CAB131/19; GEN659/1st 'The Position of the United Kingdom in World Affairs' Report by Officials, 7 July 1958, London, Public Record Office (P.R.O.), CAB130/153; D(58)24th, 5 Nov. 1958, London, Public Record Office (P.R.O.), CAB131/19.

150. D(57)7th, 2nd Aug. 1957, London, Public Record Office (P.R.O.), CAB131/18.

151. COS(57)73rd, 24 Sept. 1957, London, Public Record Office (P.R.O.), DEFE4/100.

152. COS(58)77th, 3 Sept. 1958, London, Public Record Office (P.R.O.), DEFE4/111.

153. COS(57)8th, 29 January 1957, London, Public Record Office (P.R.O.), DEFE4/94.

154. Darby, *British Defence Policy East of Suez*, p. 150.

155. CAS to Minister of Defence, 26 June 1957, London, Public Record Office (P.R.O.), AIR8/2152.

156. ACAS(P)/AUS(A) to CAS and Secretary of State for Air, 13 Nov. 1957, London, Public Record Office (P.R.O.), AIR8/2154.

157. C-in-C FEAF to VCAS, 6 Dec. 1957, London, Public Record Office (P.R.O.), AIR20/10113.

158. ACAS(P) to VCAS, 18 Sept. 1957, London, Public Record Office (P.R.O.), AIR8/2180.

159. JP(57)168(Final), 24 Dec. 1957, London, Public Record Office (P.R.O.), DEFE4/102.

160. Interview with T.C.G. James. James was a senior official based in Singapore during the Indonesian Confrontation.

161. COS(57)70th Confidential Annex, 10 Sept. 1957, London, Public Record Office (P.R.O.), DEFE4/100.

162. D(58)3rd, 20 Feb. 1958, London, Public Record Office (P.R.O.), CAB131/19.

163. C-in-C FEAF to VCAS, 6 Dec. 1957, London, Public Record Office (P.R.O.), AIR20/10113.

164. ACAS(P)/AUS(A) to CAS and Secretary of State for Air, 13 Nov. 1957, London, Public Record Office (P.R.O.), AIR8/2154.

165. COS(59)78, 9 April 1959, London, Public Record Office (P.R.O.), DEFE5/90.

166. COS(59)78, 9 April 1959, London, Public Record Office (P.R.O.), DEFE5/90.

167. ACAS(P) to CAS, 4 March 1958, London, Public Record Office (P.R.O.), AIR8/2180.

168. Benwell to Lawrence-Wilson, 14 April 1959, London, Public Record Office (P.R.O.), DEFE7/1642.

169. JP(59)17(Final), 9 Feb. 1959, London, Public Record Office (P.R.O.), DEFE4/116.

170. Interview with T. C. G. James.

171. Brown, 'The Origins and Development of the British Strategic Nuclear Deterrent Forces, 1945-1960', p. 54.

172. COS(57)95th Confidential Annex, 11 Dec. 1957, London, Public Record Office (P.R.O.), DEFE4/102.

173. Lee, *Wings in the Sun*, p. 176.

174. JP(59)107(Final), 19 August 1959, London, Public Record Office (P.R.O.), DEFE4/120.

175. ACAS(P) to CAS, 1 Jan. 1957, London, Public Record Office (P.R.O.), AIR8/2183.

176. JP(58) Note 28, 28 August 1958, London, Public Record Office (P.R.O.), DEFE4/111.

177. JP(59)107(Final), 19 August 1959, London, Public Record Office (P.R.O.), DEFE4/120.

178. Ibid.

179. 'Intolerable Acts' Paper for Meeting with Minister of Defence, 26 July 1957, London, Public Record Office (P.R.O.), AIR8/2164.

180. D(59)10th, 18 Sept. 1959, London, Public Record Office (P.R.O.), CAB131/21.

181. COS(59)65th, 20 Oct. 1959, London, Public Record Office (P.R.O.), DEFE4/121.

182. D(59)46, 24 Dec. 1959, London, Public Record Office (P.R.O.), CAB131/122.

183. Lamb, *The Failure of the Eden Government*, p. 176; Darby, *British Defence Policy East of Suez*, pp. 153-4; Carver, *Out of Step*, p. 289; Lee, *Eastward*, pp. 184-5; Healey, *The Time of My Life*, p. 287; Summary Briefing Paper - General Background, Bermuda Conference, March 1957, Washington, Library of Congress, Declassified Documents 1986, No. 000728; Recent UK Defence Developments - A Review for Ambassador Whitney (Chiefs of Mission Meeting, Paris, May 1957), Washington, National Archives; ZP15/7/G Minutes of the 15th Meeting of the Steering Committee held on May 8th, 1959, London, Public Record Office (P.R.O.), FO371/143694; JP(59) Note 38, 14 Dec. 1959, London, Public Record Office (P.R.O.), DEFE4/123; JP(59)79(Final), 9 July 1959, London, Public Record Office (P.R.O.), DEFE4/120; COS(57)8th, 29 Jan. 1957, London, Public Record Office (P.R.O.), DEFE4/94; VCAS to CAS, 22 Dec. 1958, London, Public Record Office (P.R.O.), AIR8/2183; DASB to CAS, 9 Dec. 1958, London, Public Record Office (P.R.O.), AIR8/2183.

184. Zuckerman, *Monkeys, Men and Missiles*, pp. 270-304.

185. Lee, *Wings in the Sun*, pp. 177-8.

186. Carver, *Tightrope Walking*, pp. 106-7.

187. Sir William Dickson to Sir John Slessor, 12 August 1957, Cambridge, Churchill College Archives Centre, Dickson Papers, DCKN5/2.

188. ACAS(P) to CAS, 16 Feb. 1956, London, Public Record Office (P.R.O.), AIR8/2045.

189. D.of Plans to CAS, 2 May 1956, London, Public Record Office (P.R.O.), AIR8/2045.

190. James, 'The Impact of the Sandys Defence Policy on the RAF', pp. 13-14.

191. *FRUS, 1955-1957*, IV, pp. 84-88.

192. Ibid., pp. 89-90.

193. Ibid., pp. 90-92.

194. Ibid.

195. Ibid., pp. 93-95.

196. AUS(A) to Secretary of State for Air, CAS and PUS, 21 Nov. 1956, London, Public Record Office (P.R.O.), AIR8/2065.

197. ACAS(P) to CAS, 3 July 1956, London, Public Record Office (P.R.O.), AIR8/2064.

198. Sir Frederick Brundrett to Minister of Defence, 17 July 1956, London, Public Record Office (P.R.O.), DEFE13/216.

199. COS(56)66th Confidential Annex, 6 July 1956, London, Public Record Office (P.R.O.), DEFE32/5.

200. COS(56)259, 5 July 1956, London, Public Record Office (P.R.O.), DEFE32/5.

201. Minister of Defence to Chairman, COS Committee, 3 Sept. 1956, London, Public Record Office (P.R.O.), AIR8/2065.

202. ACAS(P) to CAS, 5 Sept. 1956, London, Public Record Office (P.R.O.), AIR8/2065.

203. COS1231/4/9/56 'Draft Revised Directive to SACEUR', 4 Sept. 1956, London, Public Record Office (P.R.O.), AIR8/2065.

204. *FRUS, 1955-1957*, IV, pp. 98-99.

205. Ibid., pp. 100-102.

206. JP(56)162(Final) Annex, 26 Nov. 1956, London, Public Record Office (P.R.O.), DEFE4/92.

207. Ibid.

208. COS(56)124th, 26 Nov. 1956, London, Public Record Office (P.R.O.), DEFE4/92.

209. *FRUS, 1955-1957*, IV, pp. 123-133.

210. Note of Minister of Defence's Talk with SACEUR, 12 Dec. 1956, London, Public Record Office (P.R.O.), DEFE7/1162.

211. MISC/M(56)195 Ministry of Defence Meeting, undated [December 1956], London, Public Record Office (P.R.O.), AIR8/2046.

212. COS(56)133rd, 18 Dec. 1956, London, Public Record Office (P.R.O.), DEFE4/93.

213. Policy Review - Note by Air Ministry in reply to Minister of Defence's Directive of 21 December 1956, 10 Jan. 1957, London, Public Record Office (P.R.O.), AIR8/2046.

214. AUS(A) to Secretary of State for Air, CAS and PUS, 21 Nov. 1956, London, Public Record Office (P.R.O.), AIR8/2065.

215. Chancellor of the Exchequer to Minister of Defence, 24 Nov. 1956, London, Public Record Office (P.R.O.), AIR8/2046.

216. Directive to the NATO Military Authorities from the North Atlantic Council, Cambridge, Churchill College Archives Centre, Dickson Papers, DCKN5/2.

217. Sir Richard Powell to Minister of Defence, 16 Jan. 1957, London, Public Record Office (P.R.O.), DEFE13/237.

218. D(57)6th, 31 July 1957, London, Public Record Office (P.R.O.), CAB131/18.

219. Note by Minister of Defence, 22 Feb. 1957, London, Public Record Office (P.R.O.), AIR19/856.

220. Ibid.

221. Park, *Defending the West*, p. 49.

222. Heuser and O'Neill (eds.), *Securing the Peace in Europe, 1945-1962*, pp. 142-44, Kaiser and Roper (eds.), *British-German Defence Co-operation*, pp. 1-40 and Heller and Gillingham (eds.), *NATO*, pp. 311-331.

223. Gladwyn Jebb to Selwyn Lloyd, 1 March 1957, London, Public Record Office (P.R.O.), DEFE13/237.

224. 'Great Britain: Budget; Military Program; NATO; Western Military Posture; Germany; Bermuda Conference, 3/21-24/57; SACEUR', 10 April 1957, Washington, National Archives.

225. 'Memorandum of Conversation at British Embassy' by John Foster Dulles, 23 Oct. 1957, Abilene, Eisenhower Library, Ann Whitman-Dulles/Herter Papers, Box 7 October 57(1).

226. 'British Forces in Germany and the Support Costs Problem' C. Burke Elbrick to Secretary of State, Washington, National Archives.

227. Melissen, *The Search For Nuclear Co-operation*, pp. 93-115 argues that the American government handled the nuclearisation of NATO clumsily and alienated western European governments by its paternalistic attitude to the sharing of nuclear technology.

228. John Foster Dulles to President, 23 Oct. 1957, Abilene, Eisenhower Library, Ann Whitman-Dulles/Herter Papers, Box 7 October 57(1).

229. Desp. No.2858 American Embassy, London to Department of State, 13 May 1957, Washington, National Archives. The French government had, effectively, already decided to build nuclear weapons in 1954. In November 1957 it proposed that France, West Germany and Italy should jointly develop their own nuclear weapons. On 11 April 1958, during the dying days of the Fourth Republic, Felix Gaillard approved the first French atomic test. See Soutou, 'The French Military Program for Nuclear Energy, 1945-1981' and Barbier, 'The French decision to develop a military nuclear programme in the 1950s', pp. 103-113.

230. Melissen, *The Struggle For Nuclear Partnership*, p. 109.

231. Note of Conversation between Sir Richard Powell and SACEUR on 2nd May 1957, 6 May 1957, London, Public Record Office (P.R.O.), DEFE13/237.

232. John Foster Dulles Telephone Call to Secretary Wilson, 4 March 1957, Abilene, Eisenhower Library, John Foster Dulles Papers.

233. Note of Conversation between Sir Richard Powell and SACEUR on 2nd May 1957, 6 May 1957, London, Public Record Office (P.R.O.), DEFE13/237.

234. COS(57)11th, 8 Feb. 1957, London, Public Record Office (P.R.O.), DEFE4/94.

235. Park, *Defending the West*, p. 47.

236. COS(59)337, 24 Dec. 1959, London, Public Record Office (P.R.O.), DEFE5/98.

237. JP(57)129(Final), 6 Nov. 1957, London, Public Record Office (P.R.O.), DEFE4/101.

238. Department of State Tel.No.2972 American Embassy, London to Department of State, 9 Nov. 1957, Washington, National Archives.

239. JP(57)129(Final), 6 Nov. 1957, London, Public Record Office (P.R.O.), DEFE4/101.

240. COS(58)86th Confidential Annex, 7 Oct. 1958, London, Public Record Office (P.R.O.), DEFE4/112.

241. JP(57)129(Final), 6 Nov. 1957, London, Public Record Office (P.R.O.), DEFE4/101.

242. COS(57)11th, 8 Feb. 1957, London, Public Record Office (P.R.O.), DEFE4/94.

243. The December 1957 meeting was the first formal heads of government summit since the formation of the alliance. It considered three main issues: the creation of a NATO nuclear stockpile, the deployment of American IRBMs in Europe and the supply of nuclear information to the European allies. The United States was the main target for European criticism but Britain's insistence on its bilateral nuclear relationship with the United States and the independence of its own nuclear forces also increased tension. See Melissen, *The Search For Nuclear Co-operation*, pp. 93-115.

244. Schwartz, *NATO's Nuclear Dilemmas*, p. 35.

245. COS(57)97th, 20 Dec. 1957, London, Public Record Office (P.R.O.), DEFE4/102.

246. Carver, *Out of Step*, p. 298.

247. Park, *Defending the West*, p. 47 and Clark and Wheeler, *British Origins of Nuclear Strategy*, pp. 194-5.

248. Schwartz, *NATO's Nuclear Dilemmas*, p. 59.

249. COS(57)96th, 13 Dec. 1957, London, Public Record Office (P.R.O.), DEFE4/102.

250. COS(57)97th, 20 Dec. 1957, London, Public Record Office (P.R.O.), DEFE4/102.

251. COS(57)11th, 8 Feb. 1957, London, Public Record Office (P.R.O.), DEFE4/94.

252. 'British Aspects of Military Strategy' Lecture by MRAF Sir William Dickson to NATO Defence College, 3 Oct. 1958, Cambridge, Churchill College Archives Centre, Dickson Papers, DCKN5/10.

253. 'The UK Military Situation' Lecture by MRAF Sir William Dickson to NATO Defence College, 17 June 1959, Cambridge, Churchill College Archives Centre, Dickson Papers, DCKN5/10.

Conclusion

Retrospect and Prospect

In 1960 Britain possessed a substantial land-based nuclear air force. The backbone of the force was the V-bomber. It was intended that the V-force should be maintained at a front-line strength of 144 operational aircraft. The first V-bomber to enter service was the Vickers Valiant in 1955. 104 of these aircraft, including a strategic reconnaissance version, were produced and deliveries to the RAF were completed in 1957. The Avro Vulcan B.1 became operational in 1957 and a total of 45 were delivered between July 1957 and April 1959. The Handley-Page Victor entered squadron service in 1958 and 49 were delivered. In 1960 the Vulcan B.2 entered service and 89 had been delivered by 1964. The Victor B.2 first flew in 1959 and 34 were ordered in 1960. Deliveries were complete by 1963. These aircraft were equipped with free-fall atomic and thermonuclear weapons. The Blue Steel Mark 1 powered guided bomb did not enter service until 1963. 100 hydrogen bombs were on order for the RAF but it seems unlikely that they were all manufactured and brought into service until sometime in the 1960s. Some of the V-bombers were equipped to carry American nuclear weapons and the RAF had some access to United States stockpiles of thermonuclear and atomic weapons. The RAF was also operating 60 Thor intermediate range ballistic missiles under a dual-key system with the USAF.

The Blue Steel Mark 2 air-launched guided missile and the Blue Streak ballistic missile had been cancelled and the next development of the nuclear force was to be B.2 aircraft equipped with the American Skybolt missile carrying a British warhead. This force was to be supplemented by the TSR2 which was being designed to have the capability of directly attacking the Soviet Union. In the longer term, sometime after 1970, the options were believed to be a new bomber carrying Skybolt or the American Polaris ballistic missile launched from a submarine.

The V-force was supplemented by four squadrons of Canberra light bombers based in Germany. The first of 80 B.(I)8 variants became operational in 1956. All these aircraft were nuclear-capable. Some had been modified to carry American atomic weapons and the British 'Red Beard' atomic bomb was available from about 1958.

A further four squadrons of Canberra B.15s and B.16s were to be deployed in Cyprus. The B.15 first flew in 1960. British nuclear weapons became available in Cyprus in late 1961 and these aircraft were also capable of carrying American nuclear weapons.

The nuclear force had a wide range of roles. The V-bombers could carry out one of two primary missions. The force could attack 30 cities in the Soviet Union with hydrogen bombs or aid in the suppression of the Soviet air defence system as part of a joint Anglo-American offensive. If the need to carry out one of the primary missions was not imminent the V-force was capable of tackling a number of secondary missions. Three squadrons of V-bombers, armed with atomic bombs, were available for deployment to the Far East to resist a Chinese invasion of Malaya. The RAF also planned to disperse part of the force to the Middle East during periods of international tension. In January 1960 three squadrons of Valiants were assigned to SACEUR for missions against a Soviet invasion of Western Europe.

Canberra squadrons in Germany were also assigned to SACEUR as an atomic strike-force for use against a Soviet invasion. The Canberra squadrons in Cyprus were technically assigned to CENTO but were completely under RAF control. Their role was to launch an atomic offensive against Soviet forces invading the Middle East as part of a global war. With the exception of the V-bombers earmarked for the Far East all of these forces were intended to deter the Soviet Union from launching a large-scale nuclear or conventional offensive against Britain and Western Europe. The V-bombers would be sent to the Far East to deter China from directly attacking countries with whom Britain had defence agreements. Their use in this role would be considered even if the Soviet Union was not party to the aggression.

It seemed that Britain would continue to possess a substantial land-based nuclear air force. In 1960 Sir Thomas Pike, the newly-appointed Chief of the Air Staff, was confident that the future of the British nuclear force lay in the hands of the RAF. Sir Thomas predicted that since the choice of new weapons and delivery systems 'will rightly be decided on value for money' the nuclear force would, in the future, be smaller and cheaper. 'I think', Sir Thomas said in an address to the RAF's senior commanders, 'we shall get another airborne vehicle ... it would carry an airborne ballistic missile or missiles for the deterrent role, it could act as an air transport in more settled periods [and] it would also be capable of dropping conventional bombs if required in limited or cold war.' According to Pike such an aircraft 'would not necessarily have to fly terribly fast or high and it would not have to penetrate enemy defences in the global war role, indeed, it would only have to fly high enough and fast enough to give its ballistic missile a reasonable start.' Despite his confidence in the future of the airborne British nuclear force Sir Thomas saw a number of threats to its existence. The RAF would need to engage, as it had done in the 1950s, in constant bureaucratic struggle to beat them off. Pike was reasonably sanguine about the possibility that Britain's next strategic weapon would be a submarine-launched ballistic missile. 'The Polaris submarine', he predicted with satisfaction, 'will play itself out court on the great expense of developing both submarine and missile and the fact that it will only really be a deterrent weapon and even as a deterrent weapon it will have a limited usefulness because of the inability to recall the missile once it has been launched.'[1]

The Chief of the Air Staff sensed the ground swell of opinion against the concept of the British independent nuclear deterrent which Harold Wilson later memorably encapsulated in the jibe 'so-called independent, so-called British, so-called deterrent'.[2] Pike was concerned that 'not many people understand the full implications and pervasive effectiveness of [nuclear deterrence] ... certainly much of the press and many politicians of this country do not understand it'. More immediately, however, the RAF needed to mobilise its resources against 'a great deal of lobby in Whitehall ... that our deterrent should be combined with SAC, or be part of a NATO deterrent now that France has exploded her first device'. Sir Thomas's ringing endorsement of independence summed up a decade of thinking about its purpose, indeed it was essentially a restatement of the formula that John Slessor had committed to paper in 1952. 'The chance of our using our deterrent in any situation where we are not acting in concert with the United States is extremely remote', Pike conceded,

> but I feel that the ability to do so in extreme circumstances is the only factor which will continue to give us "big power" status in the world in our own right. It is the only factor which will make proper sense and use of the policy of interdependence with the United States i.e. the alliance of two equal partners. Our traditional position as a major power and the existence of our worldwide trading and economic interests will doubtless preserve for us the facade of influence during periods of relative international calm but if we do not possess an independent voice as a nuclear power then it would be unrealistic to suppose that in a major crisis we should be respected for anything other than our good intentions.[3]

Sir Thomas was a misguided prophet. The concept of deterrence proved remarkably durable, the existence and renewal of an independent British deterrent continued to enjoy support from key political figures in government, the correlation between nuclear weapons and great power status endured even after the withdrawal from 'East of Suez'. Pike's faith in fiscal stringency proved to be double edged. The defence budget was rigorously searched for savings but the nuclear force continued to be given priority, as the RAF had argued it should throughout the 1950s. Most significantly, of course, few could have predicted the political tergiversations which led to the Polaris deal at Nassau in 1962. Although it is true that the RAF played its part in blinding the British government to the dangers of attempting to procure Skybolt this book has attempted to explain how projections, such as those of Slessor, Pike and other RAF participants in the nuclear debate, seemed justified when they were made.

In analysing the interaction of the RAF with the rest of the defence establishment we have been concerned with two central questions. First, how far was the construction of the British nuclear force based on strategic thinking? Second, what influence did the construction of the force and the strategic debates surrounding it have on overall defence and national security policy? National security policy-making has been analysed both in terms of the individual views of senior ministers and civil servants and the interaction of defined bureaucracies, such as the service ministries, whose senior members gave defence policy their full-time attention. Each group can be seen as trying to construct armed forces in response to what it genuinely saw as external threats or it can be seen as attempting to acquire money, power and status for the organisation, or trying to gain political advantage in the case of the politicians, through a process of conflict and bargaining within the defence establishment. In the formulation of a policy for nuclear weapons the attempt to frame a coherent national strategy and the advancement of group interests interacted. The course of strategic policy-making is, therefore, unintelligible without reference to both.

The influence of particular personalities was enhanced in the aftermath of crises such as the Korean War or Suez. Such personalities could be serving officers, civil servants or ministers. In general it could be said that the Chiefs of Staff and the service staffs and ministries were very powerful between 1945 and 1952. This power was eroded between 1953 and 1956 and significantly undermined by the conduct of Duncan Sandys between 1957 and 1959. Following the initial shock of the preparation of the 1957 Defence White Paper, however, there is some evidence that the services partially recovered their control over defence policy. Power, however, was not the same as influence. Even at the nadir of service power in 1957 strategic prescriptions which had been developed by the Air Ministry in the early and mid-1950s were highly influential in the development of British nuclear forces.

Strategy, in the context of defence policy-making, can be seen as 'real' or 'advocacy'. Service planners, chiefs of staff and ministers put forward strategic arguments in which they genuinely believed and also strategic arguments which they knew to be spurious but nevertheless believed would be influential. There was, however, rarely a clear division between the two. Quite often a series of genuine and spurious arguments were combined. Even more commonly an advocate would use strategic arguments about which he had doubts in favour of a policy which had genuine strategic underpinnings. It is thus very difficult to disentangle strategic argumentation. The only way of doing so is to look at its 'producers'; in the case of this book the RAF and the Air Ministry. Even when a detailed analysis of intra- as well as inter-departmental records has been carried out many areas of uncertainty remain. Some issues can be resolved by reference to oral testimony or private papers but others remain opaque.

This kind of approach to strategy is needed if its importance for overall policy is to be properly assessed. Ideas which were of relative unimportance but were extensively stated or were a gloss on a policy decided for quite other reasons can be overstressed. Since an analysis of British defence policy does not yield a simple model of either 'bureaucratic politics' or 'rational policy-making' there is no substitute for this attention to detail.

Although it sometimes seemed that defence policy was driven, except in 1950-51, by a search for economy strategic debate remained vital throughout the period. Prime Ministers and Chancellors from Attlee and Dalton to Macmillan and Heathcoat Amory believed that defence was taking too great a proportion of national wealth and sought reductions. Yet important decision-makers had a genuine interest in national security. Ministers, civil servants and officers all wanted to act 'strategically'. If a strategic proposition was widely accepted it became difficult to dislodge. This was the case with the four propositions about nuclear weapons expounded by the RAF. The service proposed that nuclear weapons could deter all forms of war, that nuclear weapons were at the core of a stable alliance with the United States, that the possession of nuclear weapons was inextricably linked with great power status and that nuclear weapons could substitute for conventional forces.

In the period under review strategic debate was tied very closely to weapon procurement. The links between the two can be seen most clearly in the initial phases of strategic thinking about a new weapon. Nuclear weapons were a startling new element in defence planning in 1945 and were seen as such. Nevertheless, the response to the atomic bomb took place on the basis of plans already made for conventional weaponry. The RAF's formal commitment to an advanced bomber force predated the dropping of the A-bomb by at least two years. Numerous roles had been discussed for this force. In the forefront of planners' minds was the need to take part in a bomber offensive against Japan. Churchill had explicitly stated the need to compete with the United States in the prestige of advanced weaponry. Nevertheless, it had been decided in 1944 that, due to the demands of wartime production, Britain would need to jump a generation in bomber development and use American aircraft in the interim. As early as 1943 there had been mention of the need of a long-range bomber for possible use against the Soviet Union.[4] Military planners had pushed an initially reluctant Foreign Office to recognise that Russia was a likely post-war enemy. Yet the constant references to the 'big stick' behind diplomacy and a 'worldwide deterrent' and 'war-fighting tool' leads to the suspicion that a bomber force would have emerged whatever the threat assessment. As the Vice-Chief of the Air Staff commented in 1944 'an obviously strong offensive potential is a sound practical deterrent against aggression even though admittedly some countries [i.e. the Soviet Union] are less vulnerable to air attack than others.'[5]

Nevertheless, the nuclear deterrence of the Soviet Union was a significant strategic concept which emerged rapidly in the late autumn of 1945. Deterrence was a simple and appealing concept which it was hard to gainsay. Attlee had private doubts that deterrence could be anything other than a 'strategy of despair' but did not challenge the views of his military advisers on this issue. Part of the explanation for this seeming consensus was that no-one could offer any coherent alternative. The experience of the V-1 and V-2 attacks in 1944 and 1945 had conclusively shown that Britain could not be satisfactorily defended.

The influence exerted by the concept of deterrence between 1945 and 1947 should not, however, be overstated. In 1945 the Air Staff argued against planning for a short war and advocated the construction of a large fighter force as well as a nuclear bomber force. A deterrent force became its clear first priority only in 1947 largely because it proved impossible to argue for an advanced air force on the basis of immediate defence needs. The whole concept of air defence was challenged in the late 1940s and early 1950s, most notably, in the light of later developments, by the shadow Air Minister Harold Macmillan, on the grounds that such defence was pointless in an era of atomic weapons and ballistic missiles.[6] Yet the Air Staff still adhered to the position that air defence was a vital element in the prevention of nuclear blackmail. Although the Air Staff acknowledged, in 1952, that the defence of population centres was impossible, it continued to support Fighter Command as second in priority only to Bomber Command. In 1956 the Air Ministry was still arguing that Britain should maintain a significant air defence system in order to ensure that the Soviet Union could only contemplate a massive nuclear assault, to assure a second-strike capability, and to reassure the British populace that they were not defenceless. The air defence of Great Britain thus showed remarkable tenacity for a concept supposedly discredited in 1945.

It is also notable that in 1945 the Air Ministry displayed no doubts that Britain would possess the atomic bomb. Its main fear was that the RAF would be reduced to a transport and army support force by the emergence of nuclear weapons. In 1945 only a few dissenters such as distinguished wartime government scientist Patrick Blackett opposed a British bomb. Thus the decision taken by the Air Ministry in 1947 to steer the defence debate towards the need for forces nine to twelve years in the future played no part in the decision to build a nuclear force. It was of importance, however, in formally establishing deterrence rather than war-fighting as the most important yardstick for defence policy decisions. According to the Sir Frank Cooper, the former Air Ministry civil servant who later became Permanent Secretary of the Ministry of Defence, 'the crucial issue was argued by Lord Tedder who said "We have got to have a bomber strike force, and we have to have that established in the policy of the Chiefs of Staff" and ... if you look at the document produced in 1947 on future defence policy, they referred then to the supreme object of British defence being to prevent war provided that could be done without prejudice to our vital interests ... it was a major platform in the sense that the two priority tasks on a long list of tasks were, first, research and development and, secondly, the ability to strike through and provide a strong deterrent through development of air offensive forces which had got to be given high priority.'[7] Although this measure was increasingly influential, as the development of air defence shows, it took several years to be fully accepted even within the RAF.

A much greater emphasis on deterrence was achieved under the leadership of Sir John Slessor in 1951-2. In 1949 Slessor and his predecessor as Chief of the Air Staff had agreed that a nation without a nuclear force would not be a great power and both firmly upheld the view that Britain was, and should remain, a great power with global military responsibilities. Although Slessor believed that a force of 150 nuclear armed bombers would be sufficient for this purpose he was concerned that the force should have a coherent military justification; something which he believed that the Air Staff had failed to provide between 1947 and 1949.

An awareness of Britain's vulnerability to atomic attack was present in nuclear planning from 1945 onwards. Anxiety was sharpened by the appearance of the Soviet A-bomb in 1949. Consideration was therefore given to some form of counter-military targeting. Yet in 1949 the Air Staff had not adopted such a policy. Counterforce targeting, adopted in mid-1950, was a bureaucratic response to the need for a military justification for the existence of a large British bomber force in the context of a hoped for Anglo-American alliance. The proposed 240-strong medium bomber force which emerged from the discussions of the 1952 Global Strategy

Paper was calculated on the basis of an attack on forty Soviet nuclear bomber bases with six British aircraft assigned to each attack. Yet in 1949 the Air Staff had argued that 320 bombers were needed and the Air Staff's submissions for the Global Strategy Paper proposed a force of 304. It would seem that the figure of 240 was calculated more on what the Air Staff believed it could get the government to accept than on any strict military criteria. Counterforce targeting was only influential in an era when Britain had no significant nuclear capability.

Throughout this period the relationship with the United States was at the centre of British nuclear strategy. This relationship operated at two different levels in the 1940s and 1950s. First, there was the actual bilateral relationship between the two powers. Second, there was the relationship as the British desired it to be. Any detailed study of British nuclear strategy shows that the two were often elided in policy-making. USAF/RAF nuclear relations are a good measure of both levels since these two organisations provided the closest institutional links between the two defence establishments in the nuclear field. Not only were there personal contacts between senior commanders forged during World War Two but both services saw themselves as having similar interests in domestic defence debates.

USAAF involvement in Western Europe and the Middle East was actively encouraged by the wartime Chief of the Air Staff, Sir Charles Portal. Some senior USAAF officers, most notably General Carl Spaatz, were in favour of such involvement. The RAF was, however, a strong supporter of co-operation rather than of any division of labour which implied that Britain would not develop an advanced bomber force. This policy of co-operative independence continued into the nuclear age. One of the chief determinants of the course of British strategic thinking was the fear that such a division of labour, entailing British subordination, would be adopted. On the American side pressure was exerted for this to happen. In the 1940s the American government denied the British the co-operation on atomic weapon development to which they believed themselves to be entitled under the wartime Hyde Park and Quebec agreements. In addition the Americans exerted pressure on the United Kingdom not to develop its own nuclear weapons. In the late 1940s and 1950s senior American officers, especially General Curtis LeMay Strategic Air Command's commanding general and later chief of staff of the USAF, made clear that they did not regard the British bomber force as militarily important, and devoted all their attention to building up SAC. The British government chose to disregard these American pressures. Nevertheless, senior figures in the British government including the ministers Sir Stafford Cripps in the late 1940s, Reginald Maudling in 1955 and Derick Heathcoat Amory in 1958, the senior government defence scientist Sir Henry Tizard during the Attlee governments and the CIGS in the late 1950s, Sir Gerald Templer, did suggest that Britain did not need a militarily significant strategic nuclear force.

From 1945 to 1955 any strategy of nuclear deterrence was, in fact, entirely dependent on the United States. At a bilateral level this dependence was remarkably tenuous. In 1946 the RAF and the USAF had agreed that there should be American air bases in Britain. The following year the two governments recognised that Britain would help the United States gain further air bases in territory under British control. In 1948 American bombers arrived in the United Kingdom on a long-term basis. In 1950 it was agreed that Britain could terminate base rights when it chose but that the British government would have no control over the American military. Even when Churchill returned to power in 1951 the British were denied access to and even information about American nuclear planning. It was not until 1958 that the British received authoritative information and guarantees on American nuclear targeting.

British strategy for American nuclear weapons relied almost entirely on a judgement of how the Americans would act in times of crisis. Between 1945 and 1948 the Air Ministry stressed the reliability of the Americans. From 1948 onwards, by contrast, the emphasis was laid on their potential unreliability. This served to increase the importance of the British nuclear force as a fully independent and coercive instrument. Yet at the same time a countervailing process was at work. The scale of financial and technological aid directed towards the RAF habituated the British to dependence and subverted the ideal of independence. This process was symbolised by the 1954 Wilson/Alexander agreement by which the British government undertook to plan a specific role for the V-bombers in return for a dollar subsidy. There were few identifiable pro- and anti-Americans in policy-making terms. Instead it is not unusual to find the same people advocating both independence and 'interdependence'.

Between 1955 and 1960 bilateral nuclear relations became much closer. The Americans agreed to divulge targeting information, to plan joint targeting, to supply Britain with nuclear weapons in the event of war, to supply Britain with atomic and thermonuclear weapons in peacetime and offered the chance of acquiring an advanced nuclear weapon delivery system complete with warhead design. The uncertainties these developments introduced into British strategy were demonstrated by the deployment of Thor. This was supported by the Air Ministry before Suez and opposed after it. In turn this led the ministry to attempt the impossible task of backing both a British and an American air-launched guided missile between 1957 and 1960; at a time when pressure to cut both the money and the proportion of scientific resources taken up by the military research and development budget was at its height. Whereas strategy was important in building a broad politico-military coalition of support for the V-bomber it was much less important in determining what its successor system was to be. This debate was shaped by preferred service roles and the eventual decision was taken in 1960 on the basis of the system which would be available at the lowest cost.

The Anglo-American nuclear relationship, both actual and perceived, was undoubtedly the central factor in procurement decisions. Yet probably the most important consequence of strategic debate about nuclear weapons between 1945 and 1960 was the influence such debate had on the balance struck between concentrating British military power in Europe and dispersing it in the Middle and Far East.

At root the debate about the relative importance of various regions to British national security had little to do with nuclear weapons but they rapidly became an important part in the case the Chiefs of Staff made against becoming too involved in European defence. In 1945 the British defence establishment was firmly committed to disentangling the armed forces from the continent as quickly as possible and redeploying them to the Far and Middle East; a policy consistent with their pre-atomic wartime post-war planning. This policy was not initially based on perceptions of the Russian threat but on assumptions about the need for Britain to remain a colonial power. British military planners were aware of the political dimension of strategy but from 1945 to 1949 they argued vehemently against a major military commitment to the continent even as the government was constructing military alliances, the Western Union and NATO, which were meant to oppose Soviet ambitions in Europe. Two arguments were central to the Chiefs of Staff case in all these debates. First, that there was little risk of a Soviet attack on Western Europe because of American possession of nuclear weapons. Second, that it would be impossible to construct conventional forces capable of opposing the Red Army. The shock of the Soviet A-bomb and the rapid reconsideration of policy thereafter would suggest that this assessment of America's deterrent power was genuine, although it fitted in well with existing preferences.

The willingness to consider sending forces to Europe in early 1950 was based entirely on the political judgement that to do so might encourage America in the same direction. Although some officers believed that a conventional defence for Europe was conceivable there was no support for such a concept at the level of the Chiefs of Staff. A massive expansion of conventional forces was set in motion after the outbreak of the Korean War but this was seen as a political signal to guard against neutralism and defeatism in Europe and to deter Soviet adventurism. Subsequently the thought of using nuclear weapons in Europe entered military planning. Yet the whole tenor of Air Ministry planning was to concentrate on the medium bomber force. Tactical nuclear weapons were seen as little more than a technically feasible adjunct to this force which would allow more forces to be freed for use elsewhere in the world.

Forces in Europe were only regarded as politically useful. Their reduction was constrained by the desire to see some form of German integration into the West. Once this goal was achieved the economic costs of maintaining British forces in Europe began to seem more pressing than the political benefits of their presence. The Air Ministry believed that British political commitment could be signalled solely by means of a nuclear force. Between 1956 and 1960 the Air Ministry argued for a pure 'massive retaliation' strategy with a 'trip-wire' force in Europe. Although a Canberra nuclear force was built up there was no serious thought given to nuclear war-fighting in Europe. Air Ministry policy was adopted by the British government as declaratory policy in 1956. Compromises were made on political grounds not because the strategy was, arguably, inflexible and dangerous. Doubts about the policy did, however, exist outside the RAF and became important to the defence debate in the 1960s.

From 1952 until the 1960s the idea that nuclear weapons would allow Britain to reduce military commitments in Europe rather than the Middle East and South-East Asia was an important factor in military planning. Over the same period the RAF propounded the idea that conventional forces worldwide could be replaced by nuclear forces operating from secure and affordable bases. Such ideas had an important, if short-lived, influence on the reconsideration of national strategy in the late 1950s. Once more, however, it would seem that such thinking was, largely, an ex post facto justification for changes which had taken place for other reasons. The switch in emphasis in military planning from the Middle East to Europe in 1950 had little to do with nuclear weapons but subsequently such weapons did make an organisation such as the Baghdad Pact look like a useful military alliance in British eyes. It would seem that from 1955 onwards the British military establishment was convinced that nuclear weapons could be used for war-fighting overseas. At the very least it believed that the prestige accruing from the deployment of such weapons went some way to compensate for a decline in conventional force numbers. Into the 1960s the RAF was a determined opponent of any major reassessment of British national strategy. The influence of its thinking about nuclear weapons, carried out over a decade and a half, played a large part in validating such a stance.

Although nuclear weapons were seen from the outset as a revolutionary element in military strategy, discussions about their usefulness and use rapidly became normalised in the defence establishment. Nuclear strategy was not seen as a subject apart needing expert analysis. The defence establishment did, however, attempt to grapple with the problems of the nuclear age. At the same time it was faced with a relative decline in British military and economic power and status. The two issues were intertwined from the outset. Nuclear deterrence in Britain may well have been born out of an awareness of the acute vulnerability of a small, densely populated island a short distance from the coast of Europe rather than fear of imperial weakness. Yet by the time the concept of deterrence entered the mainstream of defence policy debate in 1947 it was clear that Britain could not afford nuclear weapons and the large conventional forces to support its overseas commitments. Many of the elaborations of nuclear strategy which took place after 1947 can be explained in terms of policy-makers' basic conceptions about Britain's place in the world, conceptions which were embroidered but not challenged by the defence debate within the British state. At the root of virtually all discussion was a fairly simple belief in deterrence. In September 1945 Clement Attlee, in a letter to Harry Truman, remarked that 'the only deterrent is the possibility of the victim of such an [atomic] attack being able to retort on the victor.' This dictum has had an enduring hold on the British 'official mind'. To quote Sir Arthur Hockaday, former Deputy Secretary at the Ministry of Defence, speaking in 1989 of Britain's experience with nuclear weapons: 'You've got to keep these things simple. ... Keeping it comparatively simple, the quotation ... from Clem Attlee, "the answer to an atomic bomb on London is an atomic bomb on another great city", was absolutely on the ball. And you can take that further by saying that the best deterrent to a bomb on London is the capability to deliver a bomb on somewhere else.'[8]

Notes

1. CAS's Opening Remarks at the Conference of Commanders-in-Chief, 10 March 1960, London, Public Record Office (P.R.O.), AIR8/2253.

2. Freedman, Navias and Wheeler, 'Independence in concert', p. 7.

3. CAS's Opening Remarks at the Conference of Commanders-in-Chief, 10 March 1960, London, Public Record Office (P.R.O.), AIR8/2253.

4. 'Consideration of the post-war size of the Royal Air Force', 11 Sept. 1943, London, Public Record Office (P.R.O.), AIR20/2231.

5. VCAS to ACAS(P), 27 Oct. 1944, London, Public Record Office (P.R.O.), AIR20/3158.

6. Report of Speech by Mr. Macmillan 'Biggin Hill No Safeguard', 27 Oct. 1950, London, Public Record Office (P.R.O.), AIR19/662.

7. Cooper, 'The Origins and Development of the British Strategic Nuclear Deterrent Forces, 1945-1960', p. 28.

8. Hockaday, 'The Origins and Development of the British Strategic Nuclear Deterrent Forces, 1945-1960', p. 31.

Abbreviations

A/ACAS(P)	Acting Assistant Chief of the Air Staff (Policy)
AAFCE	Allied Air Forces Central Europe
ACAS(P)	Assistant Chief of the Air Staff (Policy)
ACAS(I)	Assistant Chief of the Air Staff (Intelligence)
ACAS(Ops)	Assistant Chief of the Air Staff (Operations)
ACAS(OR)	Assistant Chief of the Air Staff (Operational Requirements)
ACAS(TR)	Assistant Chief of the Air Staff (Technical Requirements)
ADUK	Air Defence of the United Kingdom
AEC	Atomic Energy Commission (USA)
AFS	Air Force Staff
AMP	Air Member for Personnel
AMSO	Air Member for Supply and Organisation
ANZAM	Australia, New Zealand and Malaya security agreement
ANZUS	Australia, New Zealand and the United States security pact
ASM	Air-to-Surface Missile
AUS(A)	Assistant Under-Secretary (Air Staff)
AUS(G)	Assistant Under-Secetary (General)
BAFO	British Air Force of Occupation
BAOR	British Army of the Rhine
BDCC	British Defence Co-ordinating Committee
BJSM	British Joint Staff Mission
BNDSG	British Nuclear Deterrent Study Group
CAS	Chief of the Air Staff
CDS	Chief of the Defence Staff
CENTO	Central Treaty Organisation
CIGS	Chief of the Imperial General Staff
CNO	Chief of Naval Operations (USA)
COS	Chiefs of Staff Committee
CRD	Controller of Research and Development
CS(A)	Controller of Supply (Aircraft)
CSO	Chief Staff Officer
DASB	Director of Air Staff Briefing
DAT	Director of Air Training
DCAS	Deputy Chief of the Air Staff
D.of Plans	Director of Plans
D.of Policy	Director of Policy
DOR	Director of Operational Requirements
DTD	Director of Technical Development

EDC	European Defence Community
FEAF	Far East Air Force
FO	Foreign Office
FPSG	Future Policy Study Group
GOR	General Operational Requirement
GSP	Global Strategy Paper
ICBM	Inter-Continental Ballistic Missile
IRBM	Intermediate Range Ballistic Missile
JCAE	Joint Committee on Atomic Energy (USA)
JCS	Joint Chiefs of Staff (USA)
JIB	Joint Intelligence Bureau
JIC	Joint Intelligence Committee
JPS	Joint Planning Staff
LTDP	Long Term Defence Programme
MAP	Ministry of Aircraft Production
MBF	Medium Bomber Force
MEAF	Middle East Air Force
MoD	Ministry of Defence
MoS	Ministry of Supply
NATO	North Atlantic Treaty Organisation
NSC	National Security Council (USA)
OR	Operational Requirement
PRC	Policy Review Committee
PS	Private Secretary
PUS	Permanent Under-Secretary
RAF	Royal Air Force
RAFDEL	RAF Delegation
RCAF	Royal Canadian Air Force
RCM	Radar Counter-Measures
S.6	Air Staff Secretariat
SAAM	Scientific Adviser Air Ministry
SAC	Strategic Air Command (USA)
SACEUR	Supreme Allied Commander Europe
SACLANT	Supreme Allied Commander Atlantic
SEATO	South-East Asia Treaty Organisation
SHAPE	Supreme Headquarters Allied Powers Europe
TAF	Tactical Air Force
TCC	Temporary Council Committee
UKAEA	United Kingdom Atomic Energy Authority
USAAF	United States Army Air Force
USAF	United States Air Force
USN	United States Navy
VCAS	Vice-Chief of the Air Staff
VCNS	Vice-Chief of the Naval Staff
WEU	Western European Union
WUTAF	Western Union Tactical Air Force

Bibliography

Manuscript Sources

London, Public Record Office

CAB127   Private Collections: Ministers and Officials: Papers of General Ismay and Lord Normanbrook
CAB128   Cabinet Minutes
CAB129   Cabinet Memoranda
CAB130   Papers of Ad-hoc Cabinet Committees: GEN and MISC Series
CAB131   Papers of Cabinet Defence Committee
CAB134   Papers of Cabinet Committees: General Series

PREM3   Prime Minister's Office Operations Papers to 1946
PREM4   Prime Minister's Office Confidential Papers to 1946
PREM8   Prime Minister's Office: Correspondence and Papers, 1945-51
PREM11   Prime Minister's Office: Corespondence and Papers, 1951-64

DEFE4   Chiefs of Staff Committee: Minutes of Meetings
DEFE5   Chiefs of Staff Committee: Memoranda
DEFE6   Chiefs of Staff Committee: Joint Planning Staff Reports
DEFE7   Ministry of Defence Registered Files: General Series
DEFE10   Ministry of Defence Major Committees: Minutes and Papers
DEFE11   Chiefs of Staff Committee: Registered Files
DEFE13   Minister of Defence: Private Office Papers
DEFE32   Chiefs of Staff Committee: Secretary's Standard Files

T225   Treasury Defence Policy and Material Division: Files

AIR2   Air Ministry Correspondence
AIR6   Records of Meetings of the Air Council
AIR8   Papers of the Chief of the Air Staff
AIR19   Secretary of State for Air: Private Office Papers
AIR20   Air Staff Unregistered Papers

London, Ministry of Defence (Air Historical Branch)

(These papers were transferred to the Public Record Office in 1993)

Papers of Marshal of the Royal Air Force Sir John Slessor

London, Royal Air Force Museum, Hendon

Papers of Lord De L'Isle and Dudley

Cambridge, Churchill College Archives Centre

Papers of Marshal of the Royal Air Force Sir William Dickson

Bracknell, Royal Air Force Staff College

Video interviews with:

Marshal of the Royal Air Force Sir William Dickson
Marshal of the Royal Air Force Sir Dermot Boyle
Air Chief Marshal Sir Geoffrey Tuttle
Air Chief Marshal Sir David Lee

Montgomery, Albert F. Simpson Historical Research Center, Maxwell Air Force Base, Alabama

History of Headquarters Third Air Force
History of Headquarters Twelfth Air Force
History of 406th Fighter Bomber Wing
Lectures to Air War College

London, King's College Library

Papers drawn from the National Archives, Washington, D. C., the Dwight D. Eisenhower Library, Abilene and the Library of Congress, Washington, D. C. deposited by Dr. Martin Navias

Interviews

Viscount De L'Isle (Secretary of State for Air, 1951-55)
T. C. G. James (former Air Ministry civil servant and Ministry of Defence official historian)

Printed Primary Sources

Command Papers

Cmd.6923 Central Organisation for Defence

Cmd.6743 Statement Relating to Defence

Cmd.7042 Statement Relating to Defence

Cmd.7327 Statement Relating to Defence, 1948

Cmd.7332 Memorandum on Air Estimates, 1948-49

Cmd.7631 Statement on Defence, 1949

Cmd.7634 Memorandum by the Secretary of State for Air to Accompany the Air Estimates

Cmd.7883 Collective Defence under the Brussels and North Atlantic Treaties

Cmd.7894 Mutual Defence Assistance Agreement between the Government of the United Kingdom of Great Britain and Northern Ireland and the Government of the United States of America. Washington, Jan. 27, 1950

Cmd.7895 Statement on Defence, 1950

Cmd.7898 Air Estimates, 1950-51. Memorandum of the Secretary of State for Air

Cmd.8146 Defence Programme. Statement made by the Prime Minister in the House of Commons on Monday, Jan. 29, 1951

Cmd.8162 Memorandum by the Secretary of State for Air to accompany the Air Estimates

Cmd.8474 Air Estimates, 1952-53. Memorandum by the Secretary State for Air

Cmd.8475 Statement on Defence, 1952

Cmd.8768 Statement on Defence, 1953

Cmd.8771 Air Estimates, 1953-54. Memorandum by the Secretary of State for Air

Cmd.9075 Statement on Defence, 1954

Cmd.9076 Air Estimates, 1954-55. Memorandum by the Secretary of State for Air

Cmd.9289 Final Act of the Nine-Power Conference held in London Sept. 28 to Oct. 3, 1954

Cmd.9304 Documents agreed on by the Conference of Ministers held in Paris, Oct. 20 to 23, 1954

Cmd.9388 Supply of Military Aircraft

Cmd.9391 Statement on Defence, 1955

Cmd.9397 Air Estimates, 1955-56. Memorandum by the Secretary of State for Air

Cmd.9555 Agreement between the Government of the United Kingdom of Great Britain and Northern Ireland and the Government of the United States of America for Co-operation regarding Atomic Information for Mutual Defence Purposes. Washington. June 15, 1955

Cmd.9691 Statement on Defence, 1956

Cmd.9696 Air Estimates, 1956-57. Memorandum by the Secretary of State for Air

Cmnd.124 Defence. Outline of Future Policy

Cmnd.130 Defence Statistics, 1957-58

Cmnd.149 Memorandum by the Secretary of State for Air to accompany the Air Estimates

Cmnd.363 Report on Defence. Britain's Contribution to Peace and Security

Cmnd.364 Defence Statisics, 1958-59

Cmnd.366 Supply of Ballistic Missiles by the United States to the United Kingdom

Cmnd.373 Air Estimates, 1958-59. Memorandum by the Secretary of State for Air

Cmnd.406 Exchange of Notes between the Government of the United Kingdom of Great Britain and Northern Ireland and the Government of the United States of America concerning the Supply to the United Kingdom Government of Intermediate Range Ballistic Missiles. Washington, Feb. 22, 1958

Cmnd.476 Central Organisation for Defence

Cmnd.537 Agreement between the Government of the United Kingdom of Great Britain and Northern Ireland and the Government of the United States of America for Co-operation on the Uses of Atomic Energy for Mutual Defence Purposes. Washington, July 3, 1958

Cmnd.588 Exchange of Notes between the Government of the United Kingdom of Great Britain and Northern Ireland and the Federal Republic of Germany concerning Local Defence Costs of United Kingdom Forces stationed in the Federal Republic. Paris, Oct. 3, 1958

Cmnd.661 Defence Statistics, 1959-60

Cmnd.662 Progress of the Five-Year Defence Plan

Cmnd.673 Air Estimates, 1959-60. Memorandum by the Secretary of State for Air

Cmnd.859 Amendment to the Agreement between the Government of the United Kingdom of Great Britain and Northern Ireland and the Government of the United States of America for Co-operation on the Uses of Atomic Energy for Mutual Defence Purposes. Washington, May 7, 1959

Foreign Relations of the United States (FRUS)

1947 Volume III
1948 Volume II
1948 Volume III
1949 Volume I
1949 Volume IV
1950 Volume I
1950 Volume III
1951 Volume I
1951 Volume III (Part 1)
1951 Volume III (Part 2)
1952-4 Volume II (Part 1)
1952-4 Volume II (Part 2)
1952-4 Volume V (Part 1)
1952-4 Volume V (Part 2)
1955-7 Volume IV
1955-7 Volume XX
1955-7 Volume XXIV

Documents on British Policy Overseas (DBPO)

Series 1 Volume 1
Series 1 Volume 2
Series 1 Volume 3
Series 1 Volume 4
Series 1 Volume 5
Series 2 Volume 2
Series 2 Volume 3
Series 2 Volume 4

Printed Secondary Works

Books

Allen, H. R., *The Legacy of Lord Trenchard*. London, 1972.

Allison, G., *Essence of Decision*. Boston, 1971.

Armacost, M., *The Politics of Weapons Innovation: The Thor-Jupiter Controversy*. New York, 1969.

Armitage, M. J. and Mason, R. A., *Air Power in the Nuclear Age, 1945-1982*. London, 1983.

Ball, D. and Richelson, J. (eds.), *Strategic Nuclear Targeting*. Ithaca, 1986.

Barker, E., *The British Between the Superpowers, 1945-50*. London, 1983.

Barnett, C., *The Audit of War*. London, 1986.

Barraclough, G. (ed.), *Survey of International Affairs 1955-1956*. London, 1960.

Barraclough, G. (ed.), *Survey of International Affairs 1956-1958*. London, 1962.

Barraclough, G. (ed.), *Survey of International Affairs 1959-1960*. London, 1964.

Bartlett, C. J., *The Long Retreat: A Short History of British Defence Policy, 1945-1970*. London, 1972.

Baylis, J., Booth, K., Garnett, J. and Williams, P., *Contemporary Strategy*. New York, 1975.

Baylis, J. (ed.), *British Defence Policy in a Changing World*. London, 1977.

Baylis, J. *Anglo-American Defence Relations*. 2nd edn. London, 1984.

Beard, E., *Developing the ICBM: A Study in Bureaucratic Politics*. New York, 1976.

Bell, C., *Survey of International Affairs 1954*. London, 1957.

Best, R. A., *Co-operation with Like-minded Peoples: British Influences on American Security Policy, 1945-1949*. Westport, 1986.

Bialer, U., *The Shadow of the Bomber*. London, 1980.

Borowski, H., *A Hollow Threat*. Westport, 1982.

Botti, T., *The Long Wait: The Forging of the Anglo-American Nuclear Alliance*. New York, 1987.

Broadbent, E., *The Military and Government*. Basingstoke, 1988.

Brookes, A., *V-Force: The History of Britain's Airborne Deterrent*. London, 1982.

Bull, H. and Louis, W. R. (eds.), *The Special Relationship: Anglo-American Relations since 1945*. Oxford, 1986.

Bullock, A., *Ernest Bevin, Foreign Secretary*. pbk. edn. Oxford, 1985.

Bushby, J., *Air Defence of Great Britain*. London, 1973.

Cairncross, A., *Years of Recovery*. London, 1985.

Calvocoressi, P. (ed.), *Survey of International Affairs 1947-8*. London, 1952.

Calvocoressi, P. (ed.), *Survey of International Affairs 1949-50*. London, 1953.

Calvocoressi, P. (ed.), *Survey of International Affairs 1951*. London, 1954.

Calvocoressi, P. (ed.), *Survey of International Affairs 1952*. London, 1955.

Calvocoressi, P. (ed.), *Survey of International Affairs 1953*. London, 1956.

Campbell, D., *The Unsinkable Aircraft Carrier*. 2nd edn. London, 1986.

Ceadel, M., *Thinking About Peace and War*. pbk. edn. Oxford, 1989.

Carver, M., *Out of Step*. London, 1989.

Carver, M., *Tightrope Walking: British Defence Policy since 1945*. London, 1992.

Clark, I. and Wheeler, N. J., *The British Origins of Nuclear Strategy, 1945-1955*. Oxford, 1989.

Clark, I., *Nuclear Diplomacy and the Special Relationship: Britain's Deterrent and America, 1957-1962*. Oxford, 1994.

Clarke, M. and White, B. (eds.), *Understanding Foreign Policy*. Aldershot, 1989.

Cloake, J., *Templer, Tiger of Malaya*. London, 1985.

Darby, P., *British Defence Policy East of Suez, 1947-1968*. London, 1973.

Davis, V., *Postwar Defense Policy and the United States Navy*. Chapel Hill, 1966.

Davis, V., *The Admiral's Lobby*. Chapel Hill, 1967.

Darwin, J., *Britain and Decolonisation*. Basingstoke, 1988.

Deighton, A. (ed.), *Britain and the First Cold War*. London, 1990.

Dillon, G. M. (ed.), *Defence Policy Making*. Leicester, 1988.

Divine, D., *The Broken Wing*. London, 1966.

Dockrill, M., *British Defence since 1945*. Oxford, 1988.

Dockrill, M. and Young, J. W. (eds.), *British Foreign Policy, 1945-56*. Basingstoke, 1989.

Duke, S., *US Defence Bases in the United Kingdom*. Basingstoke, 1987.

Eden, A., *Full Circle*. London, 1960.

Edmonds, M. (ed.), *Central Organizations for Defense*. Boulder, 1985.

Edmonds, M. (ed.), *The Defence Equation: British Military Systems - Policy, Planning and Performance since 1945*. London, 1986.

Edmonds, R., *Setting the Mould: The United States and Britain 1945-1950*. London, 1986.

Endicott, J. and Stafford, R. (eds.), *American Defense Policy*. 4th edn. Baltimore, 1977.

Enthoven, A. C. and Smith, K. W., *How Much is Enough? Shaping the Defense Programme, 1961-1969*. New York, 1971.

Freedman, L., *The Evolution of Nuclear Strategy*. 2nd edn. Basingstoke, 1989.

Friedberg, A. L., *The Weary Titan*. Princeton, 1988.

Gilbert, M., *Never Despair: Winston S. Churchill, 1945-1965*. London, 1988.

Gorst, A., Johnman, L. and Lucas, W. S. (eds.), *Post-war Britain, 1945-64*. London, 1989.

Gowing, M., *Independence and Deterrence: Britain and Atomic Energy, 1945-52. vol. 1. Policy Making*. London, 1974 (1988 repr.).

Groom, A. J. R., *British Thinking About Nuclear Weapons*. London, 1974.

Grove, E. J., *Vanguard to Trident: British Naval Policy since WWII*. London, 1987.

Hamilton, N., *Monty The Field-Marshal, 1944-1976*. London, 1986.

Hastings, M., *Bomber Command*. London, 1979.

Hathaway, R. M., *Ambiguous Partnership: Britain and America, 1944-1947*. New York, 1981.

228

Heller, F. and Gillingham, J. R. (eds.), *NATO: The Formation of the Atlantic Alliance and the Integration of Europe.* Basingstoke, 1992.

Henderson, N., *The Birth of NATO.* London, 1982.

Healey, D., *The Time of My Life.* pbk. edn. London, 1990.

Herken, G., *The Winning Weapon.* pbk. edn. New York, 1981.

Heuser, B. and O'Neill, R. (eds.), *Securing the Peace in Europe, 1945-1962.* Basingstoke, 1992.

Horne, A., *Macmillan 1957-1986.* London, 1989.

Horne, A., *Macmillan 1894-1956.* rev. edn. London, 1990.

Howard M., *The Central Organisation of Defence.* London, 1970.

Howard M., *The Continental Commitment.* London, 1972.

Johnson, F. A., *Defence by Committee: The British Committee of Imperial Defence, 1885-1959.* London, 1960.

Johnson, F. A., *Defence by Ministry: The British Ministry of Defence, 1944-1974.* London, 1980.

Jones, N., *The Beginning of Strategic Air Power.* London, 1987.

Kaiser, K. and Roper, J. (eds.), *British-German Defence Co-operation: Partners within the Alliance.* London, 1988.

Kennedy, P., *The Realities Behind Diplomacy.* London, 1981.

Kennedy, P., *Strategy and Diplomacy.* London, 1983.

Kennedy, P., *The Rise and Fall of the Great Powers.* pbk. edn. London, 1989.

Lamb, R., *The Failure of the Eden Government.* London, 1987.

Lee, D., *Flight from the Middle East.* London, 1980.

Lee, D., *Eastward.* London, 1984.

Lee, D., *Wings in the Sun.* London, 1989.

Leffler, M. P., *A Preponderance of Power: National Security, the Truman Administration and the Cold War.* Stanford, 1992.

Lewis, J., *Changing Direction: British Military Planning for Post-War Strategic Defence, 1942-47.* London, 1988.

Lider, J., *British Military Thought After World War Two.* Aldershot, 1985.

Louis, W. R., *The British Empire in the Middle East, 1945-1951.* Oxford, 1984.

Louis, W. R. and Owen, R. (eds.), *Suez: The Crisis and its Consequences.* Oxford, 1989.

Macmillan, H., *Riding the Storm.* London, 1971.

Macmillan, H., *Pointing the Way.* London, 1973.

Mandelbaum, M., *The Nuclear Question.* Cambridge, 1979.

Mason, R. A. (ed.), *War in the Third Dimension.* Oxford, 1986.

Melissen, J., *The Struggle for Nuclear Partnership: Britain, the United States and the Making of an Ambiguous Alliance 1952-1959.* Groningen, 1993.

Menaul, S., *Countdown: Britain's Strategic Nuclear Forces.* London, 1980.

Morgan, K. O., *Labour in Power, 1945-51.* Oxford, 1984.

Murray, D. J. and Viotti, P. R. (eds.), *The Defense Policies of Nations*. Baltimore, 1982.

Navias, M., *Nuclear Weapons and British Strategic Planning, 1955-1958*. Oxford, 1991.

Norris, R. S., Burrows, A. S. and Fieldhouse, R. W. (eds.), *Nuclear Weapons Databook. vol. 5. British, French and Chinese Nuclear Weapons*. Boulder, 1994.

Osgood, R. E., *NATO: The Entangling Alliance*. Chicago, 1962.

Ovendale, R. (ed.), *The Foreign Policy of the British Labour Governments, 1945-51*. Leicester, 1984.

Ovendale, R., *The English-Speaking Alliance*. London, 1985.

Overy, R. J., *The Air War 1939-1945*. pbk. edn. London, 1987.

Paret, P. (ed.), *Makers of Modern Strategy*. Oxford, 1986.

Park, W., *Defending the West: A History of NATO*. Brighton, 1986.

Pierre, A. J., *Nuclear Politics: The British Experience with an Independent Strategic Force, 1939-1970*. London, 1972.

Ponting, C., *Breach of Promise*. pbk. edn. London, 1990.

Posen, B., *The Sources of Military Doctrine: France, Britain and Germany between the World Wars*. Ithaca, 1984.

Pringle, P. and Arkin, W., *SIOP*. London, 1983.

Reynolds, D. J. and Dimbleby, D., *An Ocean Apart*. London, 1988.

Reynolds, D. J. (ed.), *The Origins of the Cold War in Europe: International Perspectives*. New Haven, 1994.

Rosecrance, R. N., *Defense of the Realm: British Strategy in the Nuclear Epoch*. New York, 1968.

Rothwell, V., *Britain and the Cold War, 1941-1947*. London, 1982.

Schwartz, D., *NATO's Nuclear Dilemmas*. Washington, 1983.

Seldon, A., *Churchill's Indian Summer*. London, 1981.

Sherry, M., *Preparing for the Next War: American Plans for Postwar Defense, 1941-5*. New Haven, 1977.

Sherry, M., *The Rise of American Air Power*. New Haven, 1987.

Simpson, J., *The Independent Nuclear State: The United States, Britain and the Military Atom*. London, 1983.

Slessor, J., *The Central Blue*. London, 1956.

Slessor, J., *Strategy for the West*. London, 1954.

Slessor, J., *The Great Deterrent*. London, 1957.

Slessor, J., *These Remain*. London, 1969.

Smith, M., *British Air Strategy Between the Wars*. Oxford, 1984.

Smith, P. M., *The Air Force Plans for Peace, 1943-5*. Baltimore, 1970.

Snyder, W. P., *The Politics of British Defense Policy, 1945-1962*. London, 1964.

Spanier, J., *Games Nations Play*. 4th edn. New York, 1981.

Taylor, R., *Against the Bomb*. Oxford, 1988.

Tedder, A., *Air Power in War*. London, 1948.

Tedder, A., *With Prejudice*. London, 1966.

Terraine, J., *The Right of the Line: The Royal Air Force in the European War, 1939-1945*. pbk. edn. Sevenoaks, 1988.

Thetford, O., *Aircraft of the Royal Air Force since 1918*. 8th edn. London, 1988.

Thorpe, D. R., *Selwyn Lloyd*. London, 1989.

Webster, C. and Frankland, N., *The Strategic Air Offensive Against Germany. History of the Second World War: United Kingdom Military Series, 4 vols*. London, 1961.

Wiggershaus, N. and Foerster, R. G. (eds.), *The Western Security Community: Common Problems and Conflicting National Interests during the Foundation Phase of the North Atlantic Alliance*. Oxford, 1993.

Williams, P., *The Senate and US Troops in Europe*. London, 1985.

Wood, D., *Project Cancelled*. London, 1975.

Worcester, R., *Roots of British Air Policy*. London, 1966.

Wykeham, P., *Fighter Command*. London, 1960.

Wynn, H., *RAF Strategic Nuclear Deterrent Forces: Their Origins, Roles and Deployment, 1946-1969*. London, 1994.

Young, J. W. (ed.), *The Foreign Policy of Churchill's Peacetime Administration, 1951-1955*. Leicester, 1988.

Young, J. W., *France, The Cold War and the Western Alliance, 1944-49*. Leicester, 1990.

Zuckerman, S., *From Apes to Warlords*. pbk. edn. London, 1988.

Zuckerman, S., *Monkeys, Men and Missiles*. London, 1988.

Articles

Ball, S. J., 'Bomber bases and British strategy in the Middle East, 1945-1949', *Journal of Strategic Studies*, 14 (1991), 515-533.

Barbier, C., 'The French decision to develop a military nuclear programme in the 1950s', *Diplomacy and Statecraft*, 4 (1993), 103-113.

Barrett, G. G., 'The role of the RAF in the preservation of peace', *Journal of the Royal United Services Institute*, XCI (1946), 77-82.

Baylis, J., 'Britain and the Dunkirk Treaty: the origins of NATO', *Journal of Strategic Studies*, 5 (1982), 238-247.

Baylis, J., 'British wartime thinking about a post-war European security group', *Review of International Studies*, 9 (1984), 265-81.

Baylis, J., 'Britain, the Brussels Pact and the continental commitment', *International Affairs*, 60 (1984), 615-629.

Baylis, J., '"Greenwoodery" and British defence policy', *International Affairs*, 62 (1985/6), 443-457.

Baylis, J. and Macmillan, A., 'The British Global Strategy Paper of 1952', *Journal of Strategic Studies*, 16 (1993), 200-226.

Brecher, M., Steinberg, B. and Stein, J., 'A framework for research on foreign policy behavior', *Journal of Conflict Resolution*, XIII (1969), 75-101.

Buchan, A., 'The Institute for Strategic Studies', *Brasseys*, 70 (1959), 16-17.

Buzzard, A., Slessor, J. and Lowenthal, R., 'The H-bomb, Massive Retaliation and Graduated Deterrence', *International Affairs*, 32 (1956), 148-165.

Clark, I. and Angell, D., 'Britain, the United States and the control of nuclear weapons: the diplomacy of the Thor deployment 1956-58', *Diplomacy and Statecraft*, 2 (1991), 153-177.

Cowley, J., 'Future Trends in Warfare', *Journal of the Royal United Services Institute*, CV (1959/60), 4-16.

Devereux, D. R., 'Britain, the Commonwealth and the defence of the Middle East', *Journal of Contemporary History*, 24 (1989), 327-345.

Dockrill, S., 'The evolution of Britain's policy towards a European army, 1950-54', *Journal of Strategic Studies*, 12 (1989), 38-62.

Dombey, N. and Grove, E., 'Britain's thermonuclear bluff', *London Review of Books*, XIV, 20 (October 1992).

Elliot, D. C., 'Project Vista and nuclear weapons in Europe', *International Security*, 11 (1986), 163-183.

Freedman, L., Navias, M. and Wheeler, N., 'Independence in concert: the British rationale for possessing strategic nuclear weapons', *Nuclear History Program Occasional Paper*, 5 (1989).

Friedberg, A. L., 'A history of US strategic "doctrine", 1945-80', *Journal of Strategic Studies*, 3 (1980), 37-71.

Gaddis, J. L., The emerging post-revisionist synthesis on the origins of the Cold War', *Diplomatic History*, 7 (1983), 171-204.

George, A. L., 'The Operational Code: a neglected approach to the study of political leaders and decision-making', *International Studies Quarterly*, 13 (1969), 190-222.

Goldberg, A., 'The military origins of the British nuclear deterrent', *International Affairs*, 40 (1964), 600-618.

Gorst, A. and Lucas, W. S., 'Suez 1956: strategy and the diplomatic process', *Journal of Strategic Studies*, 11 (1988), 391-436.

Gott, R., 'Evolution of the British independent deterrent', *International Affairs*, 39 (1963), 238-252.

Gray, C. S., 'National style in strategy: the American example', *International Security*, 6 (1981), 21-47.

Greenwood, S., 'Return to Dunkirk: the origins of the Anglo-French treaty of March 1947', *Journal of Strategic Studies*, 6 (1983), 49-65.

Greenwood, S., 'Ernest Bevin, France and the "Western Union": August 1945 to February 1946', *European History Quarterly*, 14 (1984), 319-338.

Henrikson, A. K., 'The creation of the North Atlantic alliance, 1948-1952', *Naval War College Review*, 32 (1980), 4-39.

James, T. C. G., 'The impact of the Sandys defence review on the Royal Air Force', *Royal Air Force Historical Society Proceedings*, 4 (1988), 9-34.

Jervis, R., 'The impact of the Korean War on the Cold War', *Journal of Conflict Resolution*, 24 (1980), 563-592.

Kikuyana, K., 'Britain and short-range nuclear weapons', *Journal of Strategic Studies*, 16 (1993), 538-560.

Leffler, M. P., 'The American conception of national security and the beginning of the Cold War', *American Historical Review*, 89 (1984), 346-400.

Martin, L., 'The market for strategic ideas in Britain: the Sandys era', *American Political Science Review*, LVI (1962), 23-41.

Mastny, V., 'Stalin and the militarisation of the Cold War', *International Security*, 9 (1984/5), 109-129.

Merrick, R., 'The Russia Committee of the British Foreign Office and the Cold War', *Journal of Contemporary History*, 20 (1985), 453-468.

Myers, F., 'Conscription and the politics of military strategy in the Attlee government', *Journal of Strategic Studies*, 7 (1984), 55-73.

Navias, M., 'Terminating Conscription? The British National Service controversy, 1955-1956', *Journal of Contemporary History*, 24 (1989), 195-208.

Rahman, H., 'British post-Second World War military planning for the Middle East', *Journal of Strategic Studies*, 5 (1982), 511-530.

Rees, W., 'The 1957 Sandys White Paper: new priorities in British defence policy', *Journal of Strategic Studies*, 12 (1989), 215-229.

Reynolds, D. J., 'The origins of the Cold War: the European dimension', *Historical Journal*, XXVIII (1985), 497-516.

Reynolds, D. J., 'A "special relationship"? America, Britain and the international order since the Second World War', *International Affairs*, 62 (1985/6), 1-20.

Rosenberg, D. A., 'American atomic strategy and the hydrogen bomb decision', *Journal of American History*, 66 (1979), 66-87.

Rosenberg, D. A., '"A Smoking Radiating Ruin At The End of Two Hours" Documents on American plans for nuclear war with the Soviet Union', *International Security*, 6 (1981/2), 3-38.

Rosenberg, D. A., 'The origins of overkill: nuclear weapons and American strategy, 1945-1960', *International Security*, 7 (1983), 3-71.

Rosenberg, D. A., 'Reality and responsibility: power and process in the making of United States nuclear strategy, 1945-1968', *Journal of Strategic Studies*, 9 (1986), 35-52.

Shlaim, A., 'Britain, the Berlin blockade and the Cold War', *International Affairs*, 60 (1983/4), 1-14.

Slessor, J., 'The place of the bomber in British policy', *International Affairs*, XXIX (1953), 302-308.

Smith, R. and Zametica, J., 'The Cold Warrior: Clement Attlee reconsidered, 1945-7', *International Affairs*, 61 (1985), 237-252.

Soutou, G-H., 'The French military program for nuclear energy, 1945-1981', *Nuclear History Program Occasional Paper*, 3 (1989).

Steiner, Z., 'Decision-making in American and British foreign policy: an open and shut case', *Review of International Studies*, 13 (1987), 1-18.

Wheeler, N. J., 'British nuclear weapons and Anglo-American relations, 1945-54', *International Affairs*, 62 (1985/6), 71-86.

Wykeham-Barnes, P. G., 'The war in Korea with special reference to the difficulties of using our air power', *Journal of the Royal United Services Institute*, XCVII (1952), 149-163.

Wiebes, C. and Zeeman, B., 'Baylis on post-war planning', *Review of International Studies*, 10 (1984), 247-52.

Young, J. W., 'Churchill's "No" to Europe: the "Rejection" of European union by Churchill's post-war government, 1951-1952', *Historical Journal*, XXVIII (1985), 923-937.

Zeeman, B., 'Britain and the Cold War: an alternative approach - the Treaty of Dunkirk example', *European History Quarterly*, 16 (1986), 342-367.

Unpublished Dissertations

Converse, E. V., 'United States plans for a postwar military base system, 1942-1948', Princeton (1984).

Elliot, J. A., 'The cancellation of the Blue Streak missile system and its relevance to British nuclear thinking and strategy, 1954-1960', Cambridge (1990).

Vallance, A. G. B., 'The evolution of air power doctrine within the RAF, 1957-1987', Cambridge (1988).

Whiffen, D. E., 'Service politics and the Sandys 1957 Defence White Paper', Cambridge (1988).

Zametica, O., 'British strategic planning for the eastern Mediterranean and Middle East, 1944-1947', Cambridge (1986).

Other Sources

'A seminar on the air aspects of the Suez campaign - 1956', held at the Royal United Services Institute, London on 26 October, 1987. Participants included: Air Chief Marshal Sir David Lee; Sir Frank Cooper; Air Chief Marshal Sir Denis Smallwood; Air Chief Marshal Sir Thomas Prickett and Air Vice-Marshal Paul Mallorie. Transcript in *Royal Air Force Historical Society Proceedings*, 3 (1988), 9-65.

'Conference on the 1957 White Paper', held at King's College, London on 1 July, 1988. Participants included: Sir Richard Powell; Sir Arthur Drew; T. C. G. James; the Earl of Selkirk; Colonel K. G. Post; Julian Amery and Sir Richard Way.

'The origins and development of the British strategic nuclear deterrent forces, 1945-1960', seminar held at the Royal Air Force Museum, Hendon on 23 October, 1989. Participants included: Air Marshal Sir John Rowlands; Air Vice-Marshal W. E. Oulton; Sir Frank Cooper; Air Chief Marshal Sir Kenneth Cross and Air Commodore C. B. Brown. Transcript in *Royal Air Force Historical Society Proceedings*, 7 (1990), 7-61.

Index